D0535169

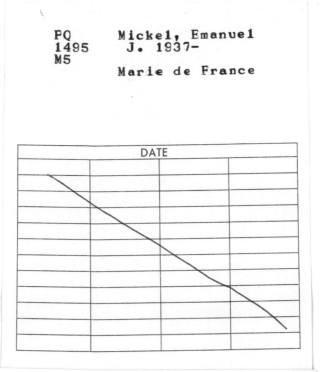

DATE		

TWAYNE'S WORLD AUTHORS SERIES

A Survey of the World's Literature

Sylvia E. Bowman, Indiana University

GENERAL EDITOR

FRANCE

Maxwell A. Smith, Guerry Professor of French, Emeritus
The University of Chattanooga
Former Visiting Professor in Modern Languages
The Florida State University

EDITOR

Marie de France

(TWAS 306)

Marie de France

Marie de France

By EMANUEL J. MICKEL, JR.

Indiana University

Twayne Publishers, Inc. :: New York

Library of Congress Cataloging in Publication Data

Mickel, Emanuel J   1937–
  Marie de France.

  (Twayne's world authors series, TWAS 306. France)
  Bibliography: p. 173.
  1. Marie de France, 12th cent.
PQ1495.M5   841'.1   73–17350
ISBN 0–8057–2591–1

In Memory of
Urban T. Holmes, Jr.
(1900–1972)

Preface

In this modest volume I have tried to keep in mind both the general reader and the student of mediaeval literature. In Chapters 1 and 5 I have attempted to present the problems concerning Marie's identity and the question of the narrative *lai* in some detail, adding extensive notes and bibliography for students interested in pursuing these subjects. Various views are presented with some critical commentary in an effort to place the different theses in perspective. Because of its nature and the limits of space, Chapter 2 is designed almost exclusively for the general reader. Chapters 3 and 4 do not pretend to be more than an introduction to Marie's translations. Because the works are translations, they are usually neglected in general studies of Marie's work. Chapters 6, 7, and 8 focus on the *Lais*. In addition to the summary of plots, Chapter 6 includes a brief discussion of the sources hypothesized for the various *lais* with indication of bibliography for further study. In Chapter 7 I offer an interpretation of the collection, followed in Chapter 8 by a consideration of some of the elements important to the structure and style of the *Lais*. Unfortunately, in a volume intended for the general reader, treatment of fascinating and complicated ideas is often brief. In these cases I have attempted to compensate by indicating references in which the subject can be pursued profitably.

The following standard abbreviations were used in the notes for frequently cited periodicals: *ZRP* (*Zeitschrift für Romanische Philologie*), *ZFSL* (*Zeitschrift für Französische Sprache und Literatur*), *MLN* (*Modern Language Notes*), *EHR* (*English Historical Review*), *SP* (*Studies in Philology*), and *PMLA* (*Publications of the Modern Language Association*).

I wish to thank my colleagues, Professors Richard Carr and Diana Guiragossian, for their careful reading of portions of the manuscript and for their helpful suggestions. I am also indebted to Miss Muriel Bertrand-Guy, who provided me with a translation of A. Ahlström's *Studier i den fornfranska lais literaturen.* Without the prompt service and warm interest of Mrs. Gail Matthews and the members of the Interlibrary Loan Department at Indiana University, a number of valuable texts might have remained unavailable to me. I am grateful to Research and Advanced Studies at Indiana University for their generous financial support. Further gratitude is due the editors of *Speculum* for permission to reprint extensively from my article "A Reconsideration of the Lais of Marie de France," and to the editors of *Studies in Philology* for permission to quote in full from a few pages of my forthcoming article, "Marie de France's Use of Irony as a Stylistic and Narrative Device." Finally, the debt of gratitude to my wife, Kathleen, can never really be expressed.

EMANUEL J. MICKEL, JR.

Indiana University

Contents

Preface

Chronology

1. Texts and Identity of Marie de France   13
2. Intellectual Background of the Twelfth Century   24
3. Fables   34
4. *Espurgatoire Saint Patriz*   41
5. The Narrative *Lai*   50
6. Plots and Sources   72
7. Marie's Concept of Love   99
8. Narrative Aspects of the *Lais*   122
9. Conclusion   141

Notes and References   143

Selected Bibliography   173

Index   185

Chronology

1066	Norman invasion of England
1096–1099	First Crusade
1122	Birth of Eleanor of Aquitaine
ca. 1125	William of Malmesbury's *De Rebus gestis regum Anglorum*
1133	Birth of Henry Plantagenet
ca. 1135	Geoffrey of Monmouth's *Historia regum Britanniae*
1137	Marriage of Louis VII and Eleanor of Aquitaine
ca. 1140	Geoffrey of Gaimar's *Estoire des Engleis*
1147–1148	Second Crusade
1152	Annulment of marriage between Louis VII and Eleanor; subsequent marriage of Henry Plantagenet and Eleanor
1154	Coronation of Henry Plantagenet as Henry II of England
1155	Wace's *Brut*
ca. 1160	*Roman d'Eneas*; *Piramus et Tisbé? Floire et Blancheflor?*
ca. 1165	Earliest of Marie's *lais? Tristan* of Thomas? *Roman de Thebes?*
1167	Beatrice de Bourgogne, wife of Frederick Barbarossa, crowned Empress on August 1
1170	Beginning of major activity of Chrétien de Troyes; murder of Thomas Becket; coronation of Henry the Young King
1173	Rebellion of Henry II's sons
1174	Incarceration of Eleanor at Salisbury
1181	Reference to Mary, Daughter of Geoffrey Plantagenet, as Abbess of Shaftesbury

1183   Death of Henry the Young King
1189   Deaths of Henry II and William of Mandeville; acces-
       sion of Richard the Lionhearted; freedom of Eleanor;
       Third Crusade
1199   Death of Richard the Lionhearted
1204   Death of Eleanor of Aquitaine
1208– Tenure of Henry, Abbot of Sartis; composition of Henry
1215   of Saltrey's *Tractatus de Purgatorio Sancti Patricii*;
       Marie's *Espurgatoire Saint Patriz*?
1215   Last reference to Mary as Abbess of Shaftesbury
1216   Death of Abbot Henry of Sartis

CHAPTER 1

Texts and Identity of Marie de France

1 Works Ascribed to Marie de France

AS an author of vernacular literature, France's first poetess, known as Marie de France, probably ranks second only to Chrétien de Troyes among the best-known writers of mediaeval French literature in the twelfth and thirteenth centuries. Most literary works which stem from this period remain anonymous and those where authorship is established leave little more than the author's name, a name which often in itself cannot be further identified with a historical personage. Celebrated as she is, Marie's own identity remains a mystery and the number of works which one may attribute to her has long been the subject of dispute, although for nearly two hundred years scholars have believed that she is the author of at least three works: (1) a group of twelve short narrative tales in verse which scholars have edited under the title *Lais*; (2) the *Fables*, a collection of fables translated from English into Old French; (3) a translation of a Latin saint's life entitled *Espurgatoire Saint Patriz*.[1]

Interest in mediaeval vernacular literature developed slowly in France and, since the texts remained in widely scattered, unedited manuscripts, knowledge of the history of this period of literary activity was slow to develop. For the most part, keen interest in the subject was awakened only in the nineteenth century and, since the early decades, great efforts have been made to provide printed editions of the unedited texts. The first reference to Marie de France, however, predates this period of activity by more than two hundred years. In the second volume of his *Recueil de l'Origine de la Langue et Poésie Françoise* (1581), Claude Fauchet first used the name Marie de France to refer to the writer who had translated a collection of fables found in the manuscript he was consulting. He coined the name from a line in the epilogue to the collection: "At the end of this text, which I have composed in romance [the vernacular], I shall name myself for the sake of posterity: Marie is my name and I am from France." [2] In the course of the next two hundred years, Marie de France, author of the *Fables*, was mentioned in a number of works. Then in 1781 Legrand d'Aussy, in the fourth volume of his *Fabliaux ou Contes du XIIe et du XIIIe siècle*, identified the translator of the Latin saint's life, the *Espurgatoire Saint Patriz*, with the same Marie who had translated the *Fables*; for, in the closing lines of the text, the writer calls herself Marie: "I, Marie, have put the book of the *Espurgatoire* into romance [the vernacular] for the sake of posterity so that it may be understood by and available to the layman." [3]

A few years earlier, in an extensive note contained in his edition of the *Canterbury Tales* (1775), Thomas Tyrwhitt, who had been studying Harley manuscript 978 in an effort to elucidate problems surrounding the origin of the Breton *lai*, suggested that the Marie named in the "Prologue" to the collection of *lais* in the manuscript was the same poetess who had translated the *Fables*. In 1800 the emigrant clergyman Abbot Gervais de La Rue (1751–1835), asserted that all three of the works mentioned should be attributed to Marie de France. [4]

Throughout the eighteenth and for most of the nineteenth century it was believed that Marie had written in the thirteenth century. To a certain extent this opinion was based on a passage from BN manuscript 1446, which contains a copy of the *Fables* as well as the text of the *Couronnement de Renard*, both written in the same hand. In the epilogue of the *Couronnement*, dedicated to Count Guillaume de Dampierre, who died in 1251, the writer (or scribe) comments that the Count Willalme mentioned in the epilogue to the *Fables* is this same Guillaume de Dampierre to whom he is dedicating the *Couronnement*. Since the text was composed for the edification of Guillaume de Dampierre's younger brother, Gui, referred to as the Marquis de Namur, it was probably written sometime between 1263, the year he became the Marquis de Namur, and 1278, the earliest suggested reference to his acquisition of the title Count of Flanders. [5]

In 1867 Eduard Mall [6] proposed that Marie de France was the Marie de Compiègne associated with the thirteenth-century satirical text *Evangile aux femmes*. Ten years later Mall renounced this identification of Marie. [7] Subsequent study of the fable manuscripts had persuaded him that Marie's language was that of the late twelfth and not that of the mid-thirteenth century. The future editor of the *Fables*, Karl Warnke, concurred, as did Gaston Paris,[8] who placed little importance on the passage in the *Couronnement de Renard*. Paris dismissed the statement in the *Couronnement* as an error of the writer, who, having a copy of the *Fables* before him, mistakenly assumed that the Count William of the *Fables* was Guillaume de Dampierre.[9] Further proof that the translator of the fables was not a Marie living in Flanders lies in her assertion that she had translated an English version of the collection.[10] It is not likely that a woman born in France and residing in Flanders would have known English nor that a manuscript of the English version should be in Flanders. It should also be remembered that the *Lais* and the *Espurgatoire*, as well as the *Vie de Seinte Audree* mentioned in the note above, are all texts signed by a Marie, and all three of them are closely linked with England.[11]

One of the most important references to a poetess named Marie comes from a contemporary writer, Denis Piramus, author of *La Vie Seint Edmund le rei*:

He who composed *Partenopeus* and who put it into verse strove to write concerning that subject how, like fables and lies, the story resembles a dream, for it could never have been. So is he considered a good master and the verse is much loved and in the rich courts praised; and likewise lady Marie who wrote in rhyme and composed the verses of *lais* which are not at all true. And so is she much praised because of it and the rhyme loved everywhere; for all love it greatly and hold it dear—counts, barons, and knights. And so they love the text and have it read and take pleasure in it and cause it often to be retold.[12]

It is clear from this text that a writer named Marie, who composed *vers de lais*, was very popular in aristocratic circles, popular enough to be identified only as "dame Marie."[13] Given the fact that women writers were not exactly commonplace, is it likely that there were four different women all with the name Marie, composing texts in the late twelfth and early thirteenth century? It is true that the name was not uncommon, yet Denis Piramus' simple reference indicates that there was only one Marie famous for her *vers de lais*. In this regard it is interesting to note certain similarities in the prologues and epilogues of these four works. In the *Lais*, the *Fables*, and the *Seinte Audree*, the poetess makes it clear that she wishes to be known to posterity as the writer. In the epilogue to the *Fables*, the translator makes it clear that she does not wish someone else to claim her work: "It is possible that a number of clerics would ascribe to themselves my work. I do not wish anyone to claim it for himself; he who is forgotten or forgets himself works badly (in vain).[14] In all the works there is the theme of "remembrance" and in three of them the phrase *se oblie* is employed. It seems unlikely that one so interested in being remembered and in not wishing someone else to gain credit for her work would call herself only Marie, if she had any notion that there were other Maries with whom she might be confused.[15]

The last has not been written on this subject, and new evidence of significance may yet be found. But, based on the material available, it is probable that the Marie of the Harley prologue is the author of the twelve *lais* which follow and that she is the same poetess mentioned by Denis Piramus.[16] In all likelihood this same Marie is the translator of the *Espurgatoire Saint Patriz* and the *Fables*. And it may well be that she is the Marie who translated *La Vie Seinte Audree*.[17]

II   *Identity and Period of Activity*

Of primary importance to any discussion concerning the identity of Marie is the line from the *Fables* where the writer asserts that she is *de France*. Except for the generally rejected thesis of Winkler that the poetess is indicating that she is a member of the royal family, it has long been held that the phrase refers to the writer's place of birth. Moreover, since it would make little sense for an author writing in France to so identify herself, scholars have postulated with reason that the phrase denotes clearly that the poetess was residing elsewhere when she composed the text. One text of the *Fables* is found in BM manuscript Harley 978 (the same manuscript which contains the twelve *lais* preceded by the prologue where Marie is named), probably copied at the Abbey of Reading. Furthermore, the author claims to have translated her text from an English version which she attributes to King Alfred, famous for his interest in learning. In addition, the *Espurgatoire* was also made from a Latin text composed in England. Based upon these facts, scholars decided that Marie was a native French woman residing in England. Exactly where she was born in

France, and when, is not easy to determine. It is always difficult to distinguish clearly the author's language from scribal influence and, even if one admits that she was writing a form of the Norman dialect, it is quite possible that she was deliberately using the popular literary language of the English court in preference to her own native speech. Gaston Paris insisted that a reference to France in this period could only refer to the Ile-de-France and adjacent districts under its dominion, the French Vexin and the "Gâtenais français." [18] Although one cannot really be sure that the phrase *de France* refers so precisely to the twelfth century political reality and not to the kingdom of France in a larger, more general sense, it is widely accepted that Marie was probably a native of the Ile-de-France area or of Norman territory in close proximity. It should be pointed out that the geographical references in the *lais*, when not borrowed from Wace, are vague and give little evidence of personal acquaintance, except for the description of the setting in *Les Deus Amanz*, where the landscape accords with reality and may represent firsthand knowledge of this Norman locale. It is also significant that her knowledge of Southern England and South Wales seems in general more precise than her knowledge of the continent.

If it is reasonably certain that Marie was writing in England, it is nonetheless difficult to establish with precision the period of her literary activity. Mall and Warnke both concluded that the language of the *Fables* is that of the late twelfth century, scarcely differing from that of Wace's *Brut* (1155). But the uncertainty of linguistic evidence in precise dating is obvious. The most reliable evidence comes from the *Tractatus de Purgatorio Sancti Patricii* (signed with the initial *H* and identified with Henricus Salteriensis), the text which Marie translated as the *Espurgatoire.* It was believed for many years that the reference to St. Malachias, canonized in 1190, provided a sound basis for establishing a *terminus a quo* for the text. F. W. Locke has pointed out, however, that the author may well have given such an honorific title before the fact and that a sounder basis for dating the Latin text is provided by the dedication to Henry, Abbot of Sartis. Locke has established that the only abbot named Henricus held the title between 1208 and 1215. It is probable, then, that the dedication was made to him while he was abbot (abbot Henry died in 1216), thus establishing that Marie's translation postdates the year 1208.[19]

Little that is certain can be stated about the period when the various *lais* were written. One can place the *lais* with reasonable certainty in the second half of the twelfth century, but less reliable is the evidence which leads scholars to date the earliest of the *lais* around 1160.[20] The reference to "dame Marie" by Denis Piramus is late twelfth century at the earliest, and nothing guarantees that he was writing prior to the early thirteenth century. Other attempts to date the *lais* have centered around Marie's relationship to her contemporary Chrétien de Troyes, whose literary activity has been located generally between 1160 and 1190. Because of his popularity, it has been argued that the lack of any influence in Marie's work from Chrétien and her failure to refer to his work in any way indicate surely that the majority of the *lais* predate Chrétien's production.[21] It has also been alleged that there is evidence that Marie's work was known to Chrétien. It is pointed out that there is reference to the composition of a *lai* in the *Joie de la cort* episode in Chrétien's *Erec*. If one accepts Lucien Foulet's thesis that Marie was entirely responsible for any notion of the *lai* and that the "composition of a *lai*" was a literary topos created solely by her, then the passage in *Erec* is significant.[22] While most accept Marie's prominence in creating the vogue of using Breton sources, few hold that she alone created the concept. Thus the *Erec* passage merely shows the same oral influences at work on Chrétien.

If one cannot establish with certainty Marie's temporal relationship to Chrétien, it seems fairly certain that Ernest Hoepffner's study of Marie's use of geographical setting indicates a reliable *terminus a quo*.[23] In his important study of Marie's sources, Hoepffner demonstrated effectively that much of the geography in the *lais* is drawn from Wace's *Brut* (1155). But this in no way indicates how soon after 1155 she began to write.

Scholars have long seen a direct relationship between Gautier d'Arras' *Ille et Galeron* and Marie's *Eliduc*. Both treat the basic folk theme of the man with two wives and, although Ille's personality and feelings toward Ganor and Galeron do not exactly parallel Eliduc's, it is striking that Ille's father is named Eliduc. Furthermore, in one of the manuscripts (ms. *P*) the writer seems to reproach some earlier *lai* for its *mençonge*, and objects to the popularity its love treatment has among "the barons." [24] The moral rectitude of Ille has led many to see in Gautier's treatment a deliberate correction of Marie's text.[25] The relationship could be important, for, in the introduction, Gautier dedicates his text to Beatrice de Bourgogne, the wife of Emperor Frederick Barbarossa, crowned Empress on August 1, 1167. Since Beatrice died in 1185, it can be assumed that Gautier's work was composed sometime between 1167 and the date of her death.[26] If, then, Gautier's text did follow Marie's, one could date the *Eliduc* sometime prior to 1185. Other bits of evidence tend to confirm that the *lais* were composed before the end of the twelfth century. In *Le Fresne* Marie makes reference to the Archbishopric of Dol, the status of which was reduced by Innocent III in 1199, and *Lanval* is mentioned in the *roman, Guillaume de Dole*, written around 1200.[27] Hence, from the evidence adduced thus far, one can say only that Marie probably composed her *Lais* after 1155 and prior to 1200.

Having established that Marie composed her *Lais* in the second half of the twelfth century and that she was writing in England, it is perhaps now possible to identify the *nobles reis* to whom she dedicated the *Lais*. Most scholars have readily accepted that the king in question must be Henry II (1133–1189). Ezio Levi rejected this notion; he argued that the adjective *nobles* could scarcely be used for the man who had Thomas Becket murdered and was known for his stingy, calculating, utilitarian spirit. He proposed instead that Marie was referring to Henry's eldest son, Henry, known as the Young King, crowned in his own right in 1170. Did not the Young King actually reign for his father in Normandy, Maine and Anjou, and was he not noted among the poets for his courtliness and patronage? [28] But the argument can be used in both ways. Foulet derided the notion that anyone could really be considered king while the powerful Henry lived, and Ahlström pointed out that the Young King became hated and an object of contempt from the period of rebellion until his abject death in June, 1183.[29] Henry himself was a well-known patron and he spoke both Latin and French, a level of learning unusual for the period. Moreover, one cannot take literally adjectives used in a dedication intended to flatter.

If there has been general agreement concerning Henry II, such has not been the case for the "cunte Willalme" mentioned in the epilogue to the *Fables*. There were literally scores of counts named William and the suggestions concerning his identity have been numerous.[30] Many have seen in this count William Longsword, illegitimate son of Henry II, who died in 1226 at Salisbury castle. Warnke pointed out that the inscription on his tomb included the Latin phrase *Flos comitum Willelmus*, a phrase close to the one Marie herself used to describe the count (*Fleurs de chevalerie*).[31] Yet William Longsword was not really a count until after 1196, and it has been pointed out that the epithet was common. Probably the most likely suggestion is that made by Sidney Painter.[32] He noted that it was strange that Marie had not taken pains to distinguish her count by more than the commonest name in England. This, he argued, was because no one of the period would have mistaken which count she meant. Painter studied the Pipe Rolls between 1167 and 1175, where debts to the king were recorded, and discovered that there was one nobleman designated only as Earl William. This was William of Mandeville, Earl of Essex from 1167 to his death in 1189, close favorite of the king and the only nonroyal Englishman listed as a patron of letters in the *Bible* of Guiot de Provins. If these two dedications are accepted, then both the *Lais* and the *Fables* were composed prior to 1189, the year when both Henry II and William of Mandeville died.

Having limited as nearly as possible the dates of the three texts commonly attributed to Marie, is it possible to identify her with a historical personage? Several suggestions have been made, but there is almost no proof to confirm any of them. Wilhelm Hertz early suggested Marie de Champagne, the famous daughter of Louis VII and Eleanor of Aquitaine, alleged patroness of mundane literature and long considered important as a proponent of the ideas associated with "courtly love." The identification was never really accepted. Marie de Champagne had never lived in England and it is unlikely that she would have referred to herself as being *de France* after 1159, by which time she had become the Countess of Champagne. One might also point out that, had such a famous person written the *Lais*, there would surely be some reference to the fact in the texts of the period.[33]

The identification which has gained widest acceptance was made in 1905 by John Fox.[34] Basically, Fox's proposal represents the selection of a lady named Marie whose identity and qualifications would accord well with the information which can be obtained from the texts. Based on the idea that the poetess in question was born in France, lived in England, knew both Latin and

English, and dedicated works to Henry II and a Count William, Fox proposed that the lady in question might be a certain Mary, Abbess of Shaftesbury, natural daughter of Geoffrey Plantagenet, the father of Henry II. Records show that she was abbess in 1181, and a document from the time of Henry III indicates that a Mary, probably the same, was still abbess in 1215.[35] Not only would this Marie have known English and Latin, but the founder of the abbey at Shaftesbury was King Alfred, to whom she attributes the English version of the *Fables* which she translated.[36] The suggestion seemed all the more appealing because the Count William of the *Fables* had been identified frequently as William Longsword, natural son of Henry II and, hence, a nephew of the abbess. It should be emphasized, however, that there is little to recommend the identity of William Longsword with the count of the *Fables* and that no evidence has been found indicating that the abbess was ever involved in literary activity.[37]

Other hypotheses concerning the identity of the poetess are even more vague. Levi suggested that she might have been a nun from the abbey at Reading. Noted as a place of literary activity, the abbey owned the best manuscript of the *Fables* and *Lais*, and was a favorite residence of the Plantagenets. Levi contended that Marie's *lais* show an unusual knowledge of monastery life, but this assertion does not seem supported by the generalities found in the texts.[38] None of the suggestions made thus far is supported by evidence which is truly persuasive. For the moment, Marie must remain anonymous.

III *Marie's Intellectual Background*

In spite of this anonymity, a good deal can be stated concerning Marie's intellectual background. Because of her unusual level of learning, she was almost certainly from an aristocratic family, and even then few men or women could boast her background. That she knew Latin well is attested by her translation of the *Espurgatoire* and from her statement in the "Prologue" to the *Lais* that she had considered translating some text from Latin. If one believes her own remarks, she knew English well enough to translate the *Fables* from English. But beyond her linguistic accomplishments, there is considerable evidence that she was well acquainted with the classics. In the "Prologue" to the *Fables* Marie indicates her awareness of the Aesopic tradition, its Greek provenance, and subsequent translation into Latin. It is true that her reference to Priscian, the sixth-century grammarian, is not correct within the context in which he was writing, yet her citation is specific enough to indicate that she may well have had firsthand knowledge of the text and that the reference was more than the simple use of a name for the sake of citing an authority. Of the classical authors, there is ample evidence that she was well acquainted with the works of Ovid. In *Guigemar* she describes at length a mural painting depicting Venus, the goddess of love, condemning and burning a work of Ovid, undoubtedly the *Remedia Amoris*, which teaches one the means of resisting love. Further Ovidian influence from the *Metamorphoses* has been noted in *Les Deus Amanz* and *Laüstic*,[39] where Marie seems to have used the Ovidian and not the twelfth-century French version of the *Piramus and Tisbe* story.

From other references in the *Lais* it is also obvious that Marie was well versed in contemporary vernacular literature. Although there is no reference to indicate a knowledge of Chrétien's work, there is ample evidence to demonstrate Marie's familiarity with Wace's *Brut*, Geoffrey of Monmouth's *Historia regum Britanniae* (1135), Gaimar's *Estoire des Engleis*, a version of the *Tristan*, and probably the *Eneas*.[40] Hoepffner argues persuasively that Marie drew the geography and physical setting of several of her works directly from Wace's *Brut*. In an effort to create the atmosphere of a remote past in which the *lais* are placed, Marie borrowed archaic place names from the *Brut*, names associated with the Arthurian period. The *Chevrefoil* text discloses her knowledge of the Tristan legend or of a lost written version in which this episode, not found in extant texts, was present. If the specific *rapprochements* made with the *Eneas* are less persuasive, it is nonetheless clear that she was familiar with the same literary traditions as the *Eneas* author. There is a close similarity in the description of the growth of love and the analysis of the emotion, as well as in the physical and spiritual portraits of the characters. From her descriptions scholars have attempted to specify from which text they were borrowed. But it is difficult to ascertain from which sources she acquired such descriptions as that of the tomb in *Yonec*, which has been compared with the description of Hector's tomb in the *Roman de Troie*, or the famous tent in *Lanval* with the eagle above it. It is true that there is such a tent in the *Roman de Thebes*, yet the passages are not so similar that one

can establish a direct link between the texts. The artistic elabora-
tions in Marie (the description of the magic bed in *Guigemar*,
the storm at sea in *Eliduc*, the use of Fortune in *Guigemar*, the
personifications of Cupid, the description of the progress of love
and its effect on the lover in *Equitan, Guigemar, Eliduc,* etc.),
rather than being proof of borrowings from the *romans antiques*,
indicate that Marie, along with the other *romanciers* of the
period, was well versed in the traditions and techniques being
used by all the writers of the time. In addition to her knowledge
of contemporary vernacular literature, Marie displays an awareness of the oral literature of the period. Many of the *lais* are
based on folk literature which she commonly attributes to the
Bretons. While it is clear that many of the folk motifs are not
specifically Breton, several of them, such as the hunt of the white
hind or boar, the magic boat, the magic bed, and the earthly paradise, are most closely associated with the Breton tradition.

It is perhaps our distance from the period and our own sim-
plistic, progressive approach to the history of literature which
makes us wonder at the "sudden" appearance of such remarkable
writers as Marie de France and Chrétien de Troyes in a period
which we often characterize as the beginning of a "renaissance"
in French letters. One must remember that the florescence of vernacular literature springs from a society whose cultural and intellectual sophistication is amply attested by the Latin literature and
the monuments of art which are extant. Marie's breadth of learning, her charming, subtle literary style, sagacious mind, and
sensitive spirit are captivating. In spite of her anonymity and the
paucity of extant texts, Marie de France emerges from the distant
twelfth century as a literary figure of signal importance and
enduring worth.

CHAPTER 2

Intellectual Background of the
Twelfth Century

F ROM this sketch of Marie's literary background, one can glimpse the range of intellectual interest for which twelfth-century Europe is renowned. The term Renaissance, which has long been applied to the period, implies a greater intellectual activity than is found in the centuries immediately preceding.[1] Latin, of course, was the primary language of written expression, but in the twelfth century there is a rather pronounced upsurge in the use of the vernacular for a large variety of subjects. Latin is by no means replaced and should not be considered an artificial language foreign to the writers of the period. Latin and French are parallel forms of expression sharing the same literary, philosophical, and cultural heritage. Although there is not the same contrast between extant and nonextant materials in Latin, the broadening of intellectual horizons is clearly evident in the Latin literature of the period. Moreover, the development of the vernacular as a medium of literary expression indicates that an increasing number of laymen were capable of reading and were interested in a wide range of subjects.

I The Crusades

Many things contributed to the broadening of intellectual horizons. One of the foremost historical factors must have been the First (1096–1099) and Second (1147–1148) Crusades. For the first time, large numbers of Europeans came into contact with the Byzantine Empire and the vague "Saracen" world which lay beyond. The success of the First Crusade established a significant European presence in the Near East for two hundred years. Since the intellectual activity in the Middle Ages is inseparably linked to the aristocracy, the importance of the event can scarcely be over-emphasized. Scholars and literati were frequently grouped around aristocratic patrons who were culturally inclined, and, because of the intermarriage on an international level, intellectual ties were closer than distances and the difficulty of travel might suggest. Many families were now associated with, and had an interest in, an area of the world which was previously only a vague realm beyond the boundaries of the Christian sphere. Documents stemming from the Crusades bear witness to the European ignorance of Byzantine civilization, its amazement before the splendor of a city as large and commercially wealthy as Constantinople, and the singular difference of perspective between the two Christian worlds concerning the crusade expedition itself. The Byzantines knew the extent of the Arab world and had come to live with the political realities of the neighboring power. The Western Europeans had no such experience with the area. For the Europeans, the Crusades meant exposure to customs, political systems, styles of art, and modes of thought different from their own. One can see Byzantine influence in the architectural features of some twelfth-century military fortifications and in certain churches.[2] There is also a noticeable awakening of interest in Greek traditions radiating from Byzantium. Literarily, a number of romances were written which have, primarily or in part, a Byzantine setting. And the First Crusade inspired the vast cycle of poems which tell of the fabulous origins of Godefroy of Bouillon, the conquests of Antioch and Jerusalem, and subsequent wars against the "courtly" Saracen leader, Saladin.

II *The Normans*

Of great importance to the extension of European horizons was the spread and growth of Norman influence.[3] The Normans in Sicily had considerable contact with Constantinople and Germany throughout the period, and the rise of Henry Plantagenet established the Normans in England and most of France. Henry was the son of the Duke of Anjou, Geoffrey Plantagenet, and Mathilda, the daughter of Henry I and rival of King Stephen for the throne of England. After more than a decade of intermittent war, Mathilda agreed to withdraw her claim to the throne in exchange for Stephen's agreement that her son, Henry, would be his successor, in the event that he should die without heir. Stephen died less than a year later in 1154 and Henry, already Duke of Anjou and Normandy, was crowned Henry II of England (1154–1189). In 1152, just two months after the annulment of her marriage of fifteen years to Louis VII of France, Henry had married Eleanor of Aquitaine. A man of intelligence and great courage, Henry gained control over Brittany in 1158 and, by 1159, he not only ruled England, but controlled virtually all of Western France from the Somme River to the Pyrenees. Vigorous and perceptive, Henry was the most powerful monarch of his day. Through the marriages of his three daughters, he acquired ties with the rulers of Saxony, Sicily, and Castile. His organizational genius and foresight led to the creation of a vast judicial and chancery procedure, including a detailed system of records and accounts.

III   Cathedral Schools and Learning

A vital factor in the intellectual awakening in France and England was the role played by the cathedral schools, the real centers of twelfth-century learning and the forerunners of the universities.[4] Here one can see an increased interest in the authors of antiquity. The schools at Chartres, Orléans (particularly in literature), Beauvais, and Tours were especially prominent. Less is known about the cathedral schools in England, but Canterbury was unsurpassed there as a center of learning. Archbishop Theobald (1138–1161), who was trained at Bec, gathered many learned men about him, as did Thomas Becket, his successor. The upsurge in interest in classical letters is manifest in the Latin as well as the vernacular literature of the period. Interest was especially keen in Virgil, the magician and necromancer, renowned for his prophetic forecast of the birth of Christ (the famous "Fourth Eclogue"), and for the wisdom revealed in the allegorical interpretations of the Aeneid. Equally important in the twelfth century was the interest in Ovid, whose preoccupation with love matched the rising philosophical interest in the subject. Some of the earliest translations into the vernacular were drawn from the Metamorphoses and there are numerous passages in the literature of the period which indicate influence from the Ars Amatoria and the Remedia Amoris. Particularly appreciated was Ovid's description of the psychological stages of love and the physical and mental transformations of the lover.

It is a characteristic of the mediaeval scholar that his interest in Latin antiquity did not stem from a desire to comprehend another society, to recreate the historical and cultural development of that society for its own sake in an effort to understand a period of history with different philosophical and social values from his own. The historical perspective of the period was rooted in the philosophical idea that Reality lay behind the events and phenomena of physical existence. To understand the true meaning of history was to perceive the importance of events in a providential perspective. In a sense, the Fall of Man and the Birth of Christ were the two historical events of real significance and divided the history of man into two distinct periods. As a result, historical events gained significance when viewed in terms of Christ's coming and in the perspective of the final judgment. Similarly, literary works were read for the "wisdom" which lay hidden within the text. Ovid was not perceived within the historical and ethical framework of the Roman civilization, but in a mediaeval philosophical and ethical context. Ovid's description of the development of love is found again and again in the *romans* of the period. The process became standard for all the great passionate loves— Pyramus and Thisbe, Aeneas and Dido, Tristan and Iseult. And, essentially, Ovid's analysis of love is reiterated in religious treatises on love in attempting to describe the effects of cupidity and the suffering (*passio*) endured when desire remains unfulfilled. In the word "love" is the paradox of the human condition seen in the historical and philosophical perspective of the Middle Ages. In that single, ambivalent word lie the epitome of sin and death, the pinnacle of goodness and salvation. The entire history of man in the truly significant sense is summed up in the gamut of human intentions and actions covered by the word "love." It is no accident that the mediaeval poets loved to juxtapose *l'amor* and *la mort* in rhyme, to play on the sound and develop the irony inherent in the mediaeval analogy. In the literature of the period and in the philosophical and theological treatises, love becomes the dominant subject. Thus, traces of Ovid in language and thought are found everywhere. But it is an Ovid seen through mediaeval eyes. He had described an aspect of love which the mediaeval man perceived and used in his own framework of moral and ethical values. This is true of the other classical writers who became favorites in the twelfth century. Horace, Cicero, Sallust, Seneca, and Terence were all appreciated more as moralists and sages than as literary figures exemplifying certain genres.

The mediaeval writer delighted in the passages of wisdom (within the mediaeval philosophical perspective) which he found in their writings.[5]

Every area of social and intellectual concern seems to show the influence of greater activity. The church went through a period of reform and self-scrutiny in the late eleventh century, the monasteries underwent the Cluniac reform and implementation of a more stringent observance of the Benedictine rule, while the monastic movement of the twelfth century underwent a spiritual transformation toward a more contemplative mode under the influence of St. Anselm and St. Bernard. At the same time, the feudal world was gradually being transformed. The growth of larger governmental units reduced enterprising individual activity of a bellicose nature, while the increased social stability saw the gradual rise in importance of the town and commercial interests.

IV *Henry II and the English Court*

But in describing the intellectual growth of an entire period, one risks losing sight of the intimate sphere in which the Renaissance in letters took place. Though international in scope and covering a wide geographical area, certain factors give the intellectual community of the period an intimate flavor. First of all, the aristocracy of importance was a relatively small class of people dotting the map of Europe. Because of intermarriage and the contact related to political affairs, these widely scattered enclaves remained in rather close intellectual proximity. In a sense there is a similarity in the situation of the church. The most important sees often included the clergymen who were most prominent, either because of their family ties or their intellectual and administrative accomplishments. Here again, though widely scattered, one finds close contact among those who have similar interests. The unity is further tightened by the close political and family relationship between the aristocracy and the church. From an intellectual standpoint, this group is even more narrowly defined by educational limits. Few clergymen and very few aristocrats became educated well enough to take an active interest in letters and learning in general. Thus the intellectual Renaissance of the period is not really national or international in a democratic sense. Essentially, the vast territory of France or England, the people of the countryside and towns, did not contribute to the intellectual awakening. It is the contribution of small groups of men and private individuals. Because of this fact, the role of the literary patron is exceedingly important. It is no accident that the bishops and members of the aristocracy who were interested in letters gathered about them learned clerks capable of furthering these interests. This is the situation one finds at the court of Henry II.

Henry was raised in the household of his uncle, Earl Robert of Gloucester, a man noted for his patronage of literature and for his large library. To him are dedicated two of the most formative historical texts of the period, William of Malmesbury's *De Rebus gestis regum Anglorum* (*ca.* 1125) and Geoffrey of Monmouth's *Historia regum Britanniae* (*ca.* 1135), both important for the Arthurian material found in them, for the growing interest being shown in British history, and, Geoffrey's text especially, for its role as a forerunner of the *roman de Bretagne*. Henry's own educational training was, from all evidence, exceptional; but, because of his personal reputation (his conduct did not reflect the qualities scholars usually admire in an enlightened man of letters), some have not accorded him the place he probably deserves in the literary Renaissance. It is true that one cannot see in his own career any of the ideals of chivalry found in the literature of the period. Both Wace and Giraldus Cambrensis complain that Henry never really paid them all that he promised, a charge which, when added to his shrewd, practical, calculating nature, has caused him to be considered parsimonious, the opposite of the ideal of *largesse*. Certainly his implication in the scandalous murder of Thomas Becket and the tumultuous dissension caused by the rebellion of his wife and sons and his subsequent wars against them make it difficult to see in him a man with strong cultural and literary interests. Moreover, he was criticized by contemporaries for his debauchery, especially for his suspected relationship with Louis VII's daughter, Alis, betrothed to his son, Richard, and kept in England by Henry in spite of requests that she be returned. But one must remember that this is a different age. Too often the refinement in the *roman* is assumed to reflect a softening in manners in this period. It should be remembered that the manners and ideals presented in the texts are placed in an ideal setting of long ago. They probably reflect far more an abstract ideal of behavior than any reality of the present. This seems confirmed when one considers a text such as Villehardouin's *Con-*

queste de Constantinople, which does not seek to create a fictive reality. Although personal honor, faith, and loyalty in oaths measure the man throughout the text, it is evident that this society of knights differs greatly in tone from that shown in the *romans.* Coarse, shrewd, violent, and ambitious, Henry was a man of his time and obviously had the qualities needed to survive and succeed. Yet one must not forget that he differed from most of his contemporaries in his intellectual interests and training. Peter of Blois had much admiration for Henry's intelligence and level of learning. According to the royal chaplain, Henry read privately, enjoyed learned conversation, and was acquainted with all the languages from the English Channel to the Jordan. The scholars and writers in his court or associated with it were among the most famous of the period. Theologians such as Ailred de Rievaulx, John of Salisbury, and William Conches either dedicated works to Henry or were associated with his family. A number of historians were commissioned by him or dedicated work to him: Among them are Giraldus Cambrensis, one of his royal chaplains, Wace, Walter Map, Henry of Huntingdon, Jordan Fantosme, and the Benoit who took over the *Roman de Rou* from Wace. In the works dedicated to Henry one finds theology, science, some vernacular poetry, and much contemporary history in both Latin and French.

But of significance here for literature is the close relationship between histories such as Wace's *Brut* and the subsequent flourishing of the *roman.* It has become increasingly clear in recent years that the Anglo-Normans and Normans were leaders in the development of the vernacular as a literary medium.[6] The trend began earlier in the reign of Henry I. Early in the twelfth century, the *Voyage of Saint Brendan* was translated into the vernacular (the earliest French text in octosyllabic rhymed couplets, the form commonly used in the *romans*) for Queen Maud, who was married to Henry I in 1100. Also associated with the English court was Philippe de Thaon, whose allegorized *Bestiaire,* dedicated to Adeliza of Louvain, enjoyed great popularity [7] and was later rededicated to Henry II's famous queen, Eleanor. Sometime just prior to 1140, Geoffrey Gaimar wrote his *Estoire des Engleis,* drawn from Geoffrey of Monmouth's *Historia.* His is the first of the Brut-type histories done in the French language and became the standard type of chronicle for the next three hundred years.

During the reign of Henry II (1154–1189) and Eleanor, the vernacular truly came into its own as a literary language both in England and on the continent.[8]

V *Vernacular Literature and Marie*

Considering that Marie was writing sometime between 1160 and 1210, it is perhaps appropriate to summarize briefly the kinds of literature being written in the vernacular at the time.[9] From what has been said thus far, it is apparent that a number of important chronicles and histories with a romance flavor had been rewritten in French just prior to the period of Marie's literary activity. Also popular from an earlier period was the saint's life, a type of literature which is itself not unrelated to the *roman* and which continued to thrive. One need only mention the *Vie de Saint Alexis*, the *Voyage de Saint Brendan* (which many consider more romance than saint's life), the lives written by Clemence of Barking and Wace, as well as the excellent contemporary work of Guernes de Pont-Sainte-Maxence, *La Vie de Saint Thomas le martyr* (*ca.* 1174). Throughout the period there was keen interest in scientific and didactic material (such as bestiaries, volucraries, and lapidaries), evident not only in the composition of such texts, but by the presence of such materials in some of the *romans*.[10] Never given enough attention, either editorially or in an interpretive sense, are the biblical commentaries, such as Sanson de Nantuil's translation and commentary of the Proverbs of Solomon made for Alice de Condet around 1150, or Peter of Blois's Latin *Compendium in Job*, written at the request of King Henry II. Such materials are by no means rare, but they are too often neglected.

More difficult to assess is the popularity of the *chanson de geste*. For the most part, scholars believe that the *chanson de geste* had already passed its period of greatest popularity. However, *chansons de geste* continued to appear; others, if they had previously been popular, were still being reworked or recopied. In fact, it is true that the large majority of texts classified as *chansons de geste* can only be substantiated in the twelfth and thirteenth centuries. It is interesting to note that much of the William of Orange cycle was probably composed in the decades just prior to Marie's own work.

Finally, in the midst of this broad literary activity, the *roman* itself developed. Among the earliest texts are the French versions of ancient Latin texts: the shorter Ovidian texts, *Narcissus* and *Piramus et Tisbe*, as well as the *Roman d'Eneas* and *Roman de Thebes*, all from the decades just after 1150. At one time much was made over the *Roman de Thebes* as a transition text between the *chanson de geste* and the *roman*. It was noted that the *roman* was closely related to the spirit of the *chanson de geste*, but that one could see the trend toward the *roman* in the slightly developed love element, not at all present in the Latin text. In the *Eneas*, which was thought to follow, one could see an increasing development toward the *roman*. Whereas the love between Dido and Eneas was already present in the Latin text, the French writer added some sixteen hundred lines in developing a love relationship between Lavinia and Eneas which was not present in the Latin. One is no longer certain that the *Thebes* precedes the *Eneas* in the chronology of the period. Both texts undoubtedly reflect the influence from Ovid in rhetoric and in substance, as well as the previously mentioned growing interest in the subject of love.[11]

In addition to these translations from Latin (and others somewhat later), there are a number of *romans* which appear sometime after 1160 and are contemporary with Marie's works. Among them one finds the Tristan story, Arthurian romances, and works with Breton and Byzantine settings. Some have dated the *Tristan* of Thomas around 1165 (others as late as 1180–1190), and it is often associated with the English court. Hue de Rotelande's *Ipomedon* and its sequel, *Protheselaus*, done for Gilbert Fitz-Baderon, Lord of Monmouth, may have been written in the 1180's. Some would date the *Floire et Blancheflor* as early as 1160. Marie's relationship with Gautier d'Arras and Chrétien de Troyes has already been discussed. Certainly there is no real evidence to support the view that Marie's *Lais* predate their period of activity. It is probably more reasonable to consider them contemporaries.

In the past scholars have tended to view Marie's work in the light of a nineteenth- and twentieth-century aesthetic perspective. Professor Foulet judged that Marie's real interest in translating the *Espurgatoire* was not because of the religious material or the saint's life, but because the adventure of Owein appealed to her.[12] Similarly, scholars have seen Marie's *Fables* and *Espurgatoire* as later works in life, suitable for one who had perhaps retired to a religious life. Implicit in this view is the judgment that didactic literature and "allegory" (in the modern use of the term) are inferior artistically to an "original" work of art such as the *Lais*.[13] What is striking is how clearly Marie's work accords with the different types of literature then appearing and with the spirit of the period. In the *Lais* one finds the subject of love treated in many contexts in a form related to the *roman* and within a didactic framework developed in the "Prologue." In her *Fables* one can see the attraction to a clearly didactic and symbolic literature much in vogue. Philosophically, the lessons contained in the individual fables reflect the values of the period seen in both the *roman* and the *chanson de geste*. In the *Espurgatoire,* which relates to the interest in saints' lives as well as to the *roman,* the principal theme of faith in God parallels closely one of the primary themes of the *chanson de geste,* while the nature of Owein's adventure is not unlike those of the heroes of the *roman.* In form, content, and variety Marie's work reflects the trends and interests which mark the twelfth-century literary Renaissance.

CHAPTER 3

Fables

S OMETIME in the second half of the twelfth century, Marie de France translated a collection of fables destined to enjoy considerable popularity. In all there are some twenty-three manuscripts extant dating from the thirteenth, fourteenth, and fifteenth centuries, and copies have been located in London, Oxford, Cambridge, York, Paris, Brussels, and Rome. Among the extant manuscripts is the complete text found in the British Museum Harley manuscript 978, in which the *Lais* are found copied in the same hand.

Marie claims to have drawn her text from an English version translated by King Alfred from a Latin collection. No English version prior to Marie is extant, but it is generally agreed that she did translate an English text, although one composed long after King Alfred's time.[1] It is curious that, in spite of the popularity of the genre, no Latin manuscript prior to Marie has come down which resembles her collection. This has caused scholars to hypothesize that the English translator may have put the collection together himself, drawing eclectically from various sources. The first forty fables are based on the collection known as the *Romulus Nilantii*, while others (67, 72, 75, 82, 85, 86, 88, 89, and 102) are from the vulgate *Romulus*. Several of the fables are of Eastern origin, (52, 57, 73, and 100), and the remainder are difficult to assess. Among them are peasant tales (41–45, 48, 56, 64, 83, 84, 94, and 95) and monks' tales (49, 53–55, and 99) resembling the *fabliau* and which may derive from an oral tradition.

I   *The Fable as a Genre*

The heterogeneous nature of Marie's collection points up the difficulty of defining the genre, of delineating it from other forms of the short narrative, a problem not unrelated to defining the nature of the *lai* (see Chapter 5). As Professor Smith notes, Aphthonius (300 A.D.) was the first to define the fable.[2] He based his definition on the kind of actors (animals, men, inanimate objects, etc.) involved: those employing men, those in which unintelligent creatures are found, and those in which both men and intelligent creatures play a role. Basically, the definition of Aphthonius is descriptive and does not provide the basis for distinguishing between certain fables employing men and other short narrative forms. Smith offers his own definition, based on the distinction between mimetic and symbolic content: ". . . a fable is a short tale, obviously false, devised to impress, by the symbolic representation of human types, lessons of expediency and morality."[3] The key element in Smith's definition, that which allows him to draw the line between a fable and a *fabliau*, is the "symbolic representation" and the didactic intent which he deems necessary to the fable. Following his definition, Professor Smith finds three basic types of fable: "(1) fables in which the actors, some or all (with the setting), and the action are both symbolic; (2) those in which only the actors (with the setting) are symbolic, while the action is that of typical human beings; and (3) those in which only the action is symbolic, while the actors consist of typical human beings."[4] Thus, it is not significant whether the actors are men or animals, but only whether there is a symbolic level inherent either in the actors or their actions.

The analysis is not without its problems, in that certain tales included within fable collections by mediaeval authors can only be classified as *fabliaux* or "observations of nature" under Smith's system. That is, when a tale contains human beings as the actors and their actions are typically human without apparent symbolic intent, it is a *fabliau*-type tale. Likewise, when a tale includes animals as the actors and their actions are suitable to the animals involved, without apparent symbolic intent, it becomes a form of short narrative in which the author is making a realistic observation on the animal world. While it is true that the vast majority of tales included in fable collections contain the recognizable symbolic and didactic elements set forth in Professor Smith's definition, it is nonetheless questionable whether those tales which do not conform to the definition should be excluded from the genre. Perhaps the problem lies in Professor Smith's aesthetic distinction between the mimetic and symbolic. In the modern aesthetic perspective it is natural to distinguish between a story which relates an interesting anecdote for its own sake and a tale where the action represents something other than what is apparent and which transcends the anecdote to a level of general human truth. From a mediaeval viewpoint, however, the anecdote and characters involved are rarely individualized in such a manner as to give the impression that the tale concerns specific people interesting because of the unique situation involved, etc. Even in the tales where the animals act as animals and the people as people, the anecdotes illustrate basic types responding to situations confronting them. Invariably, even when the actions are not symbolic and the moral not explained, the tales illustrate general human truths from which the lessons are evident, if not stated. In those animal tales where the fox acts in a way clearly appropriate to the animal itself (i.e., where he is not given specifically human traits), one still sees him shrewdly duping the other beasts. It is clearly not the personal observation of the author from a rustic scene. Even without the earmarkings of human symbolic action and the explicit moral, the mediaeval reader would have undoubtedly perceived the broad applicability in human and moral terms. In fact, it is likely that it was his aesthetic perspective which motivated him to see certain tales which we might call *fabliaux* or animal stories as fables.

The abstract definition which Professor Smith draws relates to the formal distinction we make between symbolic and mimetic action. It is a distinction based on an abstract analysis of form and neglects the unity of the substance. There is little evidence to indicate that the author carefully chose the actions based on their mimetic or symbolic appropriateness to the actors. Rather, the actions of personified inanimate objects, animals, and people are all appropriate to the situation and general truth which they serve to illustrate. The reality involved is not mimetic but poetic. It is an intellectual world in which mimesis plays an insignificant role. Where appropriate human and animal actions serve to demonstrate the point, they are used. When actions appropriate to men are assigned to beasts, it is because they are necessary to the development of the truth involved. Similarly, men are caused to act in ways which have no basis in real human behavior, but serve to illustrate human conduct in a general sense (Cf. The Man, the Boy, and the Ass). Professor Smith's analysis is helpful in perceiving the mechanism employed in most fables, but it is probably the broad descriptive definition of Aphthonius which comes nearer to the reality.[5] If a mediaeval author places what we would call *fabliaux* or *exempla* in his fable collection, it is probably because the symbolic or mimetic nature of the actors and their actions was less significant to him than his perception of the text's meaning and its substantive relationship to the other tales.

II *The Structure of the Collection*

Marie's collection comprises a "Prologue" of forty lines, a series of 102 fables, and a twenty-line "Epilogue." The "Prologue" bears a resemblance to the "Prologue" of the *Lais* in development and intent. In the first six lines Marie states that those who know how to write should put their care in the good books and writings of the *philosophe*, who wrote *par moralité* that those who read their works might benefit from them (vv. 7–11). In verses 12–16 and 17–26 Marie develops the thesis just presented by two examples: Both Romulus and Aesop wrote for didactic reasons. She further emphasizes that the tales are not merely *fable de folie*, but contain *philosophie* in the *essamples* which follow the tale. In lines 29–40 Marie explains that she is translating the text at the behest of one "who is the flower of chivalry" (v. 31) and that she will not spare *travail e peine* in her endeavor, a phrase reminiscent of lines in the prologue to *Yonec*. It is in the "Epilogue," discussed earlier, that Marie identifies herself, names her patron, and makes reference to the work of *reis Alvrez*.

The fables themselves vary in length from approximately ten lines to a few which exceed one hundred, the majority ranging from twenty to sixty. In each fable the narrative procedure is very similar. The basic situation is developed in a short narrative which leads to the crucial moment in the text, often articulated dramatically by a short dialogue between the principal actors. The process is not unlike the *Lais* themselves. It is the narrative portion of the text which places the actors in circumstances which will be resolved in the brief dialogue. In the dialogue, the nature and conduct of the actors are revealed. Here the basic human truth being illustrated becomes manifest.[6] Following the narrative resolution, there is nearly always an *essample* of four to eight lines in which the moral lesson of the text is made explicit.

In the collection there are basically three kinds of actors: animals, people, and personified inanimate objects. Nearly sixty of the fables include only animals, in eighteen men are the actors, and in nearly twenty there is a mixture of men and animals. In addition, there are several texts in which animals and objects interact, a couple where people and objects are the actors, and one in which the characters are all objects.

In the fables where only animals are involved, one finds the animals acting according to their natures and endowed with rational characteristics suitable to the roles they play within the animal hierarchy. The society is modeled on the feudal structure of the Middle Ages and mirrors the moral values of the period. Certain animals are more prominent than others and tend to acquire predictable characteristics. The animals commonly found are the lion (11), the wolf (19), the fox (12), the lamb or sheep (9), the dog (9), the mouse (5), the eagle (6), the hawk (5), the crow or raven (6), and many other animals found in one, two, or three fables. As one would expect, the hierarchy resembles the one found in the *Roman de Renard* and the lion, wolf, and fox have their traditional characteristics. The lion is the king of the animal world, castigated for his ravenous appetite (as in XI, "De leone venante," where he keeps all the spoils for himself), symbol of waning power when death is near (XIV, "De leone aegroto"), and as an example of how the powerful need the support of the weak (XVI, "De leone et mure"). In the classic fable which probably helped inspire the *Roman de Renard* (LXVIII, "De leone infirmo"), he witnesses the craftiness of the fox and presides over the flaying of the wolf, while in "De leone aegrotante" (LXX), he is completely taken in by the fox's clever sophistry. The fox himself invariably plays the role of the deceiver, but occasionally is deceived himself as in "De vulpe et gallo" (LX), in which the cock urges him cleverly to shout defiance at the chasing peasants, thereby effecting his own escape, and in "De vulpe et columba" (LXI), where the dove extricates herself from danger by a clever remark. The wolf commonly appears as a breaker of oaths, a brutal and ravenous beast (especially opposite the lamb or sheep), but thwarted often by the fox, by men, once by the hedgehog, and by his enemy, the dog. In several fables another hierarchy is evident, that involving the birds. Here the eagle is king and the hawk his villainous seneschal (Cf. LXII, "De aquila et accipitre et columbis," LXXX, "De aquila et accipitre et ardua").

[38]

Fables

Among the fables in which there is interplay between animals and humans, men play varying roles. In some fables men are present as rational creatures, clearly outside the animal world, creatures that the animals avoid and fear. In others, the animals and men communicate and associate, both belonging to the same order. Such is the case in "De leone et homine" (XXXVII), where a man and lion are companions and compare their lineage. A similar case is found in "De simiarum imperatore" (XXXIV), where two men comment differently concerning the kingdom set up by the monkeys.

It should be noted that there is a certain resemblance here between the reality presented in the *Lais* and that of the fables. In the *Lais* one perceives a poetic reality in which the natural and supernatural join to form a new order in which such distinctions lose their significance (Cf. Chapter 8). Similarly, one finds a characteristic disregard in the fables for what is possible and impossible in realistic terms. The actors in the fables are not fettered by a mimetic concern for what is realistically feasible. It is an independent poetic reality in which animals, humans, and inanimate objects interact as equals, limited only by the roles they are assigned in the tale.

Also similar to the narrative procedure in the *Lais* and in other short narrative collections is the pairing of fables which concern analogous situations. Fables XVII, "De ranarum rege," and XIX, "De columbarum rege," both concern the relationship of ruler and subjects, while fables XLIV, "De muliere et proco eius," and XLV, "Iterum de muliere et proco eius," present different perspectives of the adulterous wife. Other instances include "De rustico orante et equum petente" (LIV) and "De corvo et pullo eius" (XCII), treating the instruction of the young, and "De homine et uxore litigiose" (XCIV) and "De uxore mala et marito eius" (XCV), which develop situations involving cantankerous and contrary wives. Other pairings could be cited in which the actors are different, but where the moral theme of the text contrasts with or parallels what precedes or follows.

Finally, as Professor Francis has noted, the morality of the fables clearly reflects the feudal ethos of the twelfth century and, one might add, the ethical values found in the *Lais*.[7] The consequences of the breaking and keeping of oaths, the results of serving evil masters or associating with bad companions, the pernicious effect of self-seeking, and the misfortune that comes from pride or envy—these and many other themes common to the literature of the period are found in the collection. Particularly striking in reference to the *Lais* is the moral drawn from the well-known fable, LXVIII, "De leone infirmo," in which the wolf accuses the fox of disloyalty for not being present during the lion's sickness. Overhearing the accusation, the fox enters the scene and announces that he had been seeking a cure for the lion's illness, a search successfully concluded when a physician from Salerno prescribed that the lion must don the skin of a newly flayed wolf. In the fox's speech to the flayed wolf and in the moral of the fable, one is reminded of the proverbial comments in *Le Fresne* and *Equitan*. In the fable Marie writes, *Tels purchace le mal d'altrui, / que cil meïsme vient sur lui, / si cum li lous fist des gupil, / que il voleit metre a eissil* (vv. 57–60). Marie concludes *Equitan* with a strikingly similar passage: *Ici purreit ensample prendre: / Tel purcace le mal d'autrui / Dunt le mal [tut] vert sur lui* (vv. 308–10). Given the similarities in narrative style and form and the resemblance in ethical values, in spite of the difference between the genres, it is not difficult to see in Marie the author of both texts.

CHAPTER 4

Espurgatoire Saint Patriz

THE *Espurgatoire*, probably translated early in the thirteenth century, is now generally conceded to be the last of the three works usually attributed to Marie. Marie's translation is one of a number done in French of this version of the legend and is extant in only one manuscript, BN fr. 25407, a late thirteenth-century transcription.

I *Legend of St. Patrick's Purgatory*

The legend of St. Patrick's Purgatory emerges from the lore surrounding the revelation of Purgatory to St. Patrick. The actual site of the Purgatory is thought to have been on Station Island (in Lough Derg), formerly called Insula Purgatoria. In pre-Christian lore it had been the home of the powerful sorcerers famous in Irish myth, the Tuatha da dannan. St. Patrick preached in the area and had a monastery and church built there. However, he met with much resistance among the inhabitants, who often refused to believe his description of the afterlife and who feared reprisal from the local spirits. Disturbed by his lack of success, St. Patrick prayed to Jesus for a clear sign of God's omnipotence. Jesus appeared to the saint, blessed him, and consecrated a Bible and staff for his office. When St. Patrick arose, the stone on which he had been kneeling lifted up. He descended a long staircase and witnessed the pains of those in Purgatory as well as the blessed happiness of those in the Earthly Paradise awaiting entrance to Heaven. St. Patrick had a wall built around the pit and gave the key to the Prior of the monastery. Anyone who could spend the night in the pit and survive the ordeal would emerge purged of his sins. People made pilgrimage from far and near to visit Purgatory. Many who entered never returned. Those who survived recounted their experience and it was recorded in writing. The story of St. Patrick's

Purgatory was extremely popular in mediaeval literature for over three hundred years and there are numerous references to it in subsequent literature.

II *Henry of Saltrey's Version*

In her *Espurgatoire*, Marie translates the Latin work of a twelfth-century Cistercian monk, generally believed to have been Henry of Saltrey. Henry's text is unique in that it relates the specific adventures of a certain knight named Owein, who had survived the ordeal of St. Patrick's Purgatory. Essentially, Henry's *Tractatus de Purgatorio Sancti Patricii* is the story of Owein's experiences in Purgatory, the narration of how Purgatory was discovered serving principally as a background for the knight's adventure. Henry seems to have been the first to relate the adventure of the Irish knight, for contemporaries who discuss the legend of St. Patrick's Purgatory do not mention the adventure of Owein.[1] According to Henry, he heard the story from Gilbert of Louth, who had been sent by Gervase, the Abbot of Louth, into Ireland to acquire lands for the establishment of a monastery. Since Gilbert did not know the language, the king attached the knight Owein to him as an interpreter. Gilbert and the monks sent with him founded the monastery, Owein acting as Lay Brother. Gilbert remained some two and a half years before returning to England, where he became the Abbot of Basingwerk by 1159. Undoubtedly he learned of St. Patrick's Purgatory and of Owein's experience there from the knight himself. Gilbert retold the story often. Henry of Saltrey heard the tale and retold it to the Abbot of Sartis, who urged him to put the tale into writing. Henry's version became very popular, passing from monastery to monastery. From the surviving manuscripts it is obvious that a number of episodes were added to the original tale.

III *Manuscripts of the Latin Text*

There are more than thirty extant manuscripts which contain Henry of Saltrey's version of the legend.[2] Studies of the manuscript tradition indicate that the manuscripts fall into two basic groups. Although the specific manuscript which Marie used is not among those extant, it is clear that her text derived from the less numerous of the two groups, represented principally by three manuscripts in the British Museum (Harley 3846, Arundel 292, and Cotton, Tiberius E. i), and the versions in Bamberg and Utrecht. In fact, all but seventy-six lines of her text, excluding those lines added by Marie herself in the prologue and epilogue, can be found in the manuscripts of this group. The following outline which Professor Jenkins made illustrates the format of Marie's text and its relationship to the classes of manuscripts: [3]

Marie de France	Number of Lines	Latin Mss.
Lines 1–8	8	Marie's Prologue
9–2062	2054	Harley 3846
2063–70	8	Royal 13 B viii
2071–2116	46	Arundel 292
2117–84	68	Royal 13 B viii
2185–2296	112	Arundel 292
2297–2302	6	Marie's Epilogue

Lines 9–2062 represent the basic narrative of Gilbert de Basingwerk concerning the founding of St. Patrick's Purgatory and Owein's adventure. The remaining 240 lines contain brief tales, probably added later, which contribute to the basic theme of men harassed by demons.

IV *Résumé of Marie's* Espurgatoire

Marie begins the text with a short prologue of her own, followed by the prologue of Henry of Saltrey. Henry relates that he is composing the work at the request of a *prozdum* and that he wishes to do it as a lesson to men, to make them serve and fear God. St. Gregory gave many examples of what happens to men's souls both in and out of the body in order to give them greater devotion. Men's souls are taken by angels or devils after death. Sometimes the soul has visions of what will happen before death and sees all manner of horrible or pleasant things. Many wish to know what becomes of the soul after it leaves the body. One can be sure that the nonsinner does not suffer pains and that a bad life does not follow one that was good. Both St. Gregory and St. Augustine speak of this. Souls are kept in greater or lesser pain according to their lives. It is written that those chosen by God wait in torment in Purgatory until deliverance. Some men are shown these visions before death.

The second St. Patrick was a great man for whom God accomplished many miracles. He often preached to the people about the horrors of Hell and joys of service to God in order to lead them from the wrong path.

An old man once came to him to confess his sins. After confession, St. Patrick questioned whether or not he had ever killed a man. The old man answered that he knew of at least five men that he had killed on the spot, but that he did not realize that homicide was a sin. He is told of the gravity of such a sin and is exceedingly penitent.

Often people refused to believe St. Patrick's warnings, because they could not see the torments and joys with their own eyes. Disturbed by this, St. Patrick prayed and Jesus appeared to him, gave him the Gospel and the *bastun Deu,* which he was to carry with him when preaching to the people. God then led him to a deserted place and showed him a deep hole, which was the entrance to Purgatory. Men who were of firm belief and had confessed could enter Purgatory and witness the joys of the elect and the torments of the damned. If they could remain there an entire day and night and return, they would be cleansed of all their sins.

St. Patrick had an abbey built on the spot and enclosed the hole with a wall, so that only those who were permitted could enter the pit. Now St. Patrick was happy, believing that many would be saved by being able to see these things for themselves. The place came to be known as St. Patrick's Purgatory.

After St. Patrick's death, many men entered there: Some were lost and others returned. Those who wished to enter first confessed to the Bishop. If he were unable to dissuade them from the ordeal, he would lead them in two weeks of fasting and prayer in preparation. Finally, mass was said and the sinner was told what to expect in the pit. If he succeeded, he would remain with the monks for two weeks, during which time his story would be related and recorded in writing.

In the time of King Steven there was a knight named Owein who came to the abbey desiring to enter Purgatory and to be cleansed of his sins. After several attempts to dissuade him from his purpose, and after the customary period of preparation, Owein was allowed to enter the pit. Once in the pit, he made his way to a magnificent edifice which resembled a cloister. He was welcomed by fifteen persons dressed in white. They explained to him that he would soon be approached by horrible demons who would try to persuade him to put his faith in them instead of in God. If he agreed, they would promise to place him safely out of Purgatory. If not, they would threaten to make him suffer the torments which they would show to him. Owein was warned not to be persuaded or terrified into believing them or all would be lost. To be saved he must remember God and invoke the name of Jesus. By His name he would be delivered. Thus warned, the knight girded on the armor of the Lord: a hauberk of justice, shield of faith, helmet of firm belief, sword of the Holy Spirit, and the rest, an armor of hope.

The demons came, horrible and hideous both in form and gesture. They tried to cajole him, to offer him safe conduct with them. When they saw that he was not deceived, they tied him up, set fire all around the hall, and beat him. Owein remembered God, called the name of Jesus, and was saved. Subsequently, he was taken to four fields. In each field he witnessed sinners being tortured severely by being nailed down and beaten, by exposure to excessive cold or fire, etc. He was told that he would suffer the same unless he believed them. Each time he remembered God and was saved by invoking the name of Christ. Next he was taken to a smoke-filled building, where sinners were suffering in pits filled with molten metals; then to a mountain where many suffered from cold and were cast into a foul, frigid river; and, finally, to the mouth of Hell itself, into which the devils tried to drag him. But his faith remained strong and he was saved in each case by the name of Jesus. While he was sitting on the edge of the so-called entrance to Hell, a new group of demons arrived. They told him that this was not really the entrance to Hell, but that they would take him to the real entrance. When they arrived, Owein saw the real river of Hell, foul and fiery, filled with demons. Over it was the bridge of three perils: so slick that no one could keep his footing, so narrow that no mortal could pass, so terrifyingly high that it inspired great fear of falling. Again the demons offered to put him safely out of Purgatory, if he would only believe them. He remembered how God had delivered him in the past and set foot on the bridge. As soon as he did, it became so wide that one could have driven a loaded cart across and he passed safely to the other side, in spite of attempts by the devils to dislodge him.

At this point the author adds a Homily. The author wishes one to understand this as an example of the pains and miseries which are in the world. One must avoid them. The pains of Hell are as numerous as the pebbles in the sea. The cloistered do not know how much more severe the pains of Hell are than those of the cloister.

Having reached the other side, Owein saw a high wall. As he approached, the bejewelled door open and the fragrance which came to him from the beautiful country inside removed all his grief. A host of people of all stations in life came to him from inside the wall singing sweet, harmonious music. What he has glimpsed is the Terrestrial Paradise. They are the sinners who have passed through the torments of Purgatory and await individually their call to the Celestial Realm. They explained the conditions of Purgatory and the afterlife and pointed out to him the gate to the Celestial Paradise. A bright light suddenly descended and fulfilled them all. Owein did not wish to leave, fearing lest he never return. They told him to return the way he had come and without fear. The devils would all shrink from him. The next day the Prior found that Owein had successfully completed the ordeal of Purgatory. After his two weeks of fasting and prayer, Owein made a pilgrimage to Jerusalem. Upon his return he was attached to Gilbert as the monk's interpreter. They remained together twelve and a half years. After Owein's death, Gilbert told his story frequently. One day someone doubted that Owein had suffered physically in the Purgatory. Had he not only imagined it? Gilbert related a story concerning a monk he knew who had been carried off by devils. Three days later they returned him. The monk had many deep wounds that never healed in the fifteen remaining years of his life (at this point in the text one finds the original epilogue of Henry of Saltrey). The text continues. I asked two abbots about St. Patrick's Purgatory. One of them confirmed that there was such a place. Bishop Florentianus, nephew of the third St. Patrick, confirmed that the Purgatory was in his own diocese and told the story of a good hermit who suffered harassment from the devils. The Bishop's Chaplain also asked to tell a tale and told three stories of holy men in strife with demons. After this final tale, Marie adds her own epilogue, giving her name and reason for translating the text.

V   Henry of Saltrey's Text and Additions

It seems evident that Henry of Saltrey's text underwent several revisions. The original probably included the prologue, the theological introduction, the material concerning the preaching of the second St. Patrick,[4] the adventure of Owein, Gilbert's testimony concerning the monk with the deep wounds, and Henry's epilogue, which follows this episode in a number of manuscripts. Professor Foulet proposed that there are basically three stages to the text.[5] He surmised that Gilbert's own personal addition concerning the monk with deep wounds was popular and inspired the similar verifications concerning the two abbots and the tales related by Bishop Florentianus and his Chaplain, all designed to add credence to Owein's basic experience. Professor Foulet suggested that a third redactor added the two Homilies, placed Henry's epilogue at the end of all the adventures, and made the chapter divisions found in some manuscripts. Because Marie's text contains the first of the two Homilies, he believed that the manuscript used by Marie was made after the text had undergone its final revision. However, the Latin manuscript from which she translated retained the original position of Henry's epilogue, did not include chapter divisions, and contained only the first Homily, in all a format more in accord with the original work.

VI *Marie's Translation*

A close comparison of BM Harley ms. 3846 with Marie's translation reveals how little the French poetess altered the Latin version. Indeed, her translation is remarkably faithful. In general, when she departs from the text, it is to clarify an ambiguous Latin passage or to develop clearly what is implied in the original. One can see in these passages particularly how well she knew Latin and how sensitive she was to the subtleties of the language. In the few places where the French text omits lines found in the Latin, it is evident that the omission was deliberate, in that the omitted lines only repeat what had been written previously. On several occasions Marie adds a couplet not present in the Latin. The additions are not without interest, for they are reminiscent of the personal asides or authorial intrusions found in the *Lais*. During the account of the torments of Hell witnessed by Owein, Marie remarks: *Chaitis est cil qui en tel peine, / Par ses pechiez, se trait e meine* (vv. 1019–20).[6] And later, *Allas, que nuls deit deservir/ Qu'itel peine deüst suffrir!* (vv. 1053–54).[7] In another passage, just after Owein has seen the Terrestrial Paradise, Marie exclaims:

Or nus doint Deus ceo deservir/ Qu'a ces joies puissuns venir! (vv. 1667–68).[8]

VII   *Literary Relationships*

One of the most interesting aspects of the *Espurgatoire* is the way in which it relates to the literary genres popular in the late twelfth century. The introductory material concerning St. Patrick, the additions pertaining to the hermits, the Homilies, the theological commentary, all give the work the flavor of the saint's life. Yet the major episode of the narrative has characteristics of both the *roman* and the *chanson de geste*. Of the twenty-three hundred lines, some fifteen hundred relate the adventure of the knight Owein. Although different in intent and openly didactic, Owein's ordeal in Purgatory resembles closely the solitary adventure of the Arthurian knight and his encounter with the Other World. Just as in the episode of the *Joie de la Cort* in Chrétien's *Erec*, Owein resolutely undertakes the dangerous adventure in spite of attempts to dissuade him. The final test, in which he must cross the bridge of the three perils, is strongly reminiscent of the famous sword-bridge episode in Chrétien's *Lancelot*. Both bridges span the river of Hell and neither is suited to human passage. Moreover, in both instances the reality does not correspond with the appearance. Lancelot sees dreadful lions waiting for him on the other side. However, once he has the courage to accept the challenge, the lions literally vanish. Similarly, Owein's bridge appears so narrow and slick that none could cross. Yet, once he steps on the bridge, it seemingly expands and the perils vanish.

But if Owein's experience resembles the adventures of the Arthurian knights, there are aspects which recall the *chanson de geste*. Owein is matched against the enemies of God in a struggle for the soul. Alone he must face odds too great to be overcome by human strength. He must place himself in God's hands. God alone can give the victory. Throughout the text Owein must remember God (what Adam did not do) and he can only be saved by invoking Christ. As Owein prepares to meet the host of devils, he arms himself in knightly style, but not with human weapons. His are the weapons of the soul, the armor of the *Psychomachia*. His shield is faith, his helmet, firm belief. These are the only weapons which will count in this battle for life.

Professor Foulet believed that Marie's interest in the text lay only in the adventure of Owein. In fact, he asserted that Marie was not really comfortable in the text until she reached his adventure. However, there is no empirical evidence to support this view, probably attributable to Professor Foulet's belief in the inferiority of religious and didactic texts as opposed to romance, a form more closely associated with artistic originality in terms of nineteenth- and twentieth-century aesthetic values. Given the aesthetic values of the twelfth century and the types of literature being written, it is not difficult to see the appeal of the *Espurgatoire* to Marie, in that it includes many of the elements then popular in various genres.

CHAPTER 5

The Narrative Lai

IN approaching the narrative *lai* as a genre of twelfth- and thirteenth-century French literature, one is faced with problems similar to the ones confronting investigators studying the development of many of the genres represented in the vernacular literature. A difficult question in the study of both the *chanson de geste* and the *roman* concerns the reality of an oral tradition and the loss of written texts. Where did Geoffrey of Monmouth obtain the information which contributed to his epoch-making history? He claims to have used a certain book which had been given to him, but there is no extant copy of it and the historical records of an Arthur provide little information that would seem sufficient to stimulate such an imaginative fiction. Thus one finds in Geoffrey's text the fully developed story of an ancient legendary king whose extant historical reality is little more than that of a warrior chieftain named Arthur. Moreover, in his translation of Geoffrey's text some twenty years later, Wace adds a number of important details not found in the Latin work or anywhere else. By the end of the century, many *romans* and *contes* had been written concerning Arthurian heroes and tales purported to be from the Arthurian period. Did Geoffrey, Wace, Chrétien, and Marie have other written sources now lost, did Geoffrey create the basic Arthurian legend from his imagination, or was there a considerable tradition from which they all drew? References in Wace, Chrétien, Marie, and others have led many to believe that there was an oral literature specifically associated with the Bretons. And scholars have endeavored to trace the plots, motifs, names, and geography of the French texts back to Celtic folklore in an effort to elucidate the sources of the various genres.

I *The Term* Lai

For many years the short narrative poems written by Marie have been called *lais*. Besides the translations from Ovid (which may or may not predate Marie) and the *romans* translated from Latin, her texts are among the earliest of the period written in the vernacular. It is not certain that Marie intended her short narrative poems to be called *lais*, but later writers definitely use the term in designating similar works. As a genre it was short-lived, beginning with the collection of Marie in the second half of the twelfth century and extending to around 1270. If one includes all the texts which are called *lais*, there are approximately thirty to forty extant.[1] But if the term is used in reference to such narrative poems, it is also the name of a form of lyric poetry which flourishes from the twelfth to the fifteenth centuries. Is there a relationship between the lyric and narrative *lais*? If so, what is this relationship and how did the term come to designate two different genres?

The derivation of the term and what it meant is complicated by the lack of documents prior to the twelfth century.[2] H. d'Arbois de Jubainville early suggested that the French word *lai* comes from the Irish *loíd* (*laid*), found in a ninth-century document, where it is used to designate a genre of poetry and metaphorically to refer to *le chant des oiseaux*.[3] He further suggests that the Irish word probably has the same etymological derivation as the Latin *laus, laudis* (praise). In some ways the problem can be summed up in the difficulty of relating the twelfth-century French lyric to the Celtic lyric *lai* (which some have supposed to have been part of an oral tradition) and in their common relationship to the Latin lyric.[4] Judging from references in Northern French texts of the twelfth century, the earliest reference being that found in Wace's *Brut*, the term would seem to have been associated with the Bretons, renowned for their musical talent. However, it is not certain whether the word refers only to a tune or melody or to a song accompanied by words. Moreover, the specific Breton association has been challenged on the grounds that such references to the Bretons had become a literary fad, a stylistic feature especially in vogue in the second half of the twelfth century, and that no real proof can be offered that any of these writers had ever had any contact with Breton *jongleurs*.[5] In a recent study, Richard Baum has demonstrated that the term is found frequently in Provençal texts of the twelfth and thirteenth centuries, several of the texts predating the earliest Northern French reference. It is significant that the term rarely has anything to do with the Bretons in these texts, although it is often found in a context with "birds" meaning *chant des oiseaux* or used to designate a *chanson* of a certain rhythmic disposition. It is true, as Mr. Baum points out, that one cannot assert that the Provençal texts give the original meaning of the word, but one is not led toward a Celtic etymology from evidence in these works.[6] Over a hundred years ago, Ferdinand Wolf developed extensively the thesis that the lyric *lai* had its origin in the Latin sequence.[7] Wolf maintained that the lyric *lai* of the twelfth century, with its accompanying text, represented a later development and that the original form was purely lyric, simple melodies frequently accompanied by a stringed instrument called the *chrotta*. The essentials of this thesis have been accepted by many musicologists (such as Gennrich and Spanke), who derive the poetic strophe of romance lyric in general from liturgical origins. It was noted early that many of the same tunes used for the French lyric of the twelfth and thirteenth centuries, far from being the remains of earlier Celtic songs, were actually melodies found in earlier religious poems.

But this point of view has not been accepted by everyone. Jean Maillard believes that both the *lai* and the sequence have their origin in a popular Latin poetry brought to the attention of the poets by Celtic intermediaries. Both forms derive from the change wrought in Latin meter in an effort to accommodate the rhythms of classical Latin to the speech of the masses. He thus considers the Irish word *loîd*, cited by de Jubainville, to be merely an altered form of the low Latin *leodos* (*leudus*, itself derived from the Latin *laus*), which he believed to be a term used to indicate Latin rhythms adapted to the vernacular tongues.[8]

Maillard points out that the twelfth- and thirteenth-century lyric *lais* are of two types, those independent poems collected in the *chansonniers* of the *trouvères*, and those which were intercalated in narrative poems (such as the *Roman de la Violette*). He further notes that a number of *romans* have scenes where important characters (such as Lancelot and Tristan) are reported to have sung a *lai*. He questions whether this format should not be linked with the Irish narrative tradition where a principal character often interrupts the prose narrative to sing a narrative poem called a *laid*.[9] Professor Maillard hypothesizes that the Irish literature passed to Wales and Brittany with the missionaries who spread to England and the continent from the sixth century on.

The Celts learned it from the Irish missionaries and transmitted it to the French and Anglo-Norman courtly society.[10] Although Maillard's thesis is possible, one must view with skepticism the fragile link established between twelfth-century French or Anglo-Norman literature and this remote Irish tradition as well as the rather tenuous relationship between the sequence and Celtic intermediaries.[11]

Because of the obscurity of the origins of the term and the exact nature and provenance of the form it designates, the basic question concerning the relationship of the lyric and narrative *lais* remains doubtful. Essentially the two forms were originally compared because the same name was given to each. A closer look at the extant examples of the two types is, in this regard, beneficial.

As mentioned above, the earliest lyric *lais* are found in the second half of the twelfth century and the form continues to be in vogue down to the fourteenth century, when it became a poetry of fixed form. Basically there are two types of lyric *lai*: those inserted into Arthurian romances (usually in eight-syllable quatrains), where the interpreter is one of the famous Arthurian heroes, and those independent *lais* found in the *chansonniers* and characterized by a large number of strophes (from five to twenty-three, the longest being nearly three hundred lines) and frequently accompanied by musical notation.[12] In these the subject may or may not be Arthurian. The narrative *lai*, on the other hand, is usually in eight-syllable rhymed couplets and seems to have been in vogue only from the mid-twelfth to the second half of the thirteenth century. Since the authors of the narrative texts often refer to *lais bretons*, it was natural for scholars to link the lyric poems to the narrative genre in some way. Might not the narrative *lai* be a courtly adaptation of a Breton ballad tradition? This would account for the heroic or epic flavor in the narratives and would reflect an earlier tradition no longer present in the lyric texts.[13]

Unfortunately, there is no proof that *lais* of a ballad character existed or were accessible to the French writers, and the assumption is derived for the most part from the subject matter of the narrative texts themselves. Furthermore, there seems to be no direct common link between the two extant forms. One might postulate that the narrative *lai* represented a story version of which the lyric *lai* were only the poetic essence. This would accord with some of the statements by Marie and others where the impression is left that the Breton *lai* was a musical and poetic composition written to commemorate an extraordinary *aventure*. If this were true, one would expect to find lyric *lais* which corresponded in subject matter to some of the extant narrative poems.[14] But such has not been the case. There seems to be no common relationship between any of the extant lyrics and the narrative *lais*, although two bear titles which indicate the influence of the narrative vogue: the *Lai des Deus Amanz* and the *Lai du Chevrefueil*. Even a cursory reading of the first of these lyrics eliminates any relationship in subject matter to Marie's text. In the *Chevrefueil* there is a relationship to Marie's text in that the subject is the indissoluble love of Tristan and Iseut. However, unlike Marie's text, the love is one-sided and only Tristan dies from their separation. In addition, it should be noted that the meaning of the symbol is entirely different in the lyric text: The poet states clearly that *Chevrefueil* was chosen as a title because it is "sweeter and more fragrant than any other plant in the woods," a reason which scarcely accords with the meaning of the symbol in Marie's *lai*. It is likely that the lyric text postdates Marie's and used the title because of the narrative poem's popularity.[15] In conclusion, one must agree with Gaston Paris that there are two distinct genres called *lais* in mediaeval French literature and that their historical development is independent and unrelated, except indirectly, perhaps, in some remote past.

II *The Continental Versus Insular Origins*

Since it is widely agreed that the musical or poetic format of the twelfth-century lyric *lai* does not seem to be related directly to the Celtic oral literature to which Marie and others refer, it cannot be looked to, therefore, as a model of the *lais* which Marie and others attribute to the Bretons. Nonetheless, even if unrelated to the twelfth-century French lyric, many believe that a Breton oral literature did exist and that the *Lais* of Marie stem from this tradition. Marie attributes her sources to the Bretons or *anciens bretuns* and from her references one is led to conclude that she used oral sources (and perhaps written), although it is somewhat ambiguous whether the *lais* of the Bretons were purely musical compositions, musical compositions accompanied by text, or perhaps a musical composition preceded by a prose narrative. Marie's references, plus the fact that many of the tales are set in Brittany or Wales and include Breton folk material, have persuaded scholars that the *Lais* do stem from the Breton tradition and that an oral tradition must have been thriving in the twelfth century.

But if one accepts the Celtic origin of Marie's sources, how did she come into contact with these *jongleurs* and were they of continental or insular origin? In the nineteenth century, H. Zimmer and E. Brugger developed what came to be known as the continental theory of origin.[16] Zimmer and Brugger both argued that the only living oral tradition derived from Armorica. They held that the words *Bretagne* and *breton* referred only to Armorica and to the Armoricans in the twelfth century, and that Marie's own references can be understood then only to refer to Armorican *conteurs*. It was argued further that internal evidence leads to the same conclusion. At least seven of the *Lais* are set in Armorica,[17] and a number of the names in the text can be shown to have continental Breton etymologies.[18] One could explain the *lais* clearly set in Wales (*Yonec, Chevrefoil, Milun* [begins in Wales], and *Lanval*) by the influence of Geoffroy of Monmouth and Wace, who had made the Arthurian material and its Welsh setting popular. Marie or French predecessors had changed the original Armorican geographical setting and place-names to the literarily popular setting in South Wales.[19]

Opponents of the continental theory maintained that the twelfth-century vogue in Breton materials stemmed from the oral tradiions of both Armorica and Wales. Ferdinand Lot, while basically accepting the assertion that the terms *Bretagne* and *breton* in the twelfth century were commonly reserved for the continental Breton inhabitants and not the twelfth-century inhabitants of Wales, insisted that such was not universally the case.[20] Lot pointed out that the Latin terms *Britones, Britanni* and *gens Britannica* were used in the *Annales Cambriae* and elsewhere to refer specifically to contemporary Welshmen, and that there were many instances where the vernacular term *Bretagne* was used without a qualifying adjective to designate the island and specifically Wales. Lot suggested that the archaic literary use of the term to designate Great Britain and its inhabitants in the time of King Arthur had influenced these writers in their modern usage. He further pointed out that Marie herself referred to the *conteurs* as *li anciens bretuns* and intended to place her works in the atmosphere of an archaic past:

When the work of Geoffrey of Monmouth revealed to the courtly public the existence and deeds of the former inhabitants of the island of Britain, the word *breton* was understood in an archaic, retrospective sense. All the deeds of the Celtic heroes were related to the period of the "anciens Bretons courtois." [21]

Lot and others also pointed out that only a portion of the *lais* are actually set exclusively in Armorica. Only *Guigemar*, *Le Fresne* (Dol), *Laüstic* (Saint-Malo), and *Chaitivel* (Nantes), are clearly in Armorica. *Bisclavret* is set in *Bretagne*, but one cannot be positive that Armorica is meant. *Milun* and *Eliduc* take place both in Armorica and Great Britain, and *Les Deus Amanz* takes place in Normandy. The setting of *Equitan* has never been certain and the remaining three *lais*, *Yonec*, *Chevrefoil*, and *Lanval*, have authentic Welsh settings. In fact, only four have a specifically Armorican setting, while three are exclusively located in Wales.[22]

Because of the apparent existence of Welsh material in the *lais* and *romans* of the period, scholars who wish to limit the Celtic tradition to the continental Bretons have been forced to extreme conclusions to explain away the insular element. It is more likely that the Celtic material derives from both insular and continental sources. It has been noted that substantial numbers of continental Bretons crossed over to England with the invading force of William the Conqueror and that many received fiefs and took up residence in Monmouthshire and Gloucestershire. It is not improbable that there was a cross-fertilization of Celtic lore in the encounter between continental and Welsh *conteurs*. Undoubtedly continental Breton *conteurs* would have been keenly interested in the legendary exploits of King Arthur and their ancient Breton ancestors, and not averse to propagating and embellishing the tradition.[23] Gaston Paris attributed the spread of Breton tales to wandering Breton and Welsh *jongleurs* who made their way from castle to castle:

. . . the French public of the castles who listened to the *jongleurs* from Great Britain or Brittany greatly enjoyed their melodies and, music being a universal language, even understood them, although the public did not understand the words of these Breton *lais*. Certain French poets, notably those who used the Anglo-Norman dialect and knew both languages, had the idea of transcribing the stories of the *lais* into the current form of narrative poetry, the octosyllabic verse.[24]

Because Marie's statements sometimes seem to indicate that the Breton *lais* were musical compositions and at other times narrative tales, it was also suggested that the *jongleurs* themselves may have been bilingual and may have related the story briefly in narrative form prior to singing the Breton song.[25]

III   *Did Marie Create the Narrative Lais?*

In 1905, Lucien Foulet launched a major attack against the accepted relationship between the narrative *lai* and the Breton oral tradition. Highly skeptical of the validity of statements found in the mediaeval texts referring to the Bretons and the hypotheses which were becoming established without firm documentation, Foulet determined to review the pertinent *lais* in an effort to establish the authenticity of the tradition. From a study of the anonymous *lais*, he concluded that there was no evidence that any of the texts demonstrated a direct relationship with a Breton oral tradition. He attempted to prove that all the texts which could rightfully be called *lais* were direct imitations of Marie, including the prologues and epilogues where reference was made to the Breton sources.[26] Professor Foulet contended that whatever can be learned concerning the narrative *lai* must be sought in the works of Marie alone.

Noting that early use of the word *lai* in French is reserved for the meaning *mélodie* or *chanson*, and that the references to *jongleurs* never suggested that *lais* were narrated, Foulet asserts that Marie herself added the dimension of narration to the term and contends that a close analysis of the prologues and epilogues of the *lais* confirms the fact. Important to his argument is his belief that the "Prologue" to the collection was composed after the *lais* had been written and was placed in the position of a prologue only because of the dedication.[27] He points out that the prologue to *Guigemar* appears first in the three major manuscript collections and probably represented the original prologue to the entire collection.[28] In this regard it is significant that the term *lai* is used specifically in reference to a *chanson* or *mélodie* in the prologue to *Guigemar*, precisely in accord with the attested meaning in other early French texts. Only in later *lais* and in the "Prologue" (written later) of the entire collection does one find the word related to a meaning including narration. *Guigemar, Lanval, Les Deus Amanz, Laüstic, Eliduc, Equitan,* and *Chaitivel* are not called *lais,* but *contes* or *aventures.* One sees in the prologues to *Chevrefoil, Milun, Yonec, Bisclavret,* and *Le Fresne* how she gradually began to use the term *lai* for what she herself had written. Professor Foulet concludes that Marie and Marie alone created the genre known as the narrative *lai:*

As for the meaning, narrative poem, it is unknown before Marie; it is she who introduced it into the language. She did so without premeditation, the result of the constant confusion naturally produced by her references to the "lai breton" and the "conte français" which supposedly retraced the origin of the *lai*.[29]

He sees in Marie's use of the terms *aventure, lai,* and *conte* the natural progression of the form. The *aventure* refers to the *matière,* the ancient Breton deed or story. To commemorate the event, *lais* or Breton melodies were written which usually had the hero's name for a title. *Conte* refers to the twelfth-century French narrative which recounts the story commemorated by the *lai.* Professor Foulet's summary of his idea of the relationship between Marie and her Breton sources is worth quoting in full:

. . . formerly, in the period of the ancient Bretons, when an adventure occurred among the barons [they took pleasure in retelling it], it passed from mouth to mouth. It was then a much honored custom to make a *lai* about it to preserve the memory of the adventure. In general the *lai* was given the name of the hero of the adventure. It was a tune played on the harp or the rote and could also be sung with accompanying words. Sometimes the *lai* was composed only long after the adventure itself had taken place. Therefore it was possible for some adventures to be transmitted [to posterity] without any *lai* having been composed.[30]

Placing the composition of Breton *lais* at a time much earlier than the twelfth century, Foulet denies that Marie ever had heard any *lais* personally,[31] or that she would have known the Breton language.[32] He suggests that her sources were probably both written and oral.[33]

Although scholars recognized the importance of Foulet's study, few embraced his conclusions. None could prove that the narrative *lai* existed prior to Marie, but there was general reluctance to believe that the entire vogue of the Breton *lai* began with Marie. Most mediaevalists were likewise unwilling to accept the thesis that the Breton *lai* was a phenomenon only of a remote past. However, recent scholarship, while not agreeing with Foulet's conclusions, tends to support the questions he posed and his perspective of the issue.

For many years mediaevalists have objected to the notion that the themes and motifs in the *lais* are exclusively Breton. In fact, even in those *lais* which are generally conceded to be predominantly of Celtic inspiration (such as *Guigemar, Yonec, Lanval*, and *Chevrefoil*), major elements of the stories have only a tenuous relationship to Celtic lore.[34] Indeed, the majority of the *lais* (such as *Equitan, Le Fresne, Bisclavret, Les Deus Amanz, Milun*, and *Chaitivel*) have nothing particularly Celtic about them. It has even been observed that *Laüstic* and *Eliduc* have no link with Celtic lore, except for names or titles. Yet, whenever Marie mentions her sources, it is invariably a reference to the *bretuns* or *li anciens bretuns*.[35] The fact that Marie ascribes all her work to the Bretons has led many to doubt the authenticity of her statements. Is not the setting in *Bretagne* and the explanation concerning the manner in which *lais* were composed a stylistic feature used by the author to introduce the texts and to take advantage of a popular topos?[36] Ernest Hoepffner's study on the place-names and setting of Marie's texts might well be seen as corroborative evidence.[37] In his study of the *géographie* of the *lais*, Hoepffner demonstrates that Marie borrowed much from the settings and geography found in Wace's *Brut* and in Geoffrey of Monmouth's *Historia regum Britanniae*. He argues that the locale of Marie's stories has less to do with a real setting in the story itself than with Marie's intent to take advantage of the popularity of Breton material stimulated by Geoffrey of Monmouth and Wace. This would explain why non-Breton tales are set in Brittany or Wales. The thesis is impressive, bolstered by its reliance on extant texts and by the fact that it explains the rise of the narrative genre known as the *lai* without the need for speculation and hypothetical assumptions about an oral tradition which cannot be known with certainty. Yet, little can be written about the literary history of the period that is confirmed by solid documentary evidence. While it may be true, the dangers of the hypothesis are apparent. It forces one to deny *a priori* the authenticity of numerous references from texts of the period or to interpret them as referring only to a remote past resurrected because of a popular literary fashion.

In 1955 Martín de Riquer attempted to define some of the key terms in the controversy.[38] Accepting Marie's statements as having historical validity, Professor Riquer sought to determine the meaning and relationship of such terms as *aventure, conte,* and *lai* in an effort to establish whether or not Marie intended her own texts to be called *lais.* He begins by pointing out that there are a number of lines which refer to the Bretons as the ones who made the *lais*[39] and several texts where Marie mentions the *aventure* from which a *lai* was made.[40] From these texts it is clear that the *aventure* (the deed or event) preceded the creation of the *lai,* indicated in some texts to have been made *pur remembrance.*[41] To this point few would disagree with Professor Riquer. However, he adds, further, that between the *aventure* and the *lai* is the *conte.* That is, that the *aventure* had existed in narrative form prior to the commemoration by a *lai*:

That *aventure* was told, it could not remain unknown for long. The Bretons made from it a *lai* which is called Laüstic.[42]

Many would accept this, but not Professor Riquer's further assertion that Marie considered her own work to be *contes* based on the narrative tales stemming from the *aventure.* He attacks the traditional view that Marie called her own work *lais* by demonstrating that the two passages (in *Le Fresne* and *Bisclavret*) where she seems unequivocally to use the term *lai* for her own text are not so certain as they appear. The opening lines of *Le Fresne, Le lai del Freisne vus dirai / Sulunc le cunte que jeo sai,* seem clear enough, but Riquer points out that one manuscript (ms. S) has *Du lai del Freisne . . . etc.,* a reading which changes the meaning entirely. Marie is not going to relate *the lai*; rather she will speak *about the lai.* Hence, her own narration is not called a *lai,* but is only about a *lai.* This not only conforms to the use of the term elsewhere, it is even confirmed by the closing lines of the *lai: Quant l'aventure fu seüe/ Comment ele esteit avenue,/*

Le lai del Freisne en unt trové (*Le Fresne*, lines 515–17). Once again she is referring to the Bretons. The opening lines of *Bisclavret* (*Quant de lais faire m'entremet . . . etc.*) cannot be so easily dismissed. Riquer's arguments that the text might be corrupt (the passage is in no other manuscript) or that one might interpret *faire* to mean *dire* are not really satisfactory.[43] And his assertion that lines 315–18 contradict the opening lines and reaffirm the meaning in other texts is not indisputable:

The *aventure* which you have heard was true, do not doubt it. The *lai* was made concerning Bisclavret that it might be remembered forever.[44]

One can see the traditional interpretation in these lines. However, if one allows that Marie may have used the word *lai* for her own work, then line 317 (*De Bisclavret fu fet li lais . . .*) could well be a reference to her own text. Realizing the difficulty posed by the opening lines of *Bisclavret*, Professor Riquer urged that it would be unwise to accept the authority of one passage which contradicts so many others. He suggested that Marie's ambiguity in her use of the word *lai* probably stems from the fact that her audience knew very well what a *lai* was and that, as a consequence, there would have been no danger in their interpreting the passages in question as a reference to her own texts.[45] Those who believe in the existence of an oral tradition (including Breton *lais*) will accept most of Professor Riquer's conclusions, even if they are unwilling to go so far as to exclude Marie's use of the term *lai* for her own work. Those who believe that the statements in Marie's text refer to a remote past and are used primarily as a literary device will reject most of Professor Riquer's conclusions. It is one of those tantalizing problems which may never be resolved with certainty.

IV   *The Lai as a Narrative Genre*

It is apparent from the foregoing that not everyone agrees whether Marie called her own work *lais* or not. Yet it is clear enough from the texts which follow that there was a certain kind of narrative poetry which writers of the twelfth and thirteenth century called *lais*. It has long puzzled critics why the term ceased to be used in the late thirteenth century in France and how one might define the type of narrative poem which was called a *lai*.[46] What are the characteristics of the *lai* which distinguish it from any of the other forms of narrative poetry written in this period?

Thinking basically of the *Lais* of Marie de France, Gaston Paris described the *lai* in terms which had lasting influence:

They are tales of adventure and love in which fairies, transformations, and marvellous occurrences often play a role. More than once there is reference to the land of immortality where the fairies often lead and hold their heroes. Tristan and Arthur are mentioned and Arthur's court provides, at times, the backdrop of the action. . . . One finds there in large part the traces of an ancient mythology, ordinarily not understood and nearly unknowable. In general a melancholy, tender tone pervades the texts and there is a love sentiment not found in the *chansons de geste*. Moreover, the characters of the Celtic *contes* are transformed into knights and ladies.[47]

It is not difficult to see why this definition was successful. In general, it captures the subject matter, atmosphere and charm of the most impressive texts in the collection. But when one considers the elements of the description closely, it becomes apparent that they pertain to those *lais* which are dominated by the Breton source material. The phrase *contes d'aventures et d'amour* comes nearest to pertaining to all the texts. They are certainly all about love and the term *aventure* might fit each *lai*, if it is interpreted in its broadest sense. The remainder of the characteristics, however, concern a remarkably small number of *lais*. Strictly speaking there is only one *fée*, the fairy-mistress in *Lanval*, the only text which includes an Arthurian setting and where Avalon is actually mentioned. Tristan occurs only in *Chevrefoil*. It is true that *merveilles* play a large role, but not in all the texts: One would be hard put to find any in *Equitan*, *Le Fresne*, *Chaitivel*, *Laüstic*, and *Chevrefoil*, not to mention the problem of whether the term would apply to the swan in *Milun* or the potion in *Les Deus Amanz*. In fact, only *Guigemar*, *Yonec*, and *Lanval* seem to include a majority of the descriptive characteristics mentioned, all *lais* which are generally conceded to be of Celtic origin. The problems seen here in attempting to apply Paris' criteria to all of Marie's *lais* are similar to the ones encountered in characterizing the genre in general. The phrase *contes d'aventures et d'amour* really only excludes longer narratives, and the Breton characteristics are singularly inapplicable to the many *lais* which do not have an Arthurian setting and do not deal with the Celtic Other-World motif.[48] Of greater importance is Paris' statement that the Celtic characters are transformed into *chevaliers* and that there is a *passion inconnue aux chansons de geste.* Later writers will emphasize this transformation of folk material to twelfth-century tastes as a distinctive feature of both the *lai* and the *roman.*[49]

Besides the use of definitions of genre by content, scholars have attempted to distinguish the *lai* from other narrative forms by its external features. In addition to its length (from one hundred to twelve hundred lines), its use of octosyllabic couplets, and the prevalence of prologues and epilogues, Faral distinguishes it from the *roman* by the difference in narrative treatment:

> The *conte,* compared to the *roman,* is shorter, more quickly moving and more concisely interwoven. The few occurrences all serve to prepare the principal scene. In it lies the essential interest of the subject with all its charm or tragedy. The poetic themes, quickly treated, are never developed for their own sakes but are strictly subordinate to the action, which moves with haste toward the *dénoûment.*[50]

As much as one might agree with the distinction here made, the precise boundary between the *lai* or *conte* and the *roman* remains vague. How many lines must a text have to be called a *roman*? At one point the *Ille et Galeron,* which most would consider a *roman,* is called a *lai* and the other exterior features cited above are found in various works certainly not belonging to the same genre. If one claims that the *lai* is written in eight-syllable verse, for example, then the *Lai du Cor* with its six-syllable line does not fit. Chrétien's *Erec* has a prologue, but the *Lai de Melion* does not. If the distinction made between the *conte* and the *roman* is vague, the problem of distinguishing between the *lai* and other short narrative forms is even more complicated.

Of special importance to the *lai* is its relationship to the *fabliau,* in that the two types have many exterior features in common and their periods of development overlap. Indeed, several of the texts called *lais* have long been called *fabliaux* by modern scholars, causing one to wonder about the mediaeval writer's criteria in classifying texts. For Bédier the *lai* and *fabliau* represented types of literature written for two different social classes. The setting of the *lai* is a courtly, aristocratic society concerned with chivalric values of honor and love in an elegant environment. In contrast, the *fabliau*, which Bédier called a *conte à rire*, reflects the manners and values of the realistic bourgeois society. In the *lai*, the language and style are refined; in the *fabliau*, the style is low and the language familiar and colloquial.[51]

Because the definition of the *lai* has been based on those texts where the subject and style are refined and reflect aristocratic values, a number of works have been excluded from the genre even though they were called *lais* in the twelfth or thirteenth century. Generally, the texts have been classified as *lais* or *fabliaux* based on modern evaluations of what these terms signify. As a result, works such as the *Lai du Lecheor, Nabaret, Ignaure, Epervier, Aristote*, and *Palefroi*, though designated as *lais*, have been called refined *fabliaux*. That the basis for classifying the various shorter narrative forms is inadequate has been recognized by many scholars. Ideally one would like to arrive at a concept of the *lai* as a narrative genre which corresponds with the mediaeval man's view of the form. Recently several attempts have been made to find a definition of the *lai* broad enough to suit the many and varied narratives so designated by the mediaeval writer.

Professor Frappier has urged that the social viewpoint be abandoned in favor of a definition based on the structural principles inherent in the works themselves.[52] While conceding that the concept of genres was not nearly so developed in the mediaeval period as in the seventeenth century, he nonetheless insists that the mediaeval writer did make clear distinctions among the various narrative forms and that the modern critic should accept as *lais* the works so classified by the mediaeval writer or scribe. For Professor Frappier, the structural unity of the *lai* as a genre resides in the joining of the courtly ideal with the essentially Celtic content of the genre. He suggests that there was a natural relationship between the courtly ideal and the Celtic Other-World. The courtly elite enclosed themselves in a world forbidden to the profane on the spiritual level, not unlike the Other-World in the remains of Celtic mythology:

It is thus that one can explain the close union and synthesis, admirable in so many respects, of two mythologies in this "matière de Bretagne," the one primitive and marked by the supernatural, the other a mythology of the mind and heart.[53]

In each story there are two worlds, one common and the other ideal. Of paramount importance in the narrative development of the story is the *aventure*. It is of central importance to the plot and is the catalyst at the moment of crisis which causes the unfolding of the events:

The role of the *aventure,* of the supernatural or singular occurrence, is to allow for the passage from the lower to the higher plane or design.[54]

Thus Professor Frappier perceives a continuity of structure between the authentic Breton *lai*, the *lai mythologique*, and the *lai courtois*, the source of which is not necessarily Breton. Hence *Guigemar, Lanval,* and *Yonec* are all authentic Breton *lais* in which the hero has an encounter with the Other-World. In other *lais* which are not authentically Breton (although Marie places them in a Breton setting), the *merveilleux* tends to disappear. Nonetheless, the analogous structure remains, in the opposition of the *monde vulgaire* and *monde idéal des fins amants* to which the hero gains entrance by means of the *aventure*:

Thus there occurs nearly always in our *lais* a moment when the hero leaves the daily world to enter either a fairy world or a world of love the entry to which is permitted only to an elite. Now, for the most part, the *aventure* takes place in intermediate regions which are at the same time frontiers and crossings not without analogy to the Celtic concept of the Other-World.[55]

As an interpretive analysis, Professor Frappier's remarks are attractive and significant. However, the relationship which he seeks to establish remains only an analogy. It is perhaps our own abstraction of the concept which makes the analogy more apparent to modern sensibility. By abstraction we describe the aristocratic milieu and its refined perspective as a *monde idéal*. By a similar mental process we tend to transform the physical Other-World of Celtic lore into a spiritual realm which, in spiritual or psychological terms, seems to relate to our concept of the *monde courtois*. Professor Frappier's interpretation of the term *aventure*, similar to Elena Eberwein's,[56] appears to be strong when one analyzes the "authentic" Breton *lais* where the *aventure* is directly related to the hero's encounter with the Other-World. But in the other texts there is no specific aura of mystery, no sense of awareness that the hero is moving into another order of reality comparable to the Celtic Other-World. Professor Frappier's definition does not really serve to distinguish the *lai* as a genre. He himself admits that *Equitan, Bisclavret, Les Deus Amanz,* and *Chaitivel* do not relate to his analysis and one could add to the list. Even if one were to grant the structural relationship he sought to establish between the courtly ideal and the Celtic Other-World, there are *lais* which do not fit his structural pattern.[57]

A completely different approach to the problem is offered by Professor Tiemann.[58] Instead of viewing the *lai, fabliau, dit,* and saint's life as different genres in themselves, he sees them all as variations of the short narrative, which eventually becomes the genre known as the *novella* or short story. The significant point for Tiemann is that the short narrative developed freely, unrestricted as to form, language, and subject because it was not one of the higher forms of literature. Essentially it was an experimental form which could be used to present any subject matter. Its unity lay in the basic didactic intent, the ideal of *abréviation* in stylistic development, and the use of narrative elements in the structural development of the *exemplum* on which it was based.[59] Professor Tiemann proposed that the source of the short narrative was the Latin literature of the period and, in particular, collections such as the eleventh-century Cambridge Song Book, a potentially rich source of material for the short narrative. The disengagement from any musical relationship came with the use of the eight-syllable rhymed couplet, a common feature of the vernacular narrative. In this perspective the *Vie de Saint Alexis*, the *Piramus et Tisbé*, the new type created by Marie called *lais*, the *fabliau*, and the *dit* are all variations of a newly developing genre. Even the *lai* itself is not a homogeneous type, but an open form drawing from many different sources and including a wide variety of variations.

The thesis is attractive in that the classification of the short narrative is based on style and narrative development, elements frequently not given sufficient importance in the mediaeval creative process because of nineteenth- and twentieth-century notions concerning poetic inspiration and originality. It avoids the problem of a classification based on a modern interpretation of the contents and proposed structural similarities drawn from interpretive analogies. Yet, valid as the viewpoint may be when analyzing the origins of the *novella*, it does not focus on the different forms for their own sakes, but sees them only in a tendentious sense, as precursors of the broad genre known as the *novella*. But the mediaeval writer of the twelfth century did not know the *novella* and one is left with the problem of determining why he used the different names that he did to designate various types of short narrative.

Professor Baader's recent study focuses on the complexity of the problem.[60] In the twelfth and thirteenth centuries, the term *lai* is used to designate a number of short narratives varying in subject matter and spirit. If one is to deal with the genre in mediaeval terms, he must avoid an *a priori* modern definition which will eliminate certain of the texts. There is, in fact, no reason to assume that the term *lai* meant the same thing to the twelfth century as it did to the thirteenth, or that the works so named had to be of the same spirit. In fact, one must be sure that the term *lai* was not merely applied by a later scribe to a work which had no real affinity with the genre. It is more important, then, to pay attention to each *lai* individually and to the extant documents in reference to a developing genre than to find a general definition against which one might measure the various texts.

In many respects Professor Baader draws conclusions very similar to Lucien Foulet's concerning Marie's relationship to her folk material and to the genre known as the *lai*. For Marie the Breton lore was as remote and enigmatic as it is to us. She did not understand the motifs in reference to the mythology from which they derived nor does her combination of motifs have meaning in terms of Celtic lore. If Marie chose to retell these tales, it is because her age was fascinated by the *merveilleux* and the enigmatic nature of the stories. Marie sensed their appeal and refashioned them to suit twelfth-century tastes. It is precisely this reworking of the folktale which is distinctive of the *lai* of Marie. Thus it is that the origin of the folk-motifs is far less important than Marie's intent in using them. She deliberately created the Other-World atmosphere, an ideal past, another order of reality. It is an ideal realm in contradiction with the reality of the twelfth century.[61] In many of the *lais* the real events take place in this ideal past and the solutions are worked out in the reality of the mind. This explains why the texts which have no relationship with Breton lore are nonetheless placed in a Breton setting. Marie consciously used the Breton geographical setting for these texts to create the ideal atmosphere which Geoffrey of Monmouth and Wace had made so popular. But the key is not the fairy-tale element itself, for, in a number of the lais, the Other-World is not a factor and the *merveilleux* does not play a role. What is important is that the nonfairy-tale texts, such as *Equitan* and *Chaitivel*, have been cast in a style and in terms that are appealing to twelfth-century courtly tastes. In both texts the folk anecdote is of less importance than the question of love. In *Equitan*, for example, the description of love and the discussion of the two lovers (seen against the broader question of fidelity) are clearly manifestations of the courtly, literary tastes of the period and are as important to the text as the narrative tale itself.

But what of the texts, such as *Le Lai du Palefroi, Epervier, Nabaret, Ignaure,* and *Aristote*, which have been termed elegant *fabliaux* rather than *lais*? Can they be called *lais* and, if so, how do they relate to the genre? While recognizing the different spirit of these texts, Professor Baader maintains that they are indeed *lais* and that they reflect a very important change in the literary taste of the thirteenth century and a development in the genre itself.

That the lai declined in popularity is apparent from the distribution of texts. Of the nineteen extant manuscripts, only six are from the fourteenth century, and only one of Marie's texts, *Lanval*, is found in any of the six. Professor Baader also notes that the sense of the Breton *lai* is virtually lost, the term being used clearly to refer to the French poem itself. Only in the *Lai de Melion* and the *Lai de l'Ombre* is the fiction of the Breton *lai* maintained. As he points out, later texts sometimes omit the term *lai* altogether, as in the fourteenth-century manuscript which includes the *Conseil*. Professor Baader attributes the disappearance of the *lai* as a genre to the fact that its subject matter had become outmoded, that it no longer appealed to the taste of the period. He sees its demise in the rise of a didactic, realistic spirit no longer disposed toward the fairy tale and the fictional, courtly, idealized tales of a remote past. Does not the comment by Denis Piramus concerning Marie's "lying tales" reflect the impatience of a new period oriented toward a literature of didactic and realistic purpose? Certainly one can see such a tendency in the *fabliau*, which continued to flourish. Baader pointed out that at least two-thirds of the *fabliaux* were didactically oriented and highlighted the moral of the text. According to Professor Baader, a number of the texts called *lais* reflect this change in spirit; it is this alteration which caused them to be considered *fabliaux* for so many years.

However, even if they seem alike, it is important to note a basic difference of intent which clearly divides the two forms. The *fabliau* is in direct contrast to the *lai*. The love element, the personages, the style—all are different from the *lai*. Professor Baader adopts Nykrog's view that the *fabliau* was written for the courtly audience and ridiculed those who did not understand courtly ways.[62] Certain *lais* written when the type was falling out of favor begin to adopt general traits popular in the *fabliau*. The fairy-tale element gives way to a more realistic and didactic spirit. Some *lais* become parodies of the genre itself. But the important thing which continues to distinguish the *lai* from the *fabliau* is the courtly theme itself and the elegant style still used. Thus Professor Baader manages to explain the use of the word *lai* for texts which were often placed in the *fabliau* category, in spite of the name given by mediaeval writers. The *Lai d'Aristote* bears strong resemblance to the *fabliau* in its heavily didactic tone, but he sees the relationship to the *lai* in its theme: The *lai* seeks to teach *courtoisie* itself, that one cannot blame even the wisest when they succumb to love. The *Lai du Cor* also reminds one of the *fabliau*, but is lifted to the category of the *lai* by its refined style and Arthurian setting.[63] The *Lai du Lecheor* is seen as a parody on the courtly theme of ideal love, the *Lai d'Ignaure* a parody on the eaten-heart motif, and the *Lai de l'Epervier* is seen as a parody on the theme of the Breton *lai* itself.

Professor Baader has had the greatest success thus far in relating the broad variety of texts known as *lais* to one another and in explaining why the mediaeval writer or scribe called these different types of poems *lais*. But there are a number of considerations which should be mentioned. One of the theses of Professor Baader's developing genre concept is that the courtly theme and the fairy-tale, nonrealistic, and nondidactic nature of the *lai* soon became outmoded. Yet one could not say that *romans* with these same characteristics lost their appeal in the thirteenth or even fourteenth century. One might also question why the *fabliau* seems to have risen to popularity at the same time as the *lai*. Surely when the *lai* was in its greatest popularity, the *fabliau* would have been out of the spirit of the times. In effect, the thesis that the *lai* became outmoded is based on its demise and the rise of a short genre which seems to lack those very qualities which Professor Baader contends became outmoded. There is no real cause and effect here, and the disappearance of the *lai* might well be for other reasons.

A second problem relates to the concept of what is courtly in the *lais,* and Professor Baader's belief that a basic distinction between the *fabliau* and the *lai* lies in their different use of didactic materials. If the word "courtly," when applied to love, implies a love-service, then one must be careful to distinguish the many uses of the word "love." Marie is far from approving love-service when the primary interest is the gratification of one's desire. Love as it appears in Marie's *Lais* runs the gamut from lust (*Equitan*) to the love that turns toward God (*Eliduc*). When love dominates the reason and the will of the characters, it often leads to crime or misfortune (*Equitan, Bisclavret, Chaitivel, Deus Amanz*). When one realizes that love appears in its broadest range of meanings in Marie's works, it is difficult to see why the *Lai d'Aristote* must be seen as a *lai* which teaches *courtoisie* and not one which presents the folly of the "wisest" when they allow themselves to be governed by their desires and not their reason. Is it really that apparent that the *Lai du Lecheor* is a parody and not open condemnation of the form of love pursued by the *lecheor?*

One might also question the argument that the *Mantel mautaillié* text was never intended to be a *lai,* since it is only so named in one of four manuscripts. In deciding what the mediaeval writer considered to be a *lai,* is it not perhaps just as important to find a later scribe calling a work a *lai* as the original writer? This is especially true if one posits that the significance of the term may have changed over a period of years. It may be that the text would not have been classified a *lai* in an earlier period, but that later it fit within the limits of what would then be called a *lai.* Can one assume that a scribe would call a text a *lai* by mere association with other texts in the manuscript if he did not consider it to fall within the genre? It is probably more likely that he did not know what a *lai* was or that the text did correspond to the concept of the genre at that time. In the latter case, his use of the term for the text could be a valuable indication of the change which had taken place in the genre.

The Narrative Lai

There is much to be gained from the recent attempts to define the various short narratives. If Professor Frappier's analysis does not suffice as a means of defining the genre, it contributes to an approach to twelfth- and thirteenth-century literature being adopted by a growing number of scholars, an attempt to find the meaning of the texts within the conscious use of materials by the author. For years the thrust of scholarship had been toward discovering the meaning of episodes and motifs in terms of the mythology from which they derived. Since the concept of poetic creativity was linked with the nineteenth-century notion of originality, the mediaeval writer, with his use of traditional themes and respect for authority, was looked upon as a rather uncreative transmitter of tales. Because of the enigmatic nature of many of the texts, scholars assumed that the writers themselves had copied the tales as they had found them, content to follow the episodic narrative. Increasingly, scholars have been attempting to gain a better understanding of the mediaeval concept of originality in poetic composition. It is apparent now that the mediaeval writer did not seek to create new stories. His interest lay in the combination and elaboration of well-known themes and tales. Stylistically and intellectually, he transformed the material into an artistic narrative which had both meaning and appeal to the contemporary audience. Professor Frappier's essay attempts to explain the appeal of the Celtic Other-World by its relationship to the courtly ideal of the period.

Professor Tiemann objected to a classification of genre by content, emphasizing the intimate relationship of all short narrative forms within the mediaeval concept of style and elaboration. In so doing, however, one must not forget that the mediaeval poets did distinguish the various short narrative texts by different names. Nevertheless, his essay serves to stress the important family relationship of the short narrative in terms of style and form, something entirely too neglected in deference to a definition by content.

Professor Baader seeks to trace the rise and decline of the genre by linking the inner spirit of the genre itself to the changing spirit of the age. Although one may disagree with the various theses proposed concerning the nature of the narrative *lai* and its development as a genre, one must applaud the direction of recent studies and the results that have been obtained.

CHAPTER 6

Plots and Sources

I *Résumé* Guigemar

IN the time of King Hoilas, there was a baron named Oridials who was lord of Liun in Brittany. He had two children, a daughter named Noguent and a son called Guigemar. When the young man came of age, he was knighted and left the court to seek his fortune in Flanders. In prowess no knight was his equal and many ladies looked at him with amorous intentions. However, he was not interested in love and, as a result, strangers and friends alike doubted his masculinity. One day, after his return home, when he was engaged in his favorite pastime, hunting, he encountered a white, antlered hind. Unfortunately, when he shot the hind, his arrow rebounded and wounded him in the thigh. Before dying, the animal placed a curse on the hunter: Never would he find a cure from his wound until he should fall in love with a woman and she with him and they both should suffer so greatly that lovers everywhere would marvel at their love. Distressed by the curse, Guigemar wandered along until he came to a large river which emptied into the sea. He entered an empty boat lying in the harbor and soon found that the boat had set sail. He then lay down on a magic bed and fell asleep. The boat sailed into the harbor of a castle keep which was enclosed on three sides, but open to the sea. A jealous old man kept his young wife locked within the keep. The young lady and her companion saw the ship and went aboard. When Guigemar awakened, he saw the young lady and knew that if she did not cure him, he would never be cured. The two young people were struck by love and Guigemar remained hidden in her apartment for a year and a half. Fearing discovery, each pledged never to love another, should they be separated. As a pledge, she tied a special knot in Guigemar's shirt which only she could untie. It was agreed that, in the future, he should love only the lady who could undo the knot. Guigemar made a similar pledge, giving her a belt which he alone could undo. After they were discovered, Guigemar was permitted to leave in the same ship which had brought him. It returned him to his own country where he rejoined his family.

Meanwhile, the girl was locked in prison, where she remained for two years. One day, finding the door unlocked, she left the prison and discovered the boat in the harbor. She entered the empty boat and was taken to the castle of a certain Meriadus, who found the girl on board and planned to marry her. The girl refused his advances, referring to the task which her future lover must accomplish. Meriadus could not open the belt, nor could any other knight. After a time, Guigemar came to the castle to help Meriadus in his struggle with a neighboring lord. The two lovers met at dinner and seemed on the verge of being united. However, Meriadus angrily refused to give up his claim to her. Guigemar withdrew from the castle and besieged it with his men. Eventually the castle was taken, Meriadus killed, and the two lovers united.

II *Sources*

For those who believe that Marie's *lais* derive from a living Breton oral tradition, *Guigemar* has long been considered a tale with strong Celtic affiliations. The proper names, the setting in Brittany, and the motif of the Hunt of the White Doe are all cited as confirming evidence.

The hero's name, often written Guiomar or Guiemar, is undoubtedly derived from the Breton Wihomarch, a name held by a number of eleventh- and twelfth-century viscounts of "Lïun" (Saint-Pol-de-Léon) in Brittany. In the text King Hoilas (spelled Odels in one manuscript) is the king in Brittany, probably the same Hoël mentioned in Geoffrey of Monmouth's *Historia* and in Wace's *Brut*. There he is king of "Bretagne la Menor" and plays an important role as Arthur's faithful nephew. Meriadus is likewise considered a Breton name, perhaps identifiable with the Mardoc who is depicted abducting Winlogee (Guinevere) on the architrave of the Porta della Pescheria of the cathedral at Modena.[1]

In support of the Celtic proper names is the prominent motif in the first part of the story, the Hunt of the White Doe. The hunt appears frequently in many twelfth- and thirteenth-century texts. The anonymous *lai Graelent*, sees the hero undertake a hunt which leads him to a fairy who subsequently becomes his mistress. Guingamor (in the *lai* of the same name) pursues a white boar which leads him to a fairy mistress and the Other-World. In both the *lai Tyolet* and the so-called Wauchier continuation of the *Conte del Graal*, the hero must catch the stag, cut off its foot (the head in Wauchier), and present it to the fairy to obtain her favors. And in Chrétien's *Erec et Enide* the hunt is described as an old custom where the knight who kills the white stag bestows a kiss on the lady he considers the most beautiful of the court. Because of the hunt, Erec is eventually led to Enide.[2] All of the texts have the hunt of a white animal in common. At the end of the hunt is a young lady who becomes the knight's mistress. In some of the texts the mistress is a fairy who has deliberately sent the animal to draw the knight to her in the Other-World; occasionally the animal is the fairy herself transformed. The versions found in *Guigemar*, *Erec*, and the *Chevalier au Cygne* are seen as later variations, in that the woman at the end of the hunt is not referred to as being a fairy. Indeed, the theme as it is found in *Guigemar* is quite different. It should be noted that the hunt and the animal's prediction are intimately linked with the problem of the Hippolytus-type young man who cares nothing for love. Furthermore, it is clear from Marie's text that neither the white hind nor the magic boat is the agent of a fairy intending to draw Guigemar to her. Nor is there any indication that the young lady to whom Guigemar is taken is a fairy. The girl's situation, in fact, falls into a category of motif thought to have originated in the Orient: the inclusa motif. One can see in the variations of the theme the process of transformation inherent in storytelling as motifs are combined, changed, and used for different purposes.

In an interesting article, "Celtic Dynastic Themes and the Breton Lays,"[3] Rachel Bromwich studies the Hunt of the White Stag in the light of Irish Mythology, where it is closely associated with the theme of the Transformed Hag, a legend which had dynastic implications, ". . . the symbolical marriage of an Irish king with the deity representing the land itself."[4] In Marie's text, however, only the Hunt of the Stag motif remains, and that considerably transformed as a result of the author's tendency to ". . . substitute literary models for older popular elements in her sources."[5] Nonetheless, Miss Bromwich argues that the attachment of these tales to early Breton legendary heroes (the associa-

tion with the counts of Léon and the linking of the name Guingamor to the early Breton hero Graelemuer in Chrétien's *Erec*)
indicates that the underlying Celtic tradition of the *lais* may well
have retained the dynastic significance held in Irish mythology.
Yet, once again, as in the discussion concerning the narrative
lai, the textual link between the Irish tradition and the continental
tales is lacking. There are no extant Breton sources and the posited
Welsh intermediary is lacking as well.

R. N. Illingworth suggested that Marie's text essentially joined
two different Celtic motifs: the all-powerful fairy mistress theme
and the type where a lady is held against her will until freed by
her lover.[6] He contends that it is the joining of these two themes
which causes the radical change in the first motif, where the fairy
traditionally lures a chosen mortal to her land across the sea.[7]
In a sense, the active, forceful nature of the fairy in the first theme
would be incompatible with the passive nature of the woman in
the abduction tale, thus necessitating a change in the fairy's
character.[8]

Following the lead of Salverda de Grave and Ezio Levi, Ernest
Hoepffner sought to demonstrate the influence of the Old French
Eneas on Marie's *Lais*.[9] Among the *lais* where Professor Hoepffner
perceived the greatest influence, *Guigemar* was prominent. He
saw influence from the *Eneas* in the sumptuous descriptions, the
development of the love passion, and in analogous situations in
the two texts. Scarcely any of the passages in question is in itself
very persuasive, and Hoepffner himself stated that it was only the
number of such likenesses which gave the argument weight. In
truth, the plot situations are only vaguely similar,[10] and the resemblance in phrases and vocabulary is not so striking that one
is convinced of the direct influence. Rather, one tends to conclude
that both texts shared in the stylistic tradition then current. Proof
is seen in the fact that some of the same passages can be compared with similar ones in Wace's *Brut*, *Piramus et Tisbé*, Gaimar's
Estoire des Engleis, the *Roman de Thebes*, or even the later
Roman de Troie.

III *Résumé* Equitan

There was once a king named Equitan who was ruler of Nauns.
A man of great worth, he was esteemed by his people. His favorite
occupations were hunting and love. Equitan had a good and loyal

seneschal who had a very beautiful wife. The king had heard much about her beauty and sought to win her love even before he had seen her. Desiring to meet her as soon as possible, the king went hunting in a region near the seneschal's castle and took lodging there for the evening. The king spent a sleepless night, torn between his love for the woman and his sense of loyalty to the seneschal. The next day the king set out to hunt again, but returned shortly, feigning illness. Taking advantage of his opportunity, he disclosed his love to the seneschal's wife. After a lengthy discussion concerning the nature of honest love, the king pledged himself to the wife, offering to serve her in every way. For a long time they remained lovers until the woman began to fear that the king would soon be forced by his barons to choose a wife. When the king pointed out that he would willingly make her his wife had she not already a husband, the woman immediately urged that the seneschal be killed. It was decided that the king would suggest to the seneschal that they keep one another company during their baths after a hunting outing. The seneschal's tub would be filled with scalding water. As planned, the two tubs were prepared; however, the king and the wife foolishly became involved in love. The seneschal returned and interrupted them in their pleasures. The king tried quickly to get to the tub. In his confusion, he jumped into the wrong one. Seeing the situation, the seneschal seized his unfaithful wife and plunged her head first into the boiling water.

IV *Sources*

Except for the mediaeval German tale concerning the three monks of Kolmar,[11] and Stefan Hofer's suggested analogue in Gaimar's *Estoire des Engleis*,[12] there has been no specific folktale indicated as the likely source for this *lai*. In general it is the least favored of all the *lais*, most critics condemning it for its heavily didactic tone and resemblance to the *fabliau*. Unlike many of the *lais*, the scene of action has not been located geographically nor has the name of the king been satisfactorily explained.

Who is this "Equitan, sire de Nauns," mentioned in line twelve of the text? Most have rejected as etymologically unfeasible Warnke's suggestion that Nauns derives from the Latin Nàmnetes, which became the French Nantes. However, a variant spelling for Nauns and Equitan in BN ms. fr. 1104 (S) has caused some tantalizing speculation. In manuscript S Nauns is spelled *nains* and Equitan is written *Aquitan.* Is it not possible that the king was intended to be a certain "Aquitan, sire des nains?" In the Tristan story the dwarf who betrays the lovers is named Aquitan in the Eilhart von Oberg version and Melot petit von Aquitan by Gottfried von Strasbourg. Here the similarity ends, however, for the dwarf is killed by the hero. Nonetheless, some would see in this relationship an indication that Marie's tale was originally related to the dwarf motif so prominent in Celtic legend. Professor Delbouille points out that Béroul calls the dwarf Frocin or Frocine and that Gottfried actually names him Melot, the word Aquitan only serving to indicate his country of origin. He postulates that the spelling Aquitan is merely a scribal variant, a misreading of the original form under the influence of the more common name.[13]

Many have noted that the love debate in the text is more important than the narrative element. Of paramount importance is the discussion which eventually leads to the complete subservience of the king to the woman. Hoepffner saw an influence from the *Eneas* in the passage and considered the text to be Marie's condemnation of the new love ethic then coming into vogue.[14] Many scholars see evidence of Provençal influence in the perspective of love presented in the text.[15] More will be said of this problem in later chapters.

V Résumé Le Fresne

Formerly in "Bretaine" there dwelled two worthy knights. It happened that the wife of one of the knights became pregnant and gave birth to twins. Wishing to share his joy with his neighbor, he sent a messenger to announce the birth of the children. Jealous of the lady's good fortune, the wife of the neighboring knight maliciously slandered her neighbor in the presence of all her servants. Everyone knows, she said, that one woman cannot give birth to two infants simultaneously without having had relations with two different men. Her husband scolded her for her envious comments, but the damage had been done, for the lady's reputation suffered much from the woman's slander.

Soon the malicious woman herself became pregnant and ironically gave birth to twins. Remembering what she had said, she determined to get rid of one of her daughters before anyone could learn of the twin birth. In grief she wrapped one of the babes in a particularly elegant blanket and left a ruby ring (given to her by her husband) tied to the child's arm to indicate that she was of good family. The babe was taken by a servant, who left the child in the crook of an ash tree just outside a distant abbey. The gate-keeper found the child and gave her to his sister to raise. The girl was named Fresne (ash) for the tree in which she was found and was raised in the monastery.

Years passed and the young girl grew into a young lady. One day Gurun, the lord of Dol, visited the abbey and fell in love with Fresne. He arranged to visit the abbey frequently, but kept his love secret from the abbess. Eventually, he persuaded Fresne to leave the abbey and to come with him to Dol. The abbess gave Fresne her blanket and ring, explaining how she had been abandoned in front of the abbey. For some time Fresne lived happily with Gurun and came to be loved by all the servants of the castle. But the feudal knights of Gurun soon pressed him to marry some-one of his station who could give him an heir. They proposed the daughter of a neighboring lord, in fact the unknown twin sister of Fresne. The girl was named Codre, hazel tree, and the knights used the name to emphasize their point: The *codre* is a fruit-bearing tree, the *fresne* is not. Under pressure from his knights, Gurun agreed to put Fresne aside.

On the night of the wedding, Fresne, who still loved Gurun, visited the wedding chamber to ensure that it was fixed in a manner which would be pleasing to her lord. Dissatisfied with the bedclothes, she substituted her own blanket for the one which had been placed there by the servants. Codre's mother, who had already been touched by the concubine's noble attitude, also visited the wedding chamber and was stunned to see the blanket. After a few pertinent questions, she realized that Fresne was the daughter she had abandoned many years ago. Repentent and humbled, she sent for her husband and confessed her crime. The husband was grateful that his wife's sin was not compounded and overjoyed to discover the daughter he had never known. Magnanimously he pardoned the lady, and Fresne returned the ruby ring which her mother had given her. The Archbishop of Dol revoked the unconsummated marriage and joined Gurun and Fresne instead. Codre returned with her family and was afterwards well married to another.

[78]

VI   *Sources*

Le Fresne is one of several *lais* set in Normandy, in this case at Dol, and has no ostensible relationship with Breton lore. Because of what the heroine endures, it has frequently been compared with the patient Griselda type of story. However, there is really very little likeness in the stories, and the central aspect of testing the woman is not a feature of *Le Fresne*. It is essentially the same story found in the Scottish ballad *Fair Annie*, which seems to derive from the same folk tradition as *Le Fresne*.[16] If sources for the tale itself are lacking, the initial motif, where the woman who reproaches another for giving birth to more than one child at once suffers the same fate, and is then condemned by her own words, is rather prevalent. It has been found in the literature of Denmark, Spain, France, Italy, and elsewhere.[17]

VII   *Résumé* Bisclavret

In former times it happened that some men became werewolves. While in this state, they lived in the great forests and preyed on human flesh. The werewolf is called *bisclavret* in Breton, *garwaf* in Norman.

In "Bretaine" there once lived a noble knight who had a beautiful wife whom he loved greatly. The wife returned his love, but was disturbed by the fact that he disappeared for three days each week. Mustering her courage, she questioned him concerning his absence. Reluctantly, he told her that he turned into a werewolf during his absences. Curious about the circumstances of his transformation, she cajoled him until he revealed to her the details. He related to her how he hid his clothes beneath a bush near a chapel and that he could never recover his human form without them. No longer wishing to live with such a creature, the woman turned to a man who had long been suing for her love. She granted him her favors and plotted with him to steal the clothes.

The knight disappeared from court for good and the woman eventually married her lover. One day, when the king was hunting, he came upon the werewolf. The animal amazed the king by humbling itself before him, just as if it had human intelligence. The king ordered that the beast not be killed and adopted it as a pet. The wolf remained with the king and was always tame except for two occasions: In the first instance he attacked the lover who had married his wife; later he attacked the wife when she appeared at court and tore off her nose. Everyone was amazed by the beast's violence on these occasions and, on this second instance, were ready to kill the animal. However, one of the king's wisest men realized that the only two people attacked were those linked to the knight who had disappeared. He guessed the solution and urged the king to interrogate the wife. Under severe questioning, she confessed and produced the clothes. The animal at first showed no interest in the clothes, but when he was placed alone in a room with them, he regained the shape of a man. The knight's wife and lover were banished from the country. The woman had many children afterwards. The daughters were recognizable, because they were born noseless.

VIII Sources

Like other *lais* in the collection, *Bisclavret* is set in "Bretagne," although there is little about the folk material that would indicate any link with Breton lore. The title itself is Breton, probably deriving from *bleiz lavaret* (speaking wolf), and Marie gives the Norman equivalent, *garwaf.*

The tradition of the werewolf was well known in Greco-Roman literature and Marie's *lai* retains the features most commonly associated with the wolf-man theme, except for the relationship between his transformation and the full moon. The change from man to wolf takes place involuntarily and the wolf-man, who has removed his clothes, flees to the forest to live on prey. When he is again transformed, he returns to human society.

In his study of the sources of the *lais* and Marie's technique in using folk motifs, Professor Battaglia asserts that Marie has used two distinct tales in composing the *lai*.[18] In the first part of the story she treats the theme of the werewolf, found in Pliny's *Historia naturalis* and developed as a tale in Chapter 62 of Petronius' *Satyricon*. Battaglia notes that the second part of the tale concerns the adultery of the wife, a theme which has no particular tie with the werewolf motif and can probably be attributed to Marie's interest in the psychology of love. In concluding her story, Marie turned to a folk theme which concerned not the wolf but the dog. Battaglia believes that the docility and faithfulness of the wolf in the latter part of Marie's text are drawn from the tradition of the faithfulness of the dog and that Bisclavret's vengeance derives from the story of the dog who remembered the face of his master's assassin for many years, eventually attacking the assailant and forcing him to confess his crime. Is it an accident that the story concerning the faithful dog's vengeance appears in Book VIII of Pliny's *Historia naturalis,* the same book in which the Latin author discusses the werewolf? The solution is indeed attractive, in that docility is certainly not an attribute of the wolf and the element of vengeance is clearly present. Yet, one should be cautious. The tameness of the wolf is less the result of faithfulness than the effect of his submerged human intellect or human nature, which has been forced to reside in the bestial shape. Furthermore, the vengeance does not relate to a master nor to an animal's humanlike intelligence in remembering an offense. Bisclavret has the shape of a wolf, but the reader is well aware that his intelligence is not bestial but human. Since the crime of his wife lies in the fact that she willfully robbed her husband of his human form, the conclusion to her tale may have been suggested by this contrast rather than by any conscious fusion of the werewolf motif to the tale of the dog's vengeance.

IX *Résumé* Lanval

King Arthur had been residing at Carlysle defending his country against the ravaging attacks of the Picts and Scots. At Pentecost the king was parceling out gifts and land among his knights. In his *largesse* the king remembered everyone except the foreign knight who had served him, Lanval. Because of his bravery and generosity, many at court envied and disliked the knight. Bereft and far from his homeland, Lanval became despondent. One day he rode away from the city and came to a stream running through a meadow. He dismounted and lay down. While he was lying there, two maidens approached and announced to him that they had been sent by their mistress to bring Lanval to her tent. The knight followed and soon found himself in a luxurious tent standing before the most beautiful woman he had ever seen. The lady informed him that she loved him and had come out of her country to find him. If he should conduct himself in a worthy and courteous manner, she would make him happier than any king or count, for she loved him dearly. Struck by love for the lady, Lanval agreed to become her lover and to do all that she commanded. The lady granted her love to the knight, who remained with her the entire afternoon. Prior to his departure, the lady set down one condition which he must observe in order not to lose her love: He must never disclose to anyone that she is his love. As long as their love remains secret, he will enjoy limitless wealth. To be with her he need only wish and she will appear to him, while remaining invisible to others.

Lanval returned to the court in high spirits. His newly found wealth permitted him to be exceedingly generous. As a consequence, his reputation grew and he became one of the most popular knights. One day, later that year, Lanval joined a number of other knights for an outing in a garden outside the queen's dwelling. Seeing Lanval among the knights, she decided to join the company with her retinue. When the queen was able to speak to him privately, she opened her heart to him, offering her love. Lanval refused her, giving as a reason his unwillingness to be unfaithful to the king. Offended by his rejection, the queen accused Lanval of being more interested in men than women. Unable to contain his anger, Lanval insulted the queen in return. But in so doing, he disclosed his love for his lady, further asserting that even her humblest servant was more beautiful than the queen. Greatly angered, the queen withdrew and told her husband, King Arthur, that Lanval had insulted her and had asked for her love. The king had Lanval arrested and confronted him with the charges. Lanval denied the accusation that he had asked the queen for her love, but he admitted his comments concerning the beauty of his lady's servants. Since there were no witnesses, only the charge of having insulted the queen was prosecuted. On the day set for the trial, he must produce this beautiful woman to prove that he had stated the truth. Lanval returned to his room in despair, grieved that he had lost the privilege of seeing his mistress. On the day of the trial, the barons were all gathered to witness the judgment. Just at the moment when the king was pressing for a verdict (Lanval had produced no evidence), two ladies of extraordinary beauty rode into court. They were so beautiful that everyone was sure that they had come to vindicate Lanval. However, the knight did not know them. Again the king was pressing the barons, when two more ladies arrived at the court and told the king to prepare a room for their mistress. Finally a single lady arrived at the court. She surpassed by far the beauty of the previous maidens and was the most beautiful woman the court had seen. She announced to the king that she was Lanval's *amie*. Everyone agreed that Lanval had certainly spoken the truth. When the lady began to leave the court, Lanval leaped onto the back of her horse and they both rode off to Avalon.

X Sources

Lanval is the only *lai* in the collection which is set in the court of King Arthur. The Arthurian setting has long been considered Marie's personal invention, since the anonymous *lai Graelent*, which has essentially the same story, is not placed in Arthur's court.[19] The validity of this argument, however, rests on the belief that *Graelent* preserved the more primitive version of the original folktale, thus making the Arthurian setting an artistic embellishment developed to take advantage of the vogue started by Geoffrey of Monmouth and furthered by Wace. Recent opinion favors the conclusion of Professor Segre, however, that *Graelent* is a composite imitation of a number of Marie's works, the principal one being *Lanval*.[20] This, of course, does not preclude Marie's personal addition of the Arthurian setting, but it removes the argument that it is manifestly an addition because it was not a part of the "original" story. Hoepffner had argued that Marie had borrowed many of the exteriors from Wace's *Brut* and Geoffrey of Monmouth's *Historia:* reference to Arthur's defense against the Picts and Scots, his coronation at Pentecost, reference to the Round Table, and the important role given the Duke of Cornouaille—all common elements in the earlier texts.[21]

Professor T. P. Cross pointed out that the basic folk motif of the text was that of the "Offended Fée," a type found in the lore of many countries in Western Europe and beyond.[22] In particular, he attached it to the type of Celtic Other-World tale where the fairy leaves her realm to visit her lover.[23] In this type she remains with the lover until he violates the command (the *ges*) which she has given him. Professor Cross cites a number of Irish tales from fourteenth- and fifteenth-century manuscripts, some of which are attested in the *Book of Leinster,* dated in the mid-twelfth century, but probably attesting an earlier oral provenance.

In conjunction with this Melusine type fairy motif is the famous

"Putiphar's Wife" episode, so named for the biblical story where Joseph of Egypt is approached by the wife of Putiphar. When he refuses her love, the woman accuses him of having attempted to seduce her, thus causing his arrest and imprisonment.[24]

Hoepffner proposed that the final episode of the trial showed influence from the trial of Ganelon in the *Chanson de Roland* and the judgment of Dair le Roux in the *Roman de Thebes*. In a recent article, R. N. Illingworth argued that the trial scene was influenced by the trial of Godwine le Danois, accused of a murder he did not commit, in Gaimar's *Estoire des Engleis*. Illingworth claims the resemblance less from the charges brought than from the fact that each case is an example of an *appel de nude parole*, an accusation made without support of witness. He notes that the procedure is very similar in the two texts.[25] In truth, the substance of the trials cited by Hoepffner and Illingworth bears small resemblance to the accusation made against Lanval. Illingworth's argument concerning the resemblance in procedure is well founded, but one cannot be certain here of literary influence. E. A. Francis demonstrated some time ago that the trial in *Lanval* followed closely the customary legal procedures of the period.[26]

XI *Résumé* Les Deus Amanz

There occurred formerly in Neustria, which we call Normandy, an *aventure* which everyone came to know. It is the story of two young people and how they died together because of love. The Bretons made a *lai* from the story and called it *Deus Amanz*. In those days the king of the Pistrains, who lived in the city of Pistre, had a very beautiful daughter whom he loved dearly. Many young men wished to marry the young girl, but the king, whose wife had died, did not wish to part with her. Many looked askance at the king for his attitude and insinuated that he loved his daughter too much. To allay gossip and yet retain his daughter, the king let it be known that he would marry the girl, but only to a worthy suitor, one strong enough to carry her up the high hill just outside of town without stopping to rest. At first many young men attempted the feat, but none succeeded. Then, because of the impossibility of the task, a long time passed during which no one sought the girl's hand.

Living at the court was a young boy, the son of a count, who greatly loved the king's daughter; and she in turn loved him. Although at first content to wait until he had acquired greater strength, the boy soon grew impatient. Realizing that he was not yet strong enough, the king's daughter sent him to Salerno to obtain a strength-giving potion from her aunt, a woman versed in medicine. The boy made the trip and returned with the potion. On the day of the test, the girl fasted and wore as little clothing as possible in an attempt to help her lover. Before lifting her to begin the trek, he confided the potion to the daughter. The boy began with great enthusiasm and quickly climbed more than halfway to the summit. Soon, however, the girl felt his strength begin to wane. She counselled and then urged him to drink the potion. Unfortunately, the young man was so dominated by his love and his desire to reach the top that he refused. The couple reached the summit, but the strain was so great that it cost the boy his life. Grieved by the death of her lover, the girl cast the potion on the hillside in frustration and died from the anguish of her loss. Afterwards the hillside flourished from the strength of the potion. The king, who found the two dead lovers, fainted from grief. He buried the two children together in one coffin on the hill, which came to be known as the "Mont des Deus Amanz."

XII Sources

It has long been recognized that there is nothing particularly Breton about this tale, yet Marie attributes it to them. Hoepffner saw in this *lai* another clear example of Marie's deliberate attempt to place her works in an archaic atmosphere. One can see this in her use of the old name Neustria (*en Neüstrie/Que nos apelons Normandie*), which Hoepffner surmises may have been drawn directly from Geoffrey of Monmouth (*Neustria quae nunc Normannia dicitur*) or Wace.[27] The story seems to derive from a legend related to the Prieuré des Deux-Amants, constructed on the summit of the hill bearing the same name in the twelfth century. Apparently the priory received its name from an ecclesiastical legend recounted in Chapter 42 of Book I of Gregory of Tours' *Historia Francorum*. According to Gregory, in the time of Theodosius I (379–395 A.D.), a certain senator named Injuriosus married a rich young lady by name of Scholastica. On the night of the wedding, the young girl tells the senator that she has made a vow of chastity. Filled with love for her, the young man agrees to live with her, yet allow her to keep the vow. When she died, Injuriosus thanked God that he was able to return her to Him in the pure state in which he had found her. After his death, Injuriosus was buried in another part of the church, but a miracle caused the two separate tombs to be joined. Thus did they come to be known as the Two Lovers. J. Wathelet-Willem has suggested that the Bretons had made a *lai* from the local Norman legend. She notes that there are seemingly a few references to such a *lai* in *Guiron le Courtois, Jaufré,* and perhaps in the *Flamenca*.[28] C. Segre has demonstrated that the *lai* shows considerable influence from Ovid's *Piramus*, especially in the death scene and in the burial of the two lovers together.[29] Wathelet-Willem noted that both the twelfth-century French *Piramus* and Marie's *lai* are alike in concentrating the story on the young girl. She suggests, therefore, that the French *Piramus* postdates Marie's *lai*, a hypothesis that may well be true, given Segre's persuasive demonstration that Marie clearly borrowed from Ovid and not the French version in her several uses of the story.

XIII   *Résumé* Yonec

In the city of Carwent in "Bretagne" there lived formerly a rich, old man who had married a beautiful young girl. Because of her beauty, the old man kept her locked in a tower with his old, widowed sister as a guardian. Although other women lived in another room, the young wife was not permitted to see them without the permission of her guardian. In fact, she did not leave the tower even to see relatives or friends. For seven years the husband kept her locked up and, as a result of her sadness and lack of interest, her beauty began to fade. In that time the young lady had not given him the heir he had hoped for.

One day when she was alone, she wished that she might have a lover as the ladies of olden times were reported to have had in such circumstances. No sooner had she made the wish than a goshawk landed in the window of the tower and changed into a handsome knight. The young man tried to reassure the frightened young lady and told her that he had loved her for a long time, but had not been able to visit her until she had wished for him. Fearing that the hawk-man was evil, she sought reassurance by asking him if he believed in God. To allay her fears, he had her send for a priest to administer communion. When the priest arrived, he assumed her form and received the Host. The young lady now trusted him and granted him her love. Before departing, the hawk-man told her that she might see him whenever she wished, but that she must be prudent, lest they be discovered. Time passed and the lady saw her lover as often as she could. Soon she regained the beauty she had lost.

Noticing the change in her, the husband suspected something and told his sister to hide in the room the next day to observe what would transpire when he left on a pretended journey. The old woman saw the hawk-man come to her brother's wife and revealed to him the circumstances. He placed spikes on the ledge of the window in an effort to kill the hawk. On his next visit the hawk was mortally wounded by the spikes. Before leaving, he announced to the young wife that she would bear him a child, whom she would name Yonec, and that he would console her. Moreover, he would avenge them both. Realizing that he was dying, the lover departed quickly. In great anguish the lady leaped from the twenty-foot-high window and frantically began to follow the trail of blood left by the dying lover. She came to a hill and found an opening where the blood trail led. She entered the hill and emerged from it to see a dazzling city where everything seemed made of silver. She followed the blood into the city and straight to the palace. While she was in the city, she saw no one. Inside the palace she passed through two rooms, each one having a sleeping knight whom she did not know. In the third room, she found her dying lover. He urged her to flee, fearing reprisal for her when his people should learn of his death. Before she left, he gave her a ring and sword: The ring would make her husband forget everything that had happened and the sword was to be kept for their child until he had come of age. She was to give him the sword on a day when her husband would take them both to an abbey where they would see his tomb and hear again the story of his death. She would give her son the sword and relate to him the circumstances of his birth. Then they would see what the son would do.

The lady returned and gave birth to the predicted son. He grew to manhood and was made a knight. On the Feast of Saint Aaron the old man took his wife and her son to the abbey at Karlion. There was the tomb of Muldumarec, the boy's father. The mother called to her son, gave him the sword, and told him how the old man had killed his father. After telling her story, the mother fainted on Muldumarec's tomb and died. The boy immediately killed the old husband with the sword left to him by his father. The mother was buried with honor with the boy's father and the people proclaimed Yonec the successor to his real father's title.

XIV Sources

It has generally been accepted that the sources for *Yonec* are to be found in Celtic tradition. The *lai* is set clearly in South Wales in the area of Carwent and Carlion, and none would contest the Celtic origin of the names Muldumarec and Yonec.[30] Professor Cross isolated two basic motifs in the tale, the shape-shifting fairly lover and the inclusa motif. The first he considered clearly derived from Irish tradition and the second, the inclusa type, ultimately of Oriental provenance, he believed to have been an addition necessary for comprehension by the twelfth-century French audience.[31] Among the tales which deal with a supernatural lover, the *Togail Bruidne Da Derga,* found in a fifteenth-century manuscript, but judged to have been composed in the eleventh century from two separate oral traditions of a much earlier date, bears the closest resemblance to Marie's *Yonec.* In this tale King Cormac of Ulster puts aside his first wife, who has given him only a daughter, to marry the fairy Étain. The fairy insists that the daughter of the king's first wife be killed. The king refuses to give his daughter to Étain and servants take the girl and place her in a calf shed where she is raised. A wickerwork house with an opening at the top is made for her. While she is in the house, she is visited by a bird who becomes a man. The bird-man lies with her and predicts that she will give birth to a son who will be named Conaire. The bird-lover warns that the son must not kill birds. Afterwards the son is born and later becomes king.

There are several points of resemblance between Marie's *Yonec* and the Irish tale. A woman who has been locked away is made pregnant by a bird-lover, who then predicts the birth and announces the name of the future child. Aside from these elements of similarity, however, there are a number of important differences between the texts. In Marie's *Yonec* the woman has been locked away by her husband (the inclusa motif, common in

Oriental as well as Western literature), and it is only by her wish that the bird-lover is able to come to her. After a period of love, the bird-lover is killed by the spikes set by the husband and the wife follows the bird-lover to his land. The final motif, the vengeance of the son on his father's murderer, is likewise not in the *Togail Bruidne Da Derga,* but Professor Illingworth has linked this motif with another Middle Irish work, the *Fotha Catha Cnucha,* a twelfth-century tale.[32] Recognizing that the relationship is tenuous, only that there is a son born who takes vengeance on his father's enemies, Illingworth points out that the vengeance motif is important in this Finn saga and that the exploits of Finn were related to the reign of Cormac. He believes that Marie's work is a combination of two different stories, one which includes the bird-lover and another which concerns a son's vengeance on his father's enemies. Illingworth argues that one can see that *Yonec* is a composite of two tales from the inconsistencies present in the story.[33] As for the jealous husband and the *inclusa* setting, Illingworth follows Hoepffner in asserting that one can see the courtly influence of the *malmariée* tradition, so common in French poetry. Since no extant Celtic tale has been found which joins the two motifs in question, Illingworth proposes that Marie or some *conteur* may have been responsible for it.

While it is true that Marie's *Yonec* is far removed in time from the hypothesized ninth-century oral tradition of the Irish texts, thus making plausible the great differences between her *lai* and the proposed basic folk motifs, it is no wonder, given the slight similarities, that some have rejected the likelihood of Irish provenance. M. B. Ogle early stressed that all of the motifs in *Yonec* were accessible to Marie in classical literature.[34] He pointed to the popularity in Oriental and in classical literature of the *inclusa* motif and of the motif where a mortal or supernatural being gains access to the imprisoned woman. In this regard, Pietro Toldo had earlier cited two stories which he deemed of particular interest because of close resemblances to Marie's *lai:* the Indian story entitled *The Fan Prince* and the Russian tale *The Resplendent Falcon.*[35] Of the two, however, it is the Russian tale which is truly striking. In this tale a lady is visited in her room by a falcon who changes into a handsome knight. For a time the bird-lover goes and comes as he pleases through the window of the room. Just as in Marie's *Yonec,* the girl's beauty is enhanced by her love. Jealous of her love, her two sisters place needles, sharp knives, and broken glass on the window through which the bird enters. The falcon is wounded, but the lady, who was sleeping at the time, does not realize what has happened until she awakens to see the blood from his wound. She follows him to his kingdom, proves that she was not responsible for his wounds, and is married to him.

Clearly there is a striking resemblance between this tale and Marie's *Yonec*. But even here there are important elements which are lacking. The lady is again not being imprisoned by a jealous husband, nor does she summon the lover herself. Furthermore, no son is born to the two lovers and no vengeance is taken on anyone. It should be noted, however, that the missing elements from what is otherwise a strikingly similar tale are essentially related to the jealous husband motif lacking in this tale. Since there is no jealous husband, the summoning powers of the lady become irrelevant. And without a jealous husband, the motif of the child's birth and subsequent vengeance loses its meaning in the story. If this story bears a closer resemblance to Marie's *lai*, questions of dating and accessibility remain. How early can one date this tale, does it represent a common folktale that Marie might have heard, or was it drawn from sources which had been influenced by Marie?

Because of the names in the text, the setting, and the supernatural element, one is perhaps led too quickly to grant the Celtic origin of the *lai*. The sources indicated in extant Celtic materials are not that persuasive. There is no one tale which really resembles Marie's *lai*. It is possible that Breton storytellers adapted the tale, affording Celtic names and setting, or that Marie herself added the necessary elements to give the *lai* its Celtic flavor.

XV *Résumé* Laüstic

I shall tell you an adventure about which the Bretons made a *lai*. It is called *Laüstic*. In French the word is *russignol* and in English *nihtegale*. In a city in Seint Mallo there lived next door to one another two knights well known for their goodness and worth. The one had a beautiful wife and the other, who was unmarried, loved his neighbor's wife dearly. Although she returned his love, they conducted themselves wisely and in such a manner that none ever took notice of it. The lady was closely watched when the husband was away and a high wall separated the two dwellings. Although they were unable to come together, they could see one another from their windows and often exchanged gifts. Often the woman got up at night to go to the window, for she knew that her lover was there. Her husband noticed that she got up frequently at night and asked her the reason. She replied that she loved to hear the nightingale sing and that he who had never heard its song did not know joy. Angered by her response, the husband had traps set for the bird. Having caught the bird, he called to his wife to tell her that she would no longer have to worry about being kept awake by the bird's song. Angrily he killed the bird and threw it at his wife. Realizing that she could no longer go to the window at night, yet wishing her lover to know that her absence would not be a sign of lessening love, she decided to send him a message. She wrapped the body of the bird in a samite cloth on which she embroidered a message in gold thread. When the lover received the bird, he placed it in a little box, sealed it, and carried it with him always.

XVI   *Sources*

No specific analogue to Marie's tale has been found in earlier literature, although a number of similar stories have been found in subsequent literature.[36] Segre may well be right in relating Marie's text to Ovid's *Piramus*. He notes that fifty of the 160 lines develop the frame story, closely parallel to the Ovidian text.[37] Further support for this thesis is the similarity of the embroidered message, which R. Cargo has related to Ovid's *Philomela*.[38]

XVII   *Résumé* Milun

Milun was a native of South Wales. From the time when he had been made a knight, none had been found who could equal him in combat. His fame spread to many lands. The daughter of a baron from his country heard of his excellence and fell in love with him. She sent him a message offering her love. Thereafter, Milun became her lover and the young girl soon became pregnant. Realizing that she would be severely reproached for having a child out of wedlock, she determined to conceal the baby's birth and to send the child to be raised by her sister. When the child was born, she placed a ring around its neck and had him taken by Milun with a letter to her sister. She asked her sister to raise the child and inform him concerning his identity when he had come of age. Afterward, Milun left the country to seek his fortune. In the interim the girl was married to a baron from the region. The girl was greatly distressed by the turn of events, for she had thought that she would always remain with Milun. Milun returned from his adventures and was grief-stricken when he heard the news. Realizing that he could no longer see his loved one, he trained a swan to carry letters back and forth between them. Thus did they correspond for twenty years, seeing one another on only rare occasions.

Meanwhile, the son grew up and was told of his parents and of the great renown of his father. He decided to cross the channel into Brittany to seek his fortune. The new knight was highly successful. His fame spread both for his prowess and for his great generosity. When Milun heard of the knight's success, he determined to defeat him and then seek his son. In a tourney held at Mont-Saint-Michel, Milun met the young knight in combat. Even though he struck him squarely, he only succeeded in breaking his lance. The young man, however, unhorsed the older knight, but, in so doing, caught a glimpse of his white beard and hair. Sorry to have fought a man so much older than he, the young knight returned his horse. Milun recognized the ring on the young man's finger and questioned him concerning his identity. Both father and son were overjoyed to find one another. Milun recounted to him how much he had loved his mother and how his mother had been married to another. The son vowed to kill the man to whom his mother had been married and to unite Milun to his mother in marriage. After the two knights had recrossed the channel, they received news that the mother's husband had died. The son reunited his parents and they lived happily ever after.

XVIII Sources

Basically, the motif of the combat between father and son has been related to the frequent use of this motif in the *chansons de geste* and the folk tradition in general. In *Gormont et Isembart*, the adversary of Isembart prior to the intervention of his father was named Miles de Gailart.[39] C. Bullock-Davies has recently

[92]

claimed that the use of the swan as a love messenger relates Marie's tale to a story cycle current in South Wales and particularly in the Carwent/Carlion area.[40]

XIX *Résumé* Chaitivel

In Brittany at Nantes there was an exceedingly beautiful and refined woman. So beautiful was she that there was not a knight in the land who could resist her charm. Four knights in particular loved her and sought her love. She cared for them all equally and did not wish to give up all of them just to have one, so she led each one to believe that it was he whom she favored. One day the four knights entered a tourney. Each sought to display his prowess in hopes of winning the woman's esteem. All day they fought well, but, toward the end, they foolishly allowed themselves to become separated from their party. Their opponents fell on them, killing three and wounding one seriously. When the woman saw what had happened, she lamented her great loss. The three dead knights she buried handsomely and she had the wounded knight cared for by the best physicians. Greatly did she lament her misfortune, so that she decided to compose a *lai* and call it "Quatre Dols" in memory of her loss. When the remaining knight heard the lady's plan, he objected to the title of the proposed *lai*. He pointed out that the knights who had died were now past grief; he alone must remain alive and in misery. Daily he must live in the presence of the woman he loves without being able to love her. He maintained that the *lai* should really be called *Chaitivel*. The woman agreed. Some call it by one name, some by the other.

XX *Sources*

The *lai* does not include any of the traditional folk material. The love-question resembles the type of argument found in Andreas Capellanus' *De Amore*.

XXI *Résumé* Chevrefoil

King Mark had become very angry with his nephew, Tristan, and had banished him from his land because of Tristan's love for the queen. Tristan had gone to his homeland, South Wales, where he had remained a full year. Because of his grief, he determined to return to Cornwall to see the queen. When he arrived, he stayed with some peasants and sought news of the queen's activities. Much to his delight, he learned that she would be journeying to Tintagel for Pentecost. On the day of her journey, he went to the route that she would take and devised a plan. He cut a hazel branch, squared it, and carved his name. He knew that if the queen saw it that she would take note of it, since formerly it had so occurred. When the queen saw the stick along the road, she stopped and went into the woods. There the couple spent a few moments together, the queen expressing the hope that King Mark would soon pardon Tristan. Their parting was indeed grievous, illustrating the truth of Tristan's message to the queen that their love was like the hazel and honeysuckle; together they thrive, apart they perish. For the joy he had in seeing the queen, Tristan composed a *lai* to commemorate the event.

XXII *Sources*

This short episode concerning Tristan and Iseut has long caused scholars to question its relationship to the Tristan legend itself. If one believes Marie, it represents an authentic episode in the lore surrounding the two lovers, one meeting among others in their relationship. Yet, none of the extant versions contains the episode.

Both Hoepffner and Foulet believed that Marie's text shows signs of her having known the "primitive" Tristan story from which the later versions drew. As an indication, Hoepffner notes that Marie makes Tristan a native of Wales, in accord with the versions of Beroul and Eilhart von Oberg, believed to represent the earlier version of the *roman,* whereas Thomas has him come from the mysterious land of Ermenie near Armorica.[41] But the fact remains that the episode in question is not found in the versions believed to represent the early tradition. It has been suggested that Marie drew her inspiration for the story from the episode which Eilhart relates concerning the voyage of Tristan and Kaherdin. To justify his cool attitude toward Iseut of the White Hands, Tristan tells Kaherdin that she treats him with indifference. He adds that Iseut la Blonde treats her dog better than Iseut of the White Hands treats him. To prove his assertion, the two men make a trip to observe the actions of Queen Iseut. Tristan secretly sends a messenger ahead to inform Iseut of the circumstances and to warn her that Tristan and Kaherdin will be concealed along the route she is to travel. By a signal from

Tristan, the queen becomes aware of their presence and is able to prove the truth of Tristan's earlier statement. Did Marie borrow the exterior elements of this episode in providing the narrative frame for her own text? Foulet believed so and argued that the messenger used in the Eilhart episode clears up the ambiguity concerning the nature of the writing on the *bastun* (stick). He proposed that Marie's text implies prior communication between the lovers and that the stick served only as a signal of his presence.[42] Stefan Hofer rejects the idea that Marie's tale has any authenticity as an episode from the folk tradition. He maintains that Marie deliberately used hints and allusions from well-known Tristan events merely to lend an aura of authenticity to her anecdote. Professor Hofer bases his argument on the fact that Marie's tale does not accord with Eilhart's version, which he considers a more or less faithful rendition of the original. Given the sequence of events recounted by Eilhart, it is impossible to fit the visit by Tristan harmoniously into the context of the *roman*.[43] The inconsistencies which Hofer notes are valid, but the authenticity of Marie's text is only threatened if one grants that Eilhart von Oberg's text contained all the oral material which may have circulated about the lovers and their relationship. If there were an oral tradition, it is likely that many anecdotes were told about the lovers which would be contradictory and could not be placed logically into one narrative.

XXIII *Résumé* Eliduc

There once lived in Brittany a valiant and worthy knight named Eliduc. Because of his valor and worth, he was loved by his king. However, slanderers turned the king against him, causing him to be banished. Eliduc was grieved by the forthcoming separation from his beloved wife, Guildeluec, and he arranged for her to be well cared for in his absence. Before departing, he pledged to her that he would be faithful.

Eliduc crossed the channel and placed himself in the service of a king much beleaguered by his enemies. Because of his success in battle, the knight's fame reached the king's daughter, Guilliadun, who decided to offer the knight her love. Eliduc accepted an invitation to meet the girl and was struck by love when he saw her. Torn between his desire to love and the memory of his pledge, Eliduc did not tell the girl that he was married, yet he refrained from any actions which would violate the oath he had made to his wife. Thus did he remain in his dilemma until he was called home, pardoned by his king. Before leaving, he promised Guilliadun that he would return for her at a specified time.

Eliduc returned home and aided his king in combat. Guildeluec noticed that he was sad and questioned him, fearing that slanderers might have spread rumors about her. Eliduc feigned that his sadness resulted from his being absent from the foreign king, who needed him so badly. Thus, on the appointed day, Eliduc returned to get Guilliadun, who was overjoyed to hear of his arrival. Guilliadun departed with Eliduc for Brittany, still unaware that he had a wife. During the voyage a frightful storm arose. In their consternation, the crew began to blame the illicit affair for their misfortune. In his anger, one member disclosed to Guilliadun that Eliduc had a wife. Stunned by the revelation, Guilliadun fell unconscious. Eliduc believed that she was dead and, when they arrived in port, took her to a remote chapel, unable to bring himself to bury her. Daily he visited her and soon noticed that the condition of her body did not change. His wife, Guildeluec, grieved to see her husband so sad. One day she followed him to the chapel. Suddenly everything was clear to her. Eliduc loved the young girl lying in the chapel. Since the time of their separation, Guildeluec's interest had turned toward a life of service to God. She was moved by her husband's grief and the beauty of the young girl. At that moment a weasel ran across the unconscious girl's body and a valet killed it. The weasel's mate brought a red flower of great medicinal power and revived the dead weasel. Guildeluec seized the flower and used it to revive Guilliadun, who reproached Eliduc bitterly for his treachery. Guildeluec defended Eliduc against the girl's attack. Not long afterwards, Guildeluec withdrew to a monastery and Eliduc married Guilliadun. As time passed the two lovers likewise turned toward God. Guildeluec received Guilliadun into the monastery like a sister. They all ended their lives in the glorious service of the Lord.

XXIV *Sources*

Once again the settings and names in the text point toward a Breton origin. The opening scene is set in Brittany and Eliduc's travel across the channel follows the itinerary found in Geoffrey's *Historia* and in Wace. Except for some doubt concerning the name Guilliadun, there is general agreement that the names are of Celtic derivation. And the alternate title, "Guildeluec ha Gualadun," with its Breton conjunction *ha*, leads one to believe that Marie is drawing directly from a source with Breton affiliations. Yet the basic folktale concerning the man with two wives has no particular Celtic association. Professor Levi pointed to the similarities with *Horn, Bueve de Hamtone,* and *Ille et Galeron* (discussed in Chapter 1) and suggested that one could see in the tale the confrontation between Christian monogamy and early Celtic polygamy.[44] However, there is no text prior to Marie to establish the hypothesis. Professor Nutt's attempt to link *Eliduc* with the Snow-White type of tale and the Gaelic story of Goldtree and Silver-tree likewise lacks any early source which might add substance to his argument.[45] In the legend concerning the Count of Gleichen (sixteenth century), and in the *Histoire de Gilion de Trasegnies* (fifteenth century), the hero ends up with two wives, but the tales are both much later than Marie.[46]

As for the medicinal herb which revives the sleeping Guilliadun, numerous analogues can be found in classical literature, where the animal involved is a serpent. In mediaeval literature, reference to the weasel in such an instance occurs in Alexander Neckam's *De Naturis Rerum*, in the bestiaries of Hugh de Saint-Victor and Richart de Fournival, and in *The Topography of Ireland* of Giraldus Cambrensis.

XXV   Conclusion

In considering the collection as a whole, one must admit that the Celtic source material is neither so prominent nor so persuasive as one might expect when dealing with tales which purportedly stem from the Breton tradition. Except for *Guigemar*, *Lanval*, and *Chevrefoil*, the relationship to Celtic source material is tenuous to say the least. *Equitan, Le Fresne, Bisclavret, Les Deus Amanz, Laüstic, Chaitivel*, and *Eliduc* have no link with any demonstrable Breton folklore. The case for *Yonec* is scarcely more persuasive for the Breton sources than for an argument which leads toward a general European folk tradition, and only the love-messenger episode in *Milun* has been suggested to have Welsh origins. Yet, if only three *lais* are clearly Breton, nearly all the trappings are Celtic, either continental or insular. The settings, titles, and names of the characters, to say nothing of Marie's own consistent reference to her sources, are impressively Celtic in derivation. Hoepffner's attempt to show that Marie used literary settings and names from Geoffrey and Wace does not explain all the names nor all the geographical locations. If the Celtic material in the *lais* is authentic, one might well argue that it is only natural that a number of places and names would accord with these texts, in that these writers were all borrowing from the same tradition.

It will probably never be known for sure whether Marie's reference to the Bretons and her use of Breton settings represent a literary device or stem from a bona fide oral tradition. However, if one believes her statements, then certain conclusions might be drawn. The Bretons (both continental and insular) were known for their storytelling and their *lais*. It is likely that they retold many tales not specifically Breton and adapted them to their own tradition and time, much as Marie herself undoubtedly did in developing the *lais*.[47] This would explain the addition of exterior elements, such as names, titles, and geography, which give the texts their Celtic flavor, just as the moral issues and the chivalric customs have undoubtedly been transformed by Marie to accord with twelfth-century tastes and society. In fact, given the importance of patronage to mediaeval letters, it is not unlikely that various families (such as those cited by Miss Francis) did exercise influence in this way. The specific names and locations of some of the tales would not have been without interest to these families. A similar process can be seen in the large cycle of poems written concerning the First Crusade. The interest of the Bouillon family (and others) in attaching their heritage to the legend of the Swan-Knight is well known, a fact which may well have influenced the joining of the folktale concerning the birth of the seven swan children to the legend of the Swan-Knight and these to Godfrey of Bouillon's exaggerated role as depicted in the cycle surrounding the First Crusade. Given the paucity of extant Breton material which might otherwise establish authentic Celtic sources, it is not improbable that Breton trappings indicate the perpetual nature of the storytelling process. The storyteller constantly reuses old themes in different combinations, transposes settings and names, and changes the period, customs, and moral questions to attract the audience for which he writes.

CHAPTER 7

Marie's Concept of Love

SINCE the earliest criticism of the *Lais*, scholars have recognized that love is the unifying theme of the collection.[1] Regardless of the source of the folk motifs involved or the nature of the plot, the principal action of each *lai* concerns the subject of love. In spite of such unanimity, however, there has been wide disagreement concerning Marie's concept of love. Some have seen considerable influence from the so-called courtly love of the *troubadours*, in that the description of love in the *lai* follows patterns and uses language associated with the love lyric. Yet, if the exterior aspects of this love are present, the essential nature of the love bond seems quite different. Only in *Equitan* does one find the love-service relationship, and only in *Chaitivel* does the love resemble the rational type found in Andreas Capellanus' *De Amore*. Others have seen the kind of fatal passion associated with Tristan and Iseut. Professor Schürr stresses that fate is behind the force of love in the *Lais* and that the nature of love in the collection can be understood only when one recognizes the dominance of the fatal passion.[2]

Joseph Bédier attempted to solve the dichotomy by joining the "courtly love" with the so-called Celtic concept of love.[3] For Bédier, the love in the *Lais* represents a joining of the indigenous Celtic element with the newly arrived concepts from the South. Bédier describes the movement to the north of the "Provençal" concept of love which, he claims, changed the warrior society into the more refined society of the twelfth century. This transformation he compares to the *éclosion* of the Renaissance or Romanticism. However, this new love soon becomes less of a passion than an art form. Recognizing that this concept of love bears only an exterior resemblance to Marie's *Lais*, Bédier turned to the Celtic element to explain the "fatality" present in many of the *lais*: "To the innocent and unrefined sensuality of the old *chansons de geste* and the *galanterie* of Provençal poetry, the Breton *contes* oppose a pure idealism." [4] No longer is love a question of elegance, worth, or proper action, but an indescribable quality or bond. To the question, why does Tristan love Iseut, he answers: . . . *parce que c'est lui et parce que c'est elle. Leur passion en elle-même sa cause et sa fin.*[5] Following Bédier's analysis, Conigliani sees the *Erec* of Chrétien and the *Lais* as transition works between the early half-epic and half-romances, such as the *Roman de Troie* and *Roman de Thebes*, and later courtly literature.[6] In this early work the Breton love plays an essential role, but it is "simple" and "impulsive" and ". . . is unaware of the psychological complexities of the new school. . . ." Marie took this legendary material, ". . . inspired by a simple, violent and popular passion . . . ,"[7] and clothed it in the features of the "new" love introduced from Provence. Significantly, however, *lais* such as *Le Fresne* and *Eliduc* receive no consideration in these interpretations and the love found in *Equitan* and *Guigemar*, considered only in the light of "courtly love," is treated as if it were of the same nature as that found in *Eliduc* or *Le Fresne*.[8]

Of great importance to the discussion is the extra-marital nature of these loves. Did Marie approve of love outside of marriage? If so, is this not further proof of the influence of the "new" love ethic on her and the period? Professor Schiött notes that eight of Marie's *lais* concern an adulterous relationship.[9] Moreover, Marie clearly favors some of these loves. Yet, in other cases, such as *Bisclavret* and *Equitan*, the adulterous lovers are severely condemned and punished. Professor Schiött concludes that Marie approves extramarital love under certain circumstances: When the deceived partner has been cruel and merits deception and when the lovers are loyal to one another. However, Schiött's solution leaves many questions. Wherein does the husband in *Milun* merit deception, and is not Marie clearly sympathetic to Eliduc, even though her admiration for Guildeluec is unquestionably greater than for any heroine except, perhaps, Fresne?

To continue the study of the *Lais* in terms of Bédier's analysis or in terms of the love versus marriage controversy seems inevitably to lead to contradictions. Furthermore, with the serious challenge by contemporary critics to the concept of "courtly love" and the doubt cast on the intent of Andreas Capellanus' *De Amore*, it is perhaps altogether erroneous to analyze the *Lais* in terms of a code of love whose existence is doubtful. Similarly, seeking a fatalistic Celtic love (whose existence is essentially based on an interpretation of the love in the fragmented Tristan story) in the *Lais* is equally artificial. It is more profitable to consider only what can be found in the *Lais* and to interpret this in mediaeval terms.

It is my purpose to show that the central issue in the *Lais* is not "courtly love," not the development of the psychology of characters, but the nature of love itself, the love so often personified in mediaeval literature, so often treated as a natural force, formidable and powerful precisely because it does subvert the reason and cause man to react in a way that ultimately brings him suffering and grief. Considering love in this light causes a considerable adjustment in our modern thought processes and judgments. The nature of the love and its quality must not be judged in terms of its coincidence with marriage or with the social situation; it must not be judged evil or good based on whether or not it is adulterous.[10] To judge love in this way is to ignore its totally independent nature and strength. It is to ignore the awful reality of love, to hamper it artificially by rules which love itself does not recognize. This is only to emphasize why the mediaeval religious writer insisted that reason have primacy and that the kind of human love which causes a *passio* inevitably causes misery and suffering.

Such a consideration of love is encountered in both mediaeval secular and religious literature and in secular mediaeval commentaries and mythographies. One such work is the anonymous fourteenth-century commentary on the poem *Les Echecs amoureux*,[11] which, though late, contains much traditional material. In this work the author is careful to point out that he is considering only natural things and thus avoids any consideration of the mysteries of the sacraments and the supernatural. The author's extensive consideration of love is very helpful in analyzing the *Lais*, both in terms of his analysis of love and in terms of his (for us) strange consideration of love only as a natural phenomenon, irrespective of possible conflicts with holy institutions or secular customs.

In his treatment of love, the commentator describes the nature of Venus and her three sons, Cupid, the god of love, Iacchus, god of games and worldly solace, and Hymen, the god of harmony and amorous consideration. Throughout the remaining folios, the author concentrates on Venus and Cupid, but his brief description of Hymen is helpful in considering the *Lais*:

Hymen secretly signifies the delectation that is in marriage, in which the people are by the ordinance of the law legally joined together. And this delectation, as they say, is the greatest of them all and the least dishonored by sorrow, because one can more freely, easily and legally accomplish all these delectations in marriage.[12]

The author obviously approves of marriage and considers love in marriage not only possible but the greatest delectation of all. Yet throughout the rest of his essay on love he basically treats love outside of marriage without hint of disapproval of the love itself. This is because the love-sentiment itself is the same as that which he approved in marriage. That it should be found outside of marriage is a fact of life. And, if one reads his comments carefully, he implies that this love often leads to dishonor and sorrow. Such is the case in Marie. Love is approved when it is of high quality and condemned when it is only concupiscence or selfish love. Furthermore, because of the obstacles confronting it, the love always involves suffering and frequently ends in grief even when the love itself is approved.

However, the author's purpose is not to consider love in marriage or love within the law, but the inclination of love itself wherever it may occur. Hence he passes on to a consideration of Venus and Cupid. Venus is defined as concupiscence or the natural inclination which moves all toward carnal delight. This "inclination," he continues, is ordained by nature for the continuation and health of the species. A second inclination, a particular concupiscence, is placed in us by nature to seek a specific partner with whom love may be fulfilled most agreeably. [13] It is important that the two inclinations be joined for a lasting, unbreakable bond worthy of man. Without the joining of these two inclinations, man's interest would only be cupidity and his love more appropriate for an animal: "Thus would he take indifferently whomever he met first and would make of her his mistress if he could. Such a love would be neither reasonable nor proper. It would be a love suited to animals rather than men." [14] Finally, the commentator concludes that, in the kind of love under consideration, there are essentially two types: one cupidinous and selfish, loving only the delight ". . . without any concern for what fruit may come of it . . . ," [15] the other placing the delight after the person and pleased at the thought of the fruit which might result. Yet perhaps the most significant aspect of the entire analysis is that each love results in suffering. The love called concupiscence is bestial and demeaning in its intent to use another person selfishly. The second love, though good in itself and provider of perfect delectation in marriage, naturally causes the individuals to suffer deprivation and/or shame when there are obstacles to its natural fulfillment in marriage. [16]

I Guigemar, Equitan, Le Fresne

The first three *lais* in the text used by Professor Ewert seem to present three distinct types of love. [17] The first, *Guigemar*, presents a love which is neither charity nor cupidity, but a love begun as a *passio* and ennobled by the loyalty of the couple. The second, *Equitan*, is clearly a love of cupidity, and the third, *Le Fresne*, clearly the noblest of the three, presents a love of charity which transcends all obstacles and suffering.

Guigemar is built on the conventional motif of antithesis, in this case an ironic curse. The central figure of the *lai*, Guigemar, is the traditional Hippolytus character who has, as yet, shown no interest in love. While on a hunt, he is wounded in the thigh by a rebounding arrow which he shot into a white hind. Before dying, the white hind pronounces a curse on Guigemar: Never will he be healed from his wound until he suffers greater love for a lady and she for him than any lovers have ever endured (vv. 108–18). The ironic nature of the hind's curse is seen in the fact that Guigemar can be cured only by doing what is uninteresting to him (loving). Furthermore, the cure itself will not totally relieve Guigemar of his suffering, but will only change its nature. Love will cure his physical wound, but will add even more suffering in a spiritual sense (vv. 378–84).

The nature of the love he experiences for the lady destined to "cure" him follows the traditional lines of a *passio*. Left alone, the lover reviews his situation (vv. 399–416). Pensive and anguished, he begins to meditate on the lady and his circumstances. As he contemplates his plight, his anguish increases, for he realizes that, without gratification, he must "languish from *cest mal* forever" and "die in grief." Love so occupies his thoughts and gains hegemony over his reason that he cannot escape this suffering, *Kar [is]si fait ki me[u]s ne poet.* All night he turns over in his mind her words and her image.[18]

In lines 483 to 498, Marie comments on the nature of love: It is a sickness, an inner wound, which, because it comes from nature, endures. Many make sport of love and take their pleasure wherever they find it, boasting of their conquests. But this is not love, it is madness, evil, and lechery. Better is it to serve and love someone loyally. In this description it should be noted that suffering pertains to all "natural love." Marie condemns sheer cupidity and praises a love of a nobler quality which emphasizes loyalty and service. However, this love is not exempt from suffering, but is nobler only in that it is not totally governed by the bestial instinct.

For a time the lovers are happy, but, just as Boethius laments in the *De Consolatione Philosophiae*, those who place their hope of pleasure in the things of this life eventually must suffer the reversal of Fortune (vv. 535–42). After a brief respite, the lovers are again cast into suffering, this worse than before, since one suffers more over things lost than over things which he has never obtained.

Marie now shifts her attention to the sufferings of the woman, who, because of her love, spends two years in prison, undergoing physical privation and mental anguish. Her despair is such that she prefers death to further anguish (vv. 660–70).[19] When Guigemar again finds her, she is once more in the possession of someone else and has undergone considerable anguish because of her love for him. Only after the combat between Guigemar and Meriadus does the lovers' suffering come to an end.

It should be clear from the foregoing that the love of Guigemar and his lady fits neither the "courtly love" treated in the *De Amore* nor the imperious, fatal love which Bédier attributed to the Celtic love-tradition.[20]It is neither a love controlled by cupidity and self-interest nor a love which evades all control by the rational faculty, for the lovers mutually pledge an unending faith to one another. The knot and belt, which another person could undo only by force and violence, are symbols of their vow, a vow not made because an imperious love permitted no other solution, but because their interest was not in delight and cupidity, but in the person. It should be observed that the quality of the love between

Guigemar and his lady gains or loses nothing by her marriage. Marie's failure to punish the two lovers does not stem from a social belief that love is superior to marriage. Their relatively happy ending has little to do with adultery; it stems rather from the extraordinary quality of love and loyalty exhibited by the lovers. In every *lai* Marie deals with the nature of love. No matter what kind of love it is, the lover undergoes suffering. [21] The results of the love always depend on whether the love is in reality cupidity and self-interest or a love of higher quality.

In many ways the second *lai*, *Equitan*, presents a direct contrast with *Guigemar*. Unlike Guigemar, Equitan is described as being *mut curteis*, and whereas Guigemar loved the hunt and was essentially uninterested in love, Equitan *deduit amout e drüerie*. In the following lines, Marie strongly emphasizes the danger to one whose only interest is *deduit* and *drüerie*: "Those who have neither sense nor measure in love place their lives in great neglect. Such is the measure of love that none can keep reason in it" (vv. 17–20). It is this feature which essentially distinguishes the quality of love treated in the two *lais*. Whereas Equitan's love is entirely motivated by cupidity and carnal pleasure, Guigemar's pleasure is the natural result of a love rooted in a deeper human relationship exemplified by the lovers' voluntary commitment and loyalty to one another.

The importance of the quality of the love itself is highlighted by the fact that, in many respects, the process of love, those elements which one would see as "courtly," is essentially the same in both stories. One need only compare the passage in which Equitan is struck by love to that in *Guigemar* to see the close similarity (vv. 54–63). Like Guigemar, he is wounded by love, becomes *murnes* and *pensis*, and then falls into the reverie or *passio* in which he suffers trembling and wakeful contemplation. At this point, one should recall Marie's earlier comment on the nature and danger of love cited above. Contrary to the love in *Guigemar*, the cupidinous love of Equitan and his lady causes a subversion of the reason and leads them into *démesure* and crime.[22]

The lesion to the rational faculty which Marie emphasizes at the beginning of the *lai* is fully demonstrated in the illogical arguments of the two lovers in each passage, for the argument is invariably founded on the necessity of maintaining faith and loyalty in love.

Early in the *lai*, the king recognizes the faith he owes to the seneschal, if he expects a return in kind, and notes that what he contemplates will violate this faith (vv. 70–76). But this conclusion quickly gives way to specious reasoning formed by his desire and self-interest (vv. 77–88). He recognizes the breach of faith, but rationalizes it by arguing that it would be even worse for him to become *afolez*. Moreover, what would become of the woman's *curteisie*, if she were never to enjoy *drüerie*. He concludes by the "generous" thought that the seneschal cannot expect to have her all to himself.

Later in the *lai*, after the two have declared themselves, the seneschal's wife laments that their love cannot endure because she is not equal in station to the king: "Love is not worthy if it is not equal" (v. 137). Ironically, she argues that loyalty is a necessary ingredient in love (vv. 138–42). And she concludes that loyalty cannot be given freely when a superior partner requires love *par seignurie* (v. 148). Curiously, the king seeks to allay her fears by reasoning which is analogous to her own. Scornfully he remarks that such a consideration is merely a *bargaine de burgeis* (v. 152). Love, he asserts, is based solely on loyalty and thus excludes such base considerations (vv. 155–62). He concludes his argument with a statement whose ironic implication can scarcely be missed: "Those who are fickle and cheat in love are mocked and deceived. We have seen it happen to many" (vv. 163–66).

In the next lines, the king's inverted reasoning leads to the complete subversion of his reason and to the fulfillment of Marie's earlier statement. What began as a lament of the seneschal's wife that she is not his equal and would of necessity be subservient to him, ends by the king's complete subservience to her: "My lady, I give myself to you. Do not regard me as a king, but as your man and lover. I swear to you faithfully that I shall do your pleasure. Do not let me die for love of you. You be the lady and I the servant, you haughty and I suppliant" (vv. 169–76). It is a classic example of reason submitting to the direction of the bestial passions and opens the way for the treachery which follows. For it is now the woman who governs the king's action. Without thought he eagerly agrees to do whatever she wills whether it *turt a folie u a saveir* (v. 240). The direct result of their new relationship is clearly indicated by Marie as they made their pledge by an exchange of rings. With no little irony, Marie notes that they loved each other greatly: "Then they died and came to an end because of it" (v. 184). The evil perpetrated by the cupidity of the lovers leads to their own destruction in the boiling water while, in Marie's words, the seneschal remains *sauf e gariz* (v. 300).

By their complete loyalty, the lovers in *Guigemar* eventually overcome the obstacles which have prevented the fulfillment of their love. In *Equitan*, however, the lovers speak of loyalty and plan treachery. And because their selfishly based love leads to an act of crime, they are punished.

Just as *Equitan* presents interesting contrasts and parallels with *Guigemar*, so does the third *lai*, *Le Fresne*, bear a striking resemblance to *Equitan*. Not that the narrative or story itself is at all analogous, but the principal issues and situations are similar.

In both stories the question of unequals in love and marriage becomes crucial to the development of the story. Second, whereas *Equitan* develops the proverb that those who deceive will be deceived, *Le Fresne* illustrates a similar proverb, that those who judge will be judged. In *Le Fresne*, the mother's uncharitable accusation concerning the woman who has twins becomes self-condemnation when she herself has twins. It is the mother's malicious comments which cause Fresne to lose her heritage and nearly ruin her life. However, the nature of the love in *Le Fresne* is entirely different from that in *Equitan*. Like the love in *Guigemar* and *Equitan*, it begins as a natural love and leads to suffering, but here the similarity ends. For Fresne's love is not based on cupidity and self-interest as in *Equitan*, it is rather the transcending love or charity which includes the sacrifice of one's own happiness for the happiness of the loved one.

That Marie sought to illustrate the magnificent beauty and miraculous power of charity is clearly developed from the beginning of the story. After the mother, who had earlier accused the family friend of adultery, has given birth to twins herself, she decides that she cannot face her husband and must dispose of one of the children. She realizes the sin that she is committing, but deliberately turns from God by choosing eternal damnation over the shame of this life: "I prefer to atone for it before God than to be shamed" (vv. 93–94).

As a gift to the baby being sent away, she gives a rich blanket and the golden ruby ring given to her by her husband at their marriage. The gift of the ring should not be overlooked, in that it is again mentioned in the denouement and provides an important key to the full meaning of the *lai*. The wedding ring, the symbol of their mutual loyalty and faith, is symbolic of the pledge which the woman has forfeited and granted as a legacy to her daughter. One should also note that the ring is of pure gold, symbol of the holy and the eternal. By her own words the mother is forfeiting God's eternity, symbolized by the ring. And the ruby, well-known symbol of charity, represents the uncharitable action of the mother and her loss of that virtue. What the mother once had and lost is granted to her daughter as a legacy.

Nowhere is it clearer than in *Le Fresne* that Marie's conception of good or evil love does not depend on whether or not it is adulterous or on whether or not the relationship is carnal. The love in *Le Fresne* begins like the loves in *Guigemar* and *Equitan*. The two young people see one another, are struck by love, and soon are having relations. Although neither party is married, there is still considerable suffering involved, because their love naturally does not heed social laws and conditions. As Marie wrote in *Equitan, Tels est la mesure de amer / Que nul n'i deit reisun garder* (vv. 19–20).

Even after leaving the convent, further social circumstances present additional conflict and suffering when the king is virtually forced by his barons to tend to the business of marriage. That Fresne is not suitable is a result of her lack of identity and subsequent unequal status. The situation is grave, for it is decided that Fresne, who has been occupying the role of concubine, will even be driven from the household. That her character is pure and her conduct irreproachable is well attested by the members of the household in two separate passages (vv. 307–12 and 355–58). Even though she is recognized to be an admirable person, Fresne's fate remains unaltered.

It is at this point that Fresne's act of charity, emblematic of the nature and quality of her love, produces a miracle. Fresne's personal sacrifice of one of the two possessions she has, and one of the two links to her identity and past, for the sake of the happiness of the one she loves, literally restores to her the heritage she lost through her mother's lack of charity. In a sense, through her love Fresne restores the nobility of person and name which the mother had caused her to lose. In addition, Fresne saves her mother by moving her to confession, and the ring which she had forfeited is now regained.[23]

II   Bisclavret

In the fourth *lai*, *Bisclavret*, Marie presents a love of an entirely different nature, strikingly in contrast with the love found in *Le Fresne*. While Fresne is the perfect example of loyalty, faith, and charity, the woman in *Bisclavret* is the epitome of infidelity, treachery, and self-interest.

At the beginning of the *lai* there is virtually no indication that the woman has such a treacherous nature. Marie establishes carefully the man's worthy character and indicates that they are happily married in love (vv. 17–23). Yet from the development of the *lai*, it is clear that the statement in the last line of the quotation means little in regard to the quality of love between two individuals.

Curiously, the story develops along the lines of one of the many cases brought for judgment in Andreas Capellanus' *De Amore*. The case might be stated in the following terms: A lady loves and is loved by a knight who seems to be worthy in every respect. However, the lady learns that the knight has the unbecoming quality of turning into a werewolf at regular intervals. In view of his unbecoming habit, unknown to the lady when she granted her favors, is she not now free to turn her attentions to a second knight who has long been suing in vain for her favors? Marie emphasizes that the lady had never given any encouragement to the other knight, thus indicating that she has been faithful to her husband. Yet when she learns of his repulsive nature, she calmly turns from him and offers her love to the suitor. The coldness of her action reminds one of the judgments in the *De Amore*, where the human relationship is of little consequence and the worthiness of the knight as a lover seems the great concern.

But the crux of the matter does not seem to be the act of adultery committed by the woman, since this is only the natural consequence of her decision to be rid of this importunate husband whose presence was no longer tolerable: *Elle ne voleit mes lez lui gisir* ("She did not wish to lie next to him anymore"), v. 102.

Because of the knight's love for the woman and his faith in her, he reveals to her his secret and thus places his destiny in her hands. The woman now has the power to keep him beast (in a mediaeval sense) or man. Unlike Fresne, whose self-sacrificing love transcended great obstacles, the woman in *Bisclavret* acts purely from selfish motives. Her uncharitable act robs the knight of his human form and condemns him to a bestial existence. The punishment which she receives at the end of the story seems to have little to do with her adultery; rather it stems from her inhuman selfishness, the cupidinous nature of her love, and her cruelly uncharitable action toward her husband.

The next several *lais* all seem to illustrate, in one way or another, Marie's earlier statement that the measure of love is *démesure*. In each case, the love of the lovers is not sheer cupidity, but the lovers suffer nonetheless from the natural *démesure* of love.

III   Lanval

In some ways, *Lanval* bears a certain resemblance to *Guigemar*. In both *lais* love assuages the hero's one problem or grief. Yet, in each, love brings even greater grief to the lover. Lanval's fairy mistress removes him from the embarrassment of being in a foreign land without funds and unable to perform the usual chivalric amenities. But when Lanval is angered by the queen's accusation, he forgets his vow of silence and falls into *démesure* by revealing to the queen that he has a love (vv. 287–302). In the subsequent events it is clear that Lanval is placed in jeopardy less by the accusation that he had solicited the queen's love than by his angry boast that even his lady's maidservants are more beautiful than the queen (vv. 363–70).

Because of his *démesure*, Lanval loses his ability to "see" his lady in person and now suffers greatly, in that he has lost something he once had (vv. 337–46). It is interesting to note that, while the story has an apparently happy ending, it is only "out of this world," in "Avalun," that Lanval can find love without suffering.

IV   Les Deus Amanz

In *Les Deus Amanz*, the love of two unattached young people would seemingly face no barriers to fulfillment. However, the overweening love of the girl's father is in this case the barrier.

For a period of time the two lovers maintained their love in secrecy, even though they suffered greatly from it (vv. 63–67). The young man even exercised discretion for a time. But the pains of this love, seemingly unfulfilled unless maintained in marriage, soon pushed him beyond the bounds of reason and caused him to request that the girl run away with him.

It is at this point that the story takes a curious turn. Knowing that the boy is not strong enough to carry her to the top of the hill, the girl arranges for him to obtain a potion that will give him the necessary strength. Having returned with the potion, the boy requests from the king that he be allowed to try to carry his daughter to the top of the hill. In the ensuing lines there is considerable irony. The young man gives the potion to the girl to carry, because *Bien seit que el nel vout pas deceivre* ("Well does he know that she did not wish to deceive him"), v. 176. Yet his faith in her is not great enough to overcome his prideful *démesure*: "But I fear that it will be of little good to him, for there was in him no *mesure*" (vv. 178–79).[24] Just as in *Equitan*, the young man's *démesure* from love causes him to argue illogically against the girl's pleas that he drink the potion (vv. 189–96). He foolishly argues that he feels strong and that drinking the potion might delay him "three steps."

Of course, one cannot mistake the importance of the role of *démesure* in the outcome of *Les Deus Amanz*, and most have underscored it in their discussions of the work. However, the role of the potion has long been misunderstood, principally, I feel, because the death of the lovers and the presence of a potion have caused critics to draw a comparison between this *lai* and the Tristan story. But, in fact, the potion is here quite different. It is not the symbol of their love, nor does it represent the fatal love relationship. To the contrary, it is precisely the element which would have enabled the union of the two young people and a love of fruition. It is important to note that it is not the love of the two youths which causes the hill to flower, but the potion, which the girl spreads on the hillside in frustration. The potion, which could have given fruition to their love, nourishes flowers instead. The sentimental interpretation of a beautiful love ill-fated in a harsh world and symbolized by the eternal witness of the lovely flowers is scarcely supported by the mediaeval text. It not only neglects Marie's own comments concerning the *démesure*, but completely controverts the role of the potion. Perhaps a thought concerning the mediaeval interpretation of the story of Narcissus, a famous case of *démesure*, would be more apropos. He was turned into a flower as living witness of the futility and vanity of such love. A similar interpretation makes *Les Deus Amanz* even more tragic and more consistent than the usual interpretation. Presented with the means of obtaining a love of fruition, the young man does the very thing which will destroy them and their love. The flowers remain as reminder of the consequences of such *démesure* and of the happy fruit which would never be.

V Yonec

In *Yonec*, Marie takes great pains to outline the unfortunate circumstances under which the young girl was married and in which she must live. And when the girl expresses the wish that she be granted a lover, it is asked in the name of God (vv. 101–4). Her request is immediately answered, but further precautions are taken to ensure that her hawk-lover is not a ruse of Satan. After their love has been established and the lover must depart, the girl requests that he return often (vv. 197–98). The lover's reply is very significant, for it again emphasizes the danger of *démesure* in love and the suffering which necessarily follows. Although the girl is told that she can see the lover whenever she wishes, she must beware that they not be discovered, otherwise his death is certain.

The girl's joy is great, however, and Marie emphasizes that she wished to see her lover frequently and did so, "both night and day, late and early" (v. 222). In Marie's comment, "May God grant them long pleasure" (v. 224), added just after the passage describing the frequency of the lover's visits, one senses the implicit suggestion that such a situation cannot last. Nowhere in the text does the girl exercise the least discretion. In the passage in which they are discovered, Marie continues to emphasize the girl's eagerness and lack of forethought. Even in the style there is a sense of speed: *La dame jut; pas ne dormi,/Kar mut desire sun ami* (vv. 267–68). The lover's prediction comes true. He is killed by the husband's trap and the girl remains in misery, lamenting her lost happiness.

Yet one would be wrong to conclude that Marie's emphasis on the lady's *démesure* indicates her disapproval of the nature of the love. Throughout the *lai,* the basic goodness of the lady's character and the earnest nature of the couple's love are quite clear. So far is it from being a love of cupidity that the hawk-lover announces to her that she is pregnant with a child who will be her consolation.

After many years, when their child has grown to manhood, the lady, child, and cruel husband visit the tomb of a king who turns out to be the boy's father. It is the time of reckoning forecast by the hawk-lover. In the end, the boy kills the husband and becomes the successor to his real father. The mother dies and is buried with her lover. At this point one should note a certain similarity between this *lai* and the preceding one. In *Les Deus Amanz* the two lovers suffered and died because of the boy's *démesure.* But the potion, symbol of the possible fruition of their love, engendered the flowers, mute witness of what was lost. In *Yonec* there is an analogous situation with a different ending. The two lovers are brought to suffering and death by their love and the woman's *démesure.*[25] But the fruit of their love does not share in this suffering. It is he who avenges the evil deed of the husband, justifies the love of his parents, and then succeeds his father as king.

VI Laüstic

Laüstic is a peculiar *lai* and seems to represent that third kind of love spoken of by the commentator of the *Echecs amoureux.* The two lovers seem to derive their pleasure solely from seeing one another and never make an effort to have a physical relationship: *Delit aveient al veer,/Quant plus ne poeient aver* ("They had their joy in seeing each other since they were not able to have more") vv. 77–78. But her desire to see her lover was great, so that she frequently arose at night to keep their visual rendezvous at their windows. It is the frequency of their rendezvous which finally arouses the suspicions of the husband. When asked why she rises so often at night, she replies: *Il nen ad joië en cest mund,/Ki n'ot le laüstic chanter* ("He who does not hear the nightingale sing has no joy in this world") vv. 84–85. The husband responds angrily by killing the *laüstic.* Realizing that she would no longer be able to carry on the relationship with her lover, yet wishing him to know the reason why she would no longer keep their silent rendezvous, the lady sends him the dead bird wrapped in a cloth with a message embroidered on it. The lover understands the message and has a beautiful little coffin made. He places the bird inside and has the box well sealed.

Most commentators have made the bird and its coffin into a triumphant symbol of the two lovers. It is often said that the cruel husband could prevent their relationship, but could not destroy the undying love. Such an interpretation seems to me to misplace the emphasis of the *lai* and seems entirely out of character with the other stories. As has been shown thus far, virtually every *lai* highlights the suffering brought to lovers by their love. The suffering sometimes begins with the traditional *passio,* which can be temporarily assuaged by satisfaction. However, once the lover loses what he has once enjoyed, his suffering is greater than before. Here the bird indeed represents their love, but it should be noted that it is placed in what amounts to a coffin and is sealed in, never to be seen again (vv. 149–56). What is being emphasized here is that the lover carries around with him always the agonizing memory of his lost love, and that never again would his suffering be assuaged by the sight of his loved one, represented by the bird. One should recall the wife's words to the husband: *"Il nen ad joië en cest mund,/Ki n'ot le laüstic chanter"* (vv. 84–85). Never again will the man see the *laüstic,* yet he will carry the agonizing memory of his love with him forever.

VII Milun

The ninth *lai* of the collection, *Milun,* although similar to *Yonec* in important ways, differs from the rest of the *lai* in tone and situation. In the first place, there are seemingly no barriers to the love of the girl and her knight, since she is unattached at the beginning of the story. Second, unlike the other *lai,* love is not inspired by sight; it is initiated when the girl hears of the knight's great accomplishments. Third, it is the girl who seeks the knight's love and immediately grants her favors. Fourth, very little time is spent developing their love. There is no long description of the *passio* and the thought processes of the lovers. By line 54 the love relationship has been developed fully and the girl has become pregnant. Yet one would be deceived if he were to conclude from the hasty treatment that Marie disapproved the love because of its abrupt nature; for the rest of the story emphasizes the loyalty and good faith of the couple.

Once again, however, even though there are seemingly no barriers to the two lovers, their love comes into conflict with the situation and causes them great suffering. Because she is unmarried, her pregnancy makes her fear greatly the disgrace and misery she will undergo. Fearing torture, she resolves to have the child secretly and to send it away to be raised by her sister. While Milun is away taking the child to her sister, the girl's father arranges a marriage for her with a baron from the region. Both lovers suffer greatly from the turn of events and the girl laments her bad fortune, for she had expected always to be with her lover (vv. 139–40). For twenty years the two lovers correspond faithfully and have occasional rendezvous.

One should note here that the *lai* is really divided into three sections. The first of these, the shortest, some 54 lines in length, develops the brief initial stages of the lovers' romance and ends with the girl's pregnancy. The next part of the *lai*, some 240 lines, develops the suffering of the two lovers and their twenty years of correspondence. At this point the interest shifts to the son, who has reached manhood and has been knighted. In the remaining 244 lines, Marie relates how the boy was told who his parents were and how he set out to reunite his divided family.

It is in the last part of the *lai* that Marie is able to emphasize the high quality of love between the lady and her knight and the factor which gives love its meaning and lasting significance. When the sister tells the young man about his father, she stresses his worth as a person. Far from ashamed at the irregular nature of his birth, the young knight is pleased to have such worthy parents and determines to live up to his heritage. He sets out to seek his fortune, prove his worth, and find and unite his parents.

When father and son meet, Marie stresses the mutual love, respect, and kindness each has for the other (vv. 478–86). In his story concerning the boy's mother, the father emphasizes their strong, faithful love. Fortunately, the baron to whom the mother was married dies and the boy is able to unite his parents, as he had vowed, without bloodshed.[26] In the end, the two lovers are united happily in marriage, ending their many years of suffering. In the final scene Marie underscores the fact that it is the son who unites the parents (vv. 525–32).

The similarity between this conclusion and the conclusions of *Les Deus Amanz* and *Yonec* is striking. In *Les Deus Amanz*, the lovers suffered and died unfulfilled in their love when the boy foolishly refused the opportunity to bring their love to fruition. In *Yonec,* it is the offspring of the lovers who finally justifies the love of his parents, and flourishes as the meaningful result of their union. Similarly, in *Milun,* the joy of the parents and their meaningful union are found only in the fruition of their love. All their love and joy are in the child, who justifies their love.

VIII   Chaitivel

Of all the *lais* in the collection, perhaps it is *Chaitivel* which most reminds one of the *De Amore* of Andreas Capellanus. Not only does the love which is developed resemble the love in the *De Amore,* but the situation is analogous to one of the cases submitted to the great ladies for decision. In the story a noble lady is in a quandary, because she has four worthy lovers and cannot decide which one to choose.

At the beginning of the *lai,* one is told of a very attractive lady whose beauty captivates and enslaves all who see her. She is especially loved by four knights, all equally worthy of her love. Unlike the heroines of Marie's earlier *lais,* the lady is not drawn to any of the knights by love, but rather reacts in the manner of the ladies of the *De Amore.* It becomes an intellectual question of propriety. Which knight is worthiest and should receive her favors? Unable to decide, she leads each knight to think that he alone has been chosen, since she did not wish to lose three for the sake of one (vv. 49–62). Thus, early in the story, one becomes aware of the woman's acute selfishness and the irony in the line, *La dame fu de mut grant sens.* No *lai* more poignantly illustrates the disaster of a selfish love which has as its goal pleasure and self-gratification. One realizes that, of all the women described in the *lais,* perhaps this lady best exemplifies the courtly graces and charm. Yet nowhere are the uselessness and destructiveness of the "courtly" attitude more apparent. Such refinement scarcely masks the cruelty of a "love" which is in reality only cupidity.

In the ensuing tourney, the woman watches coquettishly from the tower as the four knights seek to display their worth before her. Ironically, fate makes the choice for her, when three of the knights are killed and one remains severely maimed. The woman faints from grief; however, after she has regained consciousness, one soon learns that her anguish is not for those who died, but for her own lost pleasure (vv. 147–56). The woman determines to nurse the wounded knight back to health and to bury the others with "loving attention." No passage in the *lai* is more ironic in its implications (vv. 159–72). The woman's care to adorn the knights *a grant amur e richement* is as "rewarding and consoling" to them as her "love" for them was in life. Marie's final comment, *Deus lur face bone merci*, highlights the irony of the passage.

Later the woman proposes to compose a *lai* concerning their love and wishes to name it "Quatre Dols." Even here the woman's gross selfishness is apparent in her emphasis on her own misery and what she has lost (vv. 193–204). Her reason for composing the *lai* is so that "her grief" will be remembered!

But the remaining knight, maimed in such a way that he can never know the fulfillment of love, sees more clearly. He rejects her proposed title on the grounds that the three dead knights are fortunate to have escaped from the suffering occasioned by their love for her. He insists, rather, that the title of the new *lai* should be *Le Chaitivel*, in that he alone must suffer the agony of his unfulfilled passion (vv. 215–26).

IX Chevrefoil

Perhaps the *lai* which best illustrates the necessary suffering brought by an unfulfilled love is *Chevrefoil*. Marie's initial summary of the work emphasizes the suffering and death which resulted from this love: "And I have put it in writing [or perhaps, I have found it written] concerning Tristram and the queen and their love which was so fine from which they had much grief. Then they died from it in one day" (vv. 6–10). Tristan has been separated from Iseut for a year. Marie's comments concerning his action after such a long separation focus attention on the central action of the *lai*: "But then he placed himself in danger of death and destruction. Do not be amazed, for he who loves loyally is in great grief when he does not have his wish" (vv. 19–24). It is this same theme which is conveyed by the symbol of the hazel tree and the honeysuckle: "It was for them the way it is with the honeysuckle which is attached to the hazel. When it is intertwined totally around the wood, both are able to live. But if they are separated, both the hazel and honeysuckle die quickly" (vv. 68–76). And this is restated again in the encounter of Tristan and

Iseut. Their meeting is joyous and reviving for them. But in the departure is grief: "Thereupon she departs, she leaves her love; but when it comes to the separation, then did they begin to weep" (vv. 102–4). Here better than in any of the previous stories is the grief or love exemplified, for, in the 118-line text, only the few lines concerning their brief visit bring any joy to the two lovers. The brevity of their encounter is completely enshrouded by the previous comments concerning the grief suffered by one unable to see his loved one and by the acute grief at parting.

X Eliduc

In many ways, the final *lai* of the collection, *Eliduc,* is the perfect conclusion to Marie's treatment of the nature of love. Just as in all the preceding *lais,* the love treated is essentially a human love and proceeds in the traditional manner. The lovers are struck by love through the eyes and undergo the physical and mental anguish so vividly portrayed in the entire collection. And just as in the other *lais* where the love is of high quality, their love is characterized by faith and loyalty, thus elevating it above the selfish motivation of delight. Essentially, the lovers are able to avoid the *démesure* which characterizes the relationship of lovers who abandon themselves blindly to their sensual appetites. As in some of the earlier *lais,* the love seems destined to end in suffering, when an act of sacrificial love allows the lovers to transcend the worldly barriers. Finally, Marie relates the quality of an honest, faithful human love to Christian charity. Indeed, the rich human love which the lovers experience is transformed, almost mystically, into a love of a much greater proportion, a love entirely devoted to the service and adoration of God.

The beginning of *Eliduc* reminds one somewhat of the situation in *Bisclavret.* Eliduc is happily married and much esteemed by his lord. Marie places great emphasis here and throughout the *lai* on the fact that the couple love one another loyally and that they are people of quality and worth (vv. 5–12). Throughout the opening passages Marie stresses Eliduc's loyalty to his king (vv. 29–32) and his tender consideration and affection for his wife. When he is preparing to leave the land, his first concern is for her safety and protection (vv. 71–74), and he pledges his faith until his return.

Just as in several of the earlier *lais,* there is seemingly no barrier to the uninterrupted continuation of their love. Already married and esteemed by the king, the lovers would seem to be safe from the usual vicissitudes which so often beset the lovers of the previous *lais*. Nevertheless, their happiness is destroyed by the meddling *losengier* (slanderer), dreaded enemy of all lovers. Without knowing why, Eliduc suddenly discovers that the king has been turned against him and that he must leave the kingdom. Hastily he departs from the realm and seeks his fortune in the service of a foreign monarch.

The foreign king's daughter hears of the great exploits and valor of the new knight and arranges to meet him. While together, the two young people are struck by the God of Love, who, in his characteristic blindness, disregards preexisting circumstances and obligations. From this moment until the miraculous events caused by the wife's extraordinary act of charity, the lovers suffer the anguish of their unfulfilled love seemingly doomed to end in frustration.

Marie develops fully the girl's *passio* from her first meeting with Eliduc through her meditations on her predicament (vv. 300–306 and 327–32). If her love remains unfulfilled, she must die (vv. 348–50).

Eliduc's situation is even more delicate and complex than Guilliadun's. For, in addition to the grief caused by his new love, he finds himself in a dilemma. Powerfully drawn to Guilliadun, he is nevertheless not unmindful of his wife and reproaches himself for his growing interest in the king's daughter (vv. 322–26). It is significant that Eliduc's reason prevails over his passions and that he is thus able to avoid the terrible *démesure* of love and its consequences. Although helpless and unable to prevent himself from loving or seeing Guilliadun, Eliduc abstains from any dishonorable action which would break the oath he had given his wife (vv. 473–77).[27] There is little doubt about the high quality of the love between Eliduc and Guilliadun. Even after pledging their love to one another, they abstain from anything which would be demeaning: "Eliduc heard the news. Much did it grieve him because of the maiden, for he loved her *anguissusement*. But between them there was *nule folie, joliveté ne vileinie . . .*" (vv. 571–76). Perhaps nowhere in the collection is there a clearer expression of the treatment of love. Recognizing the independent nature of the love attachment, Marie does not blame the lover who suddenly finds himself bound by love. Yet, for his conduct toward others, he is still held accountable. Although in great grief because of his unfulfilled love and the necessity of his departure, Eliduc resists the impulsions of a selfish love which would lead him to break the pledge he had made to his wife (vv. 585–606).[28]

In grief Eliduc departs for his homeland. His wife observes his grief, but is unable to ascertain the cause (vv. 718–26). But what one notices in the lady's reaction to Eliduc's grief is her unselfish response. Her grief is a result of his unhappiness and the thought that malicious rumor concerning her might be the cause. This aspect of Guildeluec's character is illustrated further in the scene where she is speaking to Guilliadun (vv. 1093–98). Her love for Eliduc is such that only his happiness is important to her.

Finally, there is a strong parallel between the conclusions of *Le Fresne* and *Eliduc*. In both stories Marie illustrates the miraculous power of love. In *Le Fresne*, the lady's love restores her lost nobility and overcomes the obstacles to her marriage and happiness. In *Eliduc*, Guildeluec's love virtually restores life to Guilliadun. Although technically not dead, she lies unconscious in the chapel. Clearly life is ended for her, since the obstacle which she has encountered blocks forever her marriage to Eliduc. Only Guildeluec's transcending love for both Eliduc and the girl can open the way for their happiness.

The conclusion to *Eliduc* is significant, for Marie clearly develops the relationship between human love and charity or the love of God: "Together they lived many days. Much did they have *parfit 'amur* between them. They gave much in alms and did great good until they turned toward God (vv. 1148–52)." The faith and loyal love of the couple were complemented by "good works." Their *parfit 'amur* is in itself a love of the human being without ulterior motive. The delight follows the love because it derives from the love itself. Such love naturally has its source and goal in God.

In conclusion, one should recall Marie's prologue, which is so typically mediaeval in its emphasis on the hidden significance buried in the fiction of the text and in the assertion that the hard work necessary to uncover the true meaning would add to its appreciation and to the wisdom of the reader. Those who study diligently learn to avoid the transgression contained therein.[29] Throughout the *Lais*, Marie deals with the nature of love, stressing always the suffering which accompanies it. Yet the truly important consideration is the quality of love. In *Equitan, Bisclavret,* and *Chaitivel,* the love treated is never any more than cupidity and, as one might expect of a love which considers only the selfish delights of the present, leads to various forms of crime and disaster. In *Laüstic* and *Chevrefoil,* Marie focuses on the unending suffering of human love which remains unfulfilled because the one person who could give satisfaction is unattainable. Both *Guigemar* and *Lanval* illustrate the travail attendant upon love, but in each the loyal lovers eventually overcome the obstacles and presumably any further suffering. *Les Deus Amanz, Yonec,* and *Milun,* while all developing the aspect of suffering in love, illustrate well that the lasting significance of any love is the fruition from the union.[30]

From the foregoing analysis, one can observe that Marie uses yet another well-established mediaeval technique. In the *Lais* in general, Marie initially entices the reader by appealing to a love of the senses. But, when the love is not simply cupidity, the reader is soon led to issues of a spiritual and moral nature. *Le Fresne* and *Eliduc* are excellent examples of this method. In reading these two attractive *lais,* which begin like the others with a human passion instigated by the god of love, one is gradually drawn from the sensual aspect of love to the spiritual. It becomes clear that the loyalty and faith of the true lover has as its object the consideration and happiness of the person he loves. Marie illustrates clearly the miraculous power of this love to overcome worldly suffering. Both *lais* contain charitable acts of considerable dimension. The fact that *Le Fresne* ends in earthly bliss and *Eliduc* in a union which leads toward a religious life of service and adoration serves only to illustrate that love in its true sense is of only one nature. The reader is made to see that there is only one love worthy of the name and that this love transcends suffering, in that its happiness resides not in the self, but in the happiness of another. Marie has indeed brought the reader full cycle. The suffering from what is often called love is present in every *lai,* but the means of overcoming this suffering is beautifully and subtly illustrated.

CHAPTER 8

Narrative Aspects of the Lais

IN earlier criticism there is little praise for Marie's narrative style, which was considered somewhat flat and monotonous. As a writer she was thought to lack imagination. Of primary importance in early evaluations of Marie's narrative art are the aesthetic taste of the nineteenth century and the concept of literary composition then prevalent. Marie was judged by an aesthetic standard which made a sharp distinction between imitation (inferior writers were imitators) and "originality," a distinction generally considered valid in the evaluation of artists and their work in any period. Since Marie herself constantly refers to her sources, which she proposes to put in writing or rhyme, it seemed clear that her work only preserved what had already been composed. In nineteenth-century terms, Marie was not the "original" author of the *lais*; she could not really be placed among the great "creative" writers. Essentially, Marie was not evaluated in mediaeval aesthetic terms. The artistic embellishment of the text by means of rhetoric and the transformation and ordering of materials occupies a place of less importance in the modern aesthetic than it did in the mediaeval poetic. Artistic originality was considered more a function of the "poetic imagination" than a process of the intellect. Because of the failure to consider the text in its own aesthetic terms, the critic looked for a kind of originality foreign to the mediaeval concept of literary composition. He looked for a relationship between author and text which did not exist. Marie was considered an imitator, a transmitter of someone else's work. However, if the narrative style were banal and unimaginative, the *lais* were nonetheless appreciated for their charm. In fact, what was charming about Marie's work to earlier critics can be related to nineteenth-century interest in the fairy tale, their love of the *merveilleux*, the romantic love which they saw in stories such as *Chevrefoil, Laüstic, Yonec, Deus Amanz,* etc., and what was considered Marie's enchanting *naïveté*.

Today the critical perspective is considerably altered. It is true that Marie used folktales, but in a consciously creative way, probably without understanding the episodes from folklore in their terms. From them she created stories which were aesthetically pleasing and intelligible to her twelfth-century audience. In *Guigemar*, the hunt of the white hind and the magic boat are elements found in the folktale concerning the encounter with a fairy mistress. Yet the artistic center of the story is shifted from the Celtic tale by the relationship which these episodes have to Guigemar's inner nature and the fact that he has not yet been awakened to love. It is not the episodes themselves that are important, but the inner adventure, the human crisis which they precipitate. In *Bisclavret,* Marie uses the theme of the werewolf. However, the specific transformation itself essentially provides a framework for the human problem focused upon in the text. The appearance of the hawk-man and the lady's subsequent visit to her dying lover in his "silver" city provide the basic external episodes of *Yonec*. But the dramatic center of the story concerns the situation of the imprisoned lady, her love, and the results of her adventure. In each *lai* the focus is on human relationships and their resolution. It has been noted that the sources of the *lais* are varied and include many different types of tale. Yet whether from Celtic, classical, or local tradition, and whether supernatural or realistic in nature, Marie uses them to her own purpose. The episode itself is less important than the effect it has on the characters involved in it. As in the chronicles and *romans* of the period, the events are important as configurations of the deeds of men and as agents which test man's inner substance. In this special orientation of her tales, one can see the imprint of the philosophical perspective of the period.

How much the tales have been transformed is apparent in the chivalric setting of the *lais*. Marie provides no historical perspective in our sense. She does not attempt to give each tale a social and political setting valid for the specific text. No distinction in mores or values is made between the Arthurian setting in *Lanval* and the Armorican settings of other *lais*. From a historical standpoint, all the *lais* are placed in an undifferentiated Breton past. Yet it is a past adorned with twelfth-century trappings. No matter what the ultimate folk source, Marie recasts the *lai* in a mold familiar to her own audience. Each *lai* takes place in a chivalric society of barons, kings, and knights, where the feudal relationships and values resemble those of the twelfth century. One sees the aristocratic fondness for hunting (*Guigemar, Bisclavret,* and *Equitan*), knights hiring themselves out (*Guigemar* and *Eliduc*) and seeking their fortunes (*Guigemar* and *Milun*), and the rugged nature of the earlier type of tourney as depicted in *Chaitivel.* The role of the seneschal and the responsibilities of kingship are clear in *Equitan,* and in *Le Fresne* and *Lanval* one sees the interplay between vassals and lord. In both *Lanval* and *Bisclavret,* there is a legal setting specifically related to the practices of the period.[1] Thus, in one sense, the society of the *lais* is familiar to the reader, even though the story allegedly takes place in a distant past.[2] In another sense, the society of knights and ladies represents an idealized version of twelfth-century values projected into a remote and imagined period of chivalry. Essentially, it is not a realistic portrayal that is important, but a timeless, human truth reflected in the actions of the characters against a background of ideal spiritual values.

This transformation of materials in the *roman* and *lai* poses a problem concerning the relationship of this literary reality with the sociopolitical reality of the period. Professor Köhler sees a close link between the adventurous quests depicted in the literature and social changes which had altered the role of the knight in society.[3] With the lessening of warlike activity in the twelfth century, the combative role of the knight was somewhat diminished, thus creating a situation in which the traditional function and values of the knight were at variance with the new order. Contemporary with the change is the rise in popularity of the *roman,* in which the setting and portrayal of chivalric society differ markedly from that found in the epic. The solitary, adventurous quest of the Arthurian knight represents an attempt to restore harmony and meaning to the knightly ideal. Through successful accomplishment of the adventure, the worth of the knight is restored. In the epic, the knight is portrayed as a member of a company of knights. Although individualized in his role as a leader, the hero participates in the destiny of the group as a whole. In the *roman,* the chivalric society serves as background and setting for the solitary knightly adventure. But the results of the ordeal do not concern the knight alone, for the destiny of the society hinges on the knight's success. Through his deeds, the knight transcends the private sphere, thus underscoring the importance of chivalric values and the role of the knight.

Vital to the question is the role of adventure in the *lais*.[4] Ostensibly, there are similarities between the adventures in some of the *lais* and those in the *roman*. In *Guigemar* the hero early sets out to seek his fortune and is on a hunt when he encounters the white hind. In *Milun* the father and son both set forth to seek their fortunes, as does Eliduc after the king sends him into exile. However, even in these *lais*, where there is an external similarity, there is no sense of quest or seeking of adventure in the sense that it appears in the *roman*. In *Guigemar*, the adventure occurs while the hero is merely engaging in his favorite sport. Milun and his son meet in combat as a result of both men setting forth, but the resolution is not dependent upon the successful accomplishment of an ordeal; rather, the combat simply provides the means of recognition, the first step toward reuniting the family. Eliduc's combat in exile is clearly not the real adventure; it is his fortuitous meeting with Guilliadun.

In the *lais* it is the adventure which comes to the hero. Far from setting forth on an adventurous quest, the hero of the *Lais* is essentially passive. As Professor Eberwein noted, the term *aventure* often has a meaning related to its etymological significance. In a sense, it is the adventure which seems to seek out the hero. It is an encounter which seems deliberately directed toward him, an experience which he seems destined to have and which totally transforms his existence, and at times introduces him to another order of reality.[5] Unlike the adventure in the *roman*, there is no special relationship between the destiny of society and that of the hero. Society remains unchanged by the hero's adventure. The experience is a personal one which leads to a private fulfillment and happiness. In fact, since society and social reality are often an obstacle to the hero's personal happiness, the two are actually at variance. Professor Baader sees here the importance of the fairy tale and its world of private happiness. He points out that the reality of the *lais* differs from the reality of the everyday world. It is a poetic reality, an intellectual reality where things turn out as they should, not as they do. For this reason, the heroes in Marie's *lais* can only find happiness outside of society, in a world which lies beyond.

There is a danger, however, in seeing Marie's *lais* exclusively in a perspective of the "Wunschbild," of the fairy tale. It is misleading to find an expression of ultimate happiness in all the *lais*. It is true that the *lais* are set in an idealized world governed by a poetic justice and that solutions to the circumstances in the tales are often different from what one might expect within the framework of ordinary reality. At the conclusion of *Guigemar*, the hero and his lady seemingly attain a happiness which has an unclouded horizon, in spite of the fact that the old husband remains alive and that the lady is still technically married. Fresne's happiness depends on the fortuitous recognition by her mother at a time when the marriage is retractable. Even so, Marie's solution clearly ignores the possible religious difficulties involved in such an annulment. For Lanval and his fairy mistress, future happiness lies beyond ordinary reality in Avalon. Fortunately for the lovers in *Milun*, the husband dies conveniently, thus avoiding the problems which might have arisen if the son had carried out his threat to kill the husband. And, in *Eliduc*, the final happiness of the lovers requires the extraordinary self-effacement of the wife, the miraculous medicinal flower, and complete neglect of the possible religious difficulties involved in their subsequent marriage.

Although one sees in these *lais* the attainment of happiness within a sphere of poetic reality, in the other texts the outcome is quite different. In *Equitan, Bisclavret*, and *Yonec* there is great satisfaction in seeing characters who have offended punished. And the emphasis on a resolution that is within a framework of justice focuses attention on the harmony of the conclusion. Yet, certainly in human terms, the principal characters experience anything but a gilded reality. The seneschal suffers the treachery of his wife and king, their deaths leaving him only the satisfaction of vengeance. Bisclavret loses a wife with whom he had been happily married and undergoes the harrowing ordeal perpetrated by her treachery. If Yonec triumphantly assumes his father's title and the mother enjoys the satisfaction of vengeance before dying, it is nonetheless true that a harsh reality asserts itself. Yonec's father suffered death and the mother essentially endured a life of misery waiting for her moment of exultation. In the retribution meted out to the unfaithful parties in these texts, one perceives that the *Lais* take place in an ideal world dominated by the poet's sense of justice. But there is also a strong sense of reality in the suffering of the principal characters.

One sees this even more vividly in *Les Deus Amanz, Laüstic,* and *Chevrefoil.* One can see the lovers in these *lais* as ill-starred and thwarted by society, in which case one might say that their happiness can be found only in an ideal reality. Professor Baader points out that, even in *Chevrefoil,* Marie looks forward to the future meeting of the two lovers. It seems to me that such an interpretation misplaces the emphasis of the texts, which stress the grief present in these loves. Viewed in conjunction with the conclusions of *Guigemar, Lanval, Le Fresne, Milun,* and *Eliduc,* one can see a very realistic pattern in the collection. In each case the lovers find obstacles to their happiness. In some *lais* they are able to overcome them, in others they are not. Curiously, only in *Lanval* do the lovers actually go beyond reality to find their happiness. In the other texts, the harmony is established within the society itself. Furthermore, in *Les Deus Amanz* and *Laüstic* there is really an emphasis on grief and the termination of the love, not a consoling thought regarding the ability of love to transcend life.[6] Marie's is a real world where fate and circumstances play a major role and can lead to both joy and grief. It is idealized in that the personal conduct of the characters influences their destinies so decisively, even to the extent of overcoming physical obstacles. In the sense that Marie sets aside residual difficulties left unanswered in the text (*Guigemar, Eliduc, Le Fresne*), there is operative a poetic justice in an ideal reality. It is not a gilded reality, but an intellectual reality in which the rational choices of the characters lead to the inexorable consequences of their acts. Within the narrative structure of the tales, happenstance, or perhaps destiny, plays a major role in the lives of the characters. Forces beyond their control place them in dilemmas or precipitate inner human crises. Ultimately, however, it is their conduct which determines their fate more frequently than impersonal factors beyond their control.

I *Unifying Patterns*

A number of scholars have sought to uncover unifying factors in the collection as a whole. Based on her statement in the "Prologue," Professor Spitzer believed that Marie was conscious of her role as *poeta philosophus et theologus.*[7] Far from being simply fairytales, Marie's *lais* contained serious problems which she articulated poetically by means of key symbols in the text. Not every *lai* incorporates such a symbolic device, but in a number of *lais* certain objects are prominent in the resolution of the plot and are symbolic of the meaning. One recalls the belt and knotted shirt in *Guigemar,* symbolic of the lovers' pledge of faith and an important factor in the scene where they are reunited. In *Le Fresne,* the ring and blanket play a central role in the denouement and, at the same time, symbolize the spiritual problem of the text. The potion of *Les Deus Amanz* provides the possibility of a successful conclusion to the conflict in the *lai,* and also symbolizes the potential fulfillment of happiness. The dead nightingale in *Laüstic* informs the lover of the unhappy events of which he was unaware and symbolizes their love. The story ends when the lover seals the dead bird in the reliquary, symbol of the termination of their love and of the grief which he will carry with him the rest of his life. Perhaps the most famous of all is the image of the hazel and the honeysuckle in *Chevrefoil.* In the image and in the well-known lines which express the relationship of the two plants (vv. 68–78), one perceives the essence of the story itself. The intertwined hazel and honeysuckle symbolize the lovers; but, in noting that the two plants cannot live apart, Tristan foreshadows the well-known conclusion of their love. More immediately, he stresses the agony which they have experienced in being apart and the grief of their forthcoming separation. In terms of the symbol, the difficult separation of the lovers represents the first agonies of approaching death.

Within the collection various thematic groupings are apparent. *Guigemar, Lanval,* and *Yonec* all concern a love which is involved with the supernatural. There are mysterious elements in *Bisclavret* (the werewolf), *Les Deus Amanz* (the potion), *Milun* (the swan-messenger), and *Eliduc* (the medicinal flower), but only in *Guigemar, Lanval,* and *Yonec* does one see two distinct worlds. In fact, one of the mysterious aspects of the *Lais* is the juxtaposition of ordinary reality and realistic detail with the supernatural. Basically, extraordinary encounters are accepted as if they were a part of ordinary reality. Guigemar hears the speech of the white hind and is dismayed by the curse, but not once does he express any shock in having heard an animal speak. When he finds the magic boat, he ponders over the fact that he has never heard of boats being able to come to that harbor. When the empty boat mysteriously sets sail, he is again dismayed, but does not question how this could be. Similarly, when the girl finds the same boat waiting for her two years later, after her escape from confinement, she does not question the boat's presence, nor in any of these instances does Marie offer an explanation for these mysterious circumstances. In fact, her comment concerning Guigemar's first voyage only adds mystery to the meaning of *aventure:* "It is not surprising if he [Guigemar] is dismayed, for he has great grief from his wound; it is necessary for him to suffer the adventure" (vv. 197–99). Why did the boat take Guigemar back to his own land and later take the girl to the land of Meriadus? From a narrative standpoint one can see that this allows for the test of their mutual vows. In terms of the supernatural intervention, no explanation is offered. Nowhere in the *lai* does the author offer an explanation for these events, so vital to the development of the narrative. Moreover, the encounter with the supernatural ends as mysteriously as it had begun.

A similar situation is found in *Yonec*. The girl fears that the hawk-man is a partisan of the devil and assures herself by having him take communion.[8] Not once does she question how a man could change into a hawk. Nor does Marie explain why he could not appear to her until she had wished for him. Later the girl follows him through the hole in the *hoge* and emerges before the "silver city." The dying lover gives her a magic ring which causes the jealous husband to forget the entire affair. But, as in *Guigemar*, the supernatural element vanishes as abruptly as it had appeared. There is no suggestion that Yonec has any of the supernatural qualities of his father and, in the conclusion of the tale, the son assumes his father's title, his dominion appearing to be merely a neighboring region.

The same acceptance of the extraordinary and the intermingling of reality and the *merveilleux* is true in other *lais*. If Bisclavret's wife is horrified by his transformation, she nonetheless accepts the reality of it, as do the king and the members of his court at the conclusion of the story.[9] There is no speculation concerning the reasons for his periodic change, nor does Marie indicate at the end of the tale whether he continues to undergo such transformations. The extraordinary potion given the young lover in *Les Deus Amanz*, the curative powers of the flower in *Eliduc*, and the unusual abilities of the swan in *Milun* are all accepted within the fabric of reality in tales which otherwise have nothing super-natural about them. Lanval and his fairy mistress ride off to Avalon as if they were merely going to another country. In this total integration of the *merveilleux* and reality, there is a narrative parallel to the poetic reality mentioned earlier in reference to the idealization of the twelfth-century values. In narrative terms, the *lais* are placed in an autonomous poetic reality where distinctions between what is real and not real lose their importance. The nat-ural and supernatural blend to create an independent fictional world.

Other *lais* resemble one another in the treatment of similar themes or by analogy in circumstances. *Guigemar, Le Fresne, Lanval, Milun,* and *Eliduc* all share the theme of search and ful-fillment of love. In *Les Deus Amanz, Laüstic, Chaitivel,* and *Chevrefoil,* one sees love temporarily or permanently denied. In *Equitan, Bisclavret,* and *Yonec,* vengeance is wreaked upon the disloyal and cruel.[10] *Guigemar, Yonec,* and *Laüstic* all contain the theme of the wife closely guarded by a jealous husband. Although it is clear that Marie dislikes the jealous husband, only one is punished for his acts: the husband in *Yonec.* In *Guigemar,* the old husband is abandoned and disappears from the story. The hus-band in *Laüstic* triumphs brutally over his wife. In these three conclusions one again sees that the poetic justice of the *Lais* is nonetheless tempered by reality.

Some of the *lais* seem to have rather close counterparts. *Le Fresne* and *Milun* both present a situation in which children are abandoned only to recover their own parents at the conclusion of the story. However, *Le Fresne* may be closer in substance to *Eliduc,* in that both *lais* involve a woman willing to sacrifice her-self for her love; while *Milun* and *Yonec* may be more closely related, in that both involve offspring conceived out of marriage who reunite their father and mother. In these pairings and parallel groupings Marie further unifies the collection. By this means she is able to develop similar situations in varying circumstances and with different human responses, thereby presenting other facets of the problem.

II *Narrative Development*

Something has already been said concerning Marie's use of prologues and epilogues in the *Lais*. Basically, each *lai* has a brief prologue which variously makes reference to the Bretons and their *lais*, declares Marie's purpose in composing them, and/or sets the text in the ancient Breton past. The epilogues often restate that the Bretons had made a *lai* of the story and repeat again its title.

In between these brief introductions and conclusions is a narrative which is both carefully and economically developed. The narratives fall into three groups of varying lengths: (1) *Guigemar* (886 vv.) and *Eliduc* (1184 vv.); (2) *Le Fresne* (518 vv), *Lanval* (646 vv), *Yonec* (554 vv.), and *Milun* (536 vv.); (3) *Equitan* (314 vv.), *Bisclavret* (318 vv), *Deus Amanz* (244 vv.), *Laüstic* (160 vv), *Chaitivel* (240 vv.), and *Chevrefoil* (118 vv.). Consideration of the texts involved discloses that the length of the *lai* is directly related to the subject matter and the outcome of the text. Both the longer and middle-length *lais* concern the *development* of a love through a series of episodes, eventually culminating in fulfillment. In *Guigemar* there are two parts to the development: The first involves Guigemar's own change, his first encounter with love, and the subsequent description of his and the lady's suffering, thus fulfilling the prediction; the second episode relates their further suffering in separation and tests the strength of their love for one another. *Eliduc* likewise has two broad developments: After a brief prelude which describes Eliduc happily married, Marie develops his encounter with Guilliadun, the growth of their love, and Eliduc's dilemma and the subsequent happiness of the three people involved.

In each of the middle-length *lais*, Marie develops a love relationship which is temporarily thwarted but ultimately resolved. The economy of Marie's narrative is evident in *Le Fresne*. Marie briefly but unhurriedly develops the circumstances of Fresne's birth, her abandonment, and subsequent upbringing in the abbey. In a few lines Fresne is fully grown, has fallen in love with Gurun, and goes to live with him at Dol. It is at this point that her happiness is suspended by the intervention of the barons. The remainder of the text reveals Fresne's own loving nature and the ultimate restoration of her birthright. The first part of *Lanval* concerns his encounter with the fairy mistress and the rectification of his financial and social discomfort. The episode with the queen causes Lanval to lose his mistress temporarily. In the remaining episode of the *lai* one sees Lanval regain his mistress and the happiness of love. Both *Yonec* and *Milun* follow similar patterns.

In the shorter *lais* the loves are all thwarted. Essentially the process of development is unimportant. These *lais* are centered around the denouement of the text. Each *lai* is like a vignette, in that there is one scene in which the plot is resolved. All the action in these *lais* leads directly to the principal episode.

After a brief introduction which sets the scene, Equitan immediately moves toward his encounter with the seneschal's wife. The dialogue in which they pledge faith to one another is followed by a period when they carry on an affair. However, Marie does not develop the action in this period of time. Essentially, the bargain has been made, the stage has been set for their treacherous agreement and subsequent death. In *Laüstic* everything prepares one for the scene when the husband confronts his wife with the nightingale and the principal scene in *Chevrefoil*, the brief meeting and agonizing separation of the lovers, is restated in the opening passage when Tristan prepares the famous *bastun*.

Both *Bisclavret* and *Les Deus Amanz* offer the possibility of more episodes. However, Marie again moves quickly to the principal episode. Once the werewolf's clothes have been stolen, Marie briefly describes the wolf's encounter with the king and how he became his pet. What is important is the initial treachery of his wife and the later scenes at court when the truth becomes known. In *Les Deus Amanz* Marie spends little time describing the nascent love of the two lovers, even though their liaison lasts some time before the boy decides to attempt the feat, nor does she relate any details concerning his trip to Salerno to obtain the potion. Only at the moment when the boy attempts to carry the girl up the hill does the narrative pace relent. It is interesting to note how well the brevity of these texts accords with the subject. In each case the story ends in misery for the lovers. By abridging the description of their developing love and the moments of their happiness, Marie emphasizes the fleeting nature of their love, thereby stressing their grief. The finality of the conclusion is heightened by the abrupt nature of the moment when the lovers come to grief. Those which do not end in death (*Bisclavret*,

Laüstic, Chaitivel, and *Chevrefoil*) focus on a future of misery and grief.[11]

It is clear from the economy of Marie's narratives that *abréviation* is the rhetorical figure which dominates her style. The characters in the *Lais* are described briefly and incidents not related to the primary adventure, but which are necessary to establish a character's background or reputation, receive only the attention necessary. Tristan remains near the court for some time, yet we hear little of his activities. In *Yonec* and *Milun,* many years pass from the time the son is born until the *lai's* resolution. Marie comments little about these years in *Yonec* and, in *Milun,* she describes briefly the continuity of their correspondence.

Even description, a favorite twelfth-century stylistic embellishment, is used sparingly. For the most part, when Marie indulges in an extended description, her purpose and the importance of the description are obvious. Marie describes the boat which Guigemar boards in detail, in order to establish the magic nature of the vessel and to prepare one for the role it plays in the remainder of the *lai.* In *Lanval* she describes the tent of the fairy mistress at length, again to establish the other-worldly encounter and the wealth of the fairy. Lanval's subsequent rise in popularity and prominence is directly related to the wealth which he obtains from his fairy mistress. If the procession of damsels is dwelled upon at the conclusion, it is to prove the truth of Lanval's assertion that the least of the fairy's maidservants is more beautiful than the queen. Otherwise, descriptions are neither numerous nor extended. In the introductory passage of *Laüstic,* the important description of the two houses is very brief, only enough information being given to set the scene for the story.

More important to the substance of the text is Marie's use of monologue and dialogue. As mentioned earlier, it is not the external adventure which is important, but the internal crisis which it provokes. Thus one sees the real issue developed in the character's meditation or in the conversations between two of the personages. In these passages the text becomes more leisurely as Marie focuses her attention on the central issue. In *Guigemar* there is emphasis placed on Guigemar's meditation concerning his love for the girl and Marie refers to the fact that the girl undergoes the same experience. This, of course, illustrates that the love developing between the two is fulfilling the requirements for Guigemar's cure set forth in the hind's curse. Equitan's long meditation concerning his love for the seneschal's wife develops clearly the extent to which he is driven by his desire and the treachery which he tries to justify by his contorted logic. On several occasions Eliduc ponders over his situation, each time illustrating his dilemma and his attempt to be faithful and yet maintain his love.

It has been recognized that twelfth-century fascination with monologue can be seen in its nascent form in Marie's *lais*. However, too little importance has been given to her use of dialogue, perhaps even more adroitly used. In the dialogue between Equitan and the seneschal's wife, one sees the treachery of the couple clearly demonstrated in their ironic discussion. One cannot miss the humor of their discussion concerning loyalty in love and the nobility of love between equals. The seneschal's wife masterfully maneuvers the king into a position of weakness and then boldly proposes the murder of her husband. Also cleverly articulated is the dialogue between Bisclavret and his "beloved" wife in the opening scenes of the text. Playing upon the idea that he should trust her, the wife elicits the information needed in order to betray him. The climax of·*Laüstic* occurs when the husband confronts his wife with the ensnared bird. The real meaning of what he says is clear in his actions, although he sarcastically states that he has done her a favor. She will no longer be kept awake by the bird's singing. In *Deus Amanz*, the resolution of the text comes out of the dialogue between the girl and her young lover during the climb. She urges him repeatedly to listen to her, to drink the potion. He, too, uses specious arguments to contradict her good advice. As a final example, the discussion between the woman and the remaining lover in *Chaitivel* not only determines the title to be given the *lai*, but their contradictory views of the situation highlight the central issue of the *lai* and point out the mainspring of the misfortune.

In the past, Marie has been admired for the psychological portrayal of her characters, especially her women. There is, to be sure, a misunderstanding here if one thinks of character analysis in the modern sense. There is certainly little probing of the personalities in a Balzacian or Proustian sense. At most there is revelation of the moral qualities of the characters.

Essentially, all the lovers are described in similar terms. They are handsome, refined, noble, brave—in short, they have the usual attributes of the Arthurian knight. Even Equitan is described in these terms. What is added to his description is the moral failing of loving *deduit* too much. It is notable that certain situations might allow for speculation concerning the personal reasons responsible for a character's action, but virtually nothing is offered. Eliduc faces a dilemma and reacts to it in a way which might provoke some commentary. Yet, one has the distinct impression that his reaction to the situation is not peculiar to his own personality; rather, one senses that several of the other men in the *lais* might well have reacted in a similar fashion. Marie does not reproach him for it, nor does she relate his reaction to Eliduc's specific personality. Gurun does not support Fresne, nor does he resist the judgment of the barons. One might see in this a weakness in him, or one might expect the author to explain the reasons for his actions in terms of his own personality. No such explanation is forthcoming. In fact, there is no suggestion that he might have reacted differently. In reality, he is not involved as a personality. The situation is accepted as a reality which concerns Fresne alone. Even the servants, who have come to love her, only lament her misfortune. It is not seen as a situation which can be influenced by the psychological reactions of the persons involved. What seems essentially hopeless is transformed by the selfless deed, which unlocks the secret that had fixed Fresne's destiny so many years before. It is true that Lanval reacts too violently and discourteously to the queen's offer, but Marie does not link this to any character trait peculiar to the knight. And, except for the fact that he is probably the youngest of the lovers, no specific explanation is given for the lover's impetuosity in *Deus Amanz*. Rather, his actions are ascribed to the force of "love" itself.[12] Among the lesser male characters, there are three husbands who play a role. There is really very little to distinguish one jealous husband from another. Is the action of the husband in *Laüstic* distinctive? One might expect a similar reaction from the husband in *Yonec*. Both of the husbands in *Yonec* and *Guigemar* are jealous and act as "jailers" for their wives. Beyond this, they are not provided with distinctive personality.

Among the heroines there is considerably more variation in tone. However, it is within the moral sphere that one sees the distinction. One does not really see a variation in personality in the sense that they are shown to have different interests or that one heroine is more serious or thoughtful in comparison with another who is more frivolous in personality. Of course, one might deduce certain qualities that would probably be present in the personalities of Guildeluec and Fresne as opposed to the seneschal's wife or the wife of Bisclavret. However, such deductions would only be based on the revelation of their reaction to the situations and the assumption that a reflective nature is more in accord with the selfless acts of Guildeluec and Fresne. What really distinguishes the women in *Guigemar*, *Yonec*, or *Milun*? Can one say that the wife in *Milun* would be out of character if placed in the role of Guigemar's lady? Actually, the distinctive tone of each woman is more the result of the situation in which she finds herself, of her own moral nature, and of her reaction to the circumstances of the text. The women in *Equitan* and *Bisclavret* are both treacherous. Both are given the usual physical characteristics. One cannot really see that one woman is essentially different from the other. Guildeluec and Fresne both have a great capacity for self-sacrifice. Yet, can one say that, because of acutely different personalities, the women of *Guigemar*, *Milun*, and *Deus Amanz* would not have acted so charitably in similar circumstances? In the *Lais*, the tone of the character is created by the moral reaction of that person to the particular situation in which the character finds himself or herself. If the heroines are more distinctive in the *Lais*, it is because the situations in the texts call for action from them more frequently than from the men. One should not expect personality, for, to the mediaeval man, the deeds of man cannot be explained in terms of his milieu or psychological makeup; rather they depend upon the presence or absence of a harmonious alliance and judicious governance of his will and reason.

III *Marie's Use of Irony*

Important to the collection, both structurally and stylistically, is Marie's use of irony.[13] It is scarcely possible to read the *Lais* without being charmed by the many gently ironic passages. However, irony is present not only in incidental passages, it is a basic element inherent in several of the plots and contributes prominently to an understanding of the collection. The importance of irony in the *Lais* is demonstrated by the fact that only *Milun* and *Chevrefoil* seem entirely free of the figure.

In the second *lai* of the collection, the title, *Equitan,* is also the name of the king, described as being "of great worth" and "much loved in his land" (vv. 13–14). In the next two lines these qualities are somewhat modified by the author's reference to the king's intense love of *deduit* (pleasure) and *drüerie* (love). His other great interest is hunting. Given the common mediaeval association of amorous conquest and the image of the hunt, it is not unlikely that Marie deliberately joined these two loves in the king's character and appropriately named him Equitan, a name etymologically suggestive of horsemanship. The play on the king's name and his "two" interests continues throughout the text. It should be recalled that the king's first intimate conversation with the seneschal's wife is the result of a hunting expedition. In the lines immediately preceding his departure, one is told that the king "coveted" the seneschal's wife, and the hunting trip takes him straight to her. In verse 48 ("When he returned from his pleasure"), the nature of the hunt is apparent. In returning from the *deduit* of the hunt, he begins the *deduit* of another "hunt." The irony is compounded when he himself becomes the prey of the God of Love whose arrow subdues the lover. The next day Equitan, suffering from his love-wound, again sets out to hunt, but returns quickly. Essentially, the king is no longer the hunter; he has become the prey. From this point the king is a slave to his love. Willingly he obeys the seneschal's wife even to the extent of plotting his vassal's murder. Finally, the resolution of the plot develops against the background of the hunt, when the wife and king plan the setting for the seneschal's death. The king is to undertake another hunting trip in the vicinity of the seneschal's home. On the third day he will propose the fatal bath. The ironic overtones of the hunt motif are multiple. The king begins the story hunting the seneschal's wife and the pleasure of love. During the hunt he himself becomes the prey of love and is wounded. In the final scene he begins another hunt, this one directed by the wife, a deadly hunt with the seneschal as the prey.

If Equitan's name is ironic because it suggests the nature of the king's character, Fresne's name becomes ironic because it is the antithesis of all that she is. Abandoned by her mother at birth, Fresne receives her name from those who found her in a basket left under an ash tree. At the moment when she is named, one is unaware of the significance of the word. However, in the resolution of the *lai*, several important overtones become apparent. The barons insist that the king put aside his concubine, Fresne, and take a wife who may give him a legitimate heir to the throne. The barons suggest the daughter of a neighboring lord as a worthy wife. Ironically, the girl is actually Fresne's sister and has been named coincidentally after a tree, *Codre*. The barons take advantage of the two names to illustrate the wisdom of their advice: "In the Codre there is fruit and pleasure; Fresne never bears fruit" (vv. 339–40). That the concubine should have been named after a nonbearing tree is ironic in itself. But the irony is yet more poignant. In one sense there is a bitter truth in the name, caused by the mother's own uncharitable action. If Fresne is unable to bear fruit, it is because the mother's deed has left her "nameless," robbed of her noble identity and unable, therefore, to become the king's wife. In a sense, the name is symbolic of the result of slander and selfishness. But in the conclusion of the text is the contradiction of all that the name implies. Fresne's inner nature is completely antithetical to the "sterility" imposed on her by the uncharitable attitude of her mother and, in the end, it is Fresne's love which bears fruit. Through her unselfish love and tender concern for the king's happiness, Fresne miraculously overcomes her own forlorn situation and saves her mother from sin.

In a few of the *lais*, the plot itself is constructed on an ironic situation. The opening lines of *Guigemar* introduce a young knight admirable in every way, but, like Hippolytus, uninterested in love. After the introduction suggesting the knight's nature, Marie introduces the Celtic motif, the hunt of the white doe. During the hunt, Guigemar is wounded in the thigh by his own rebounding arrow. Before dying, the wounded doe pronounces an ironic curse. Several elements in this situation should be noted. Guigemar's wound is actually self-inflicted, reflecting his own failure to love another, and his cure can come only in doing what is least interesting to him—loving a woman. Marie continues the irony inherent in Guigemar's situation through the portion of the *lai* which develops Guigemar's first love. Guigemar's physical cure can come only by his acquiring the spiritual suffering for another.

In two other *lais* the central irony of the plot is contained in a proverb which the story illustrates. In *Equitan*, when the king and the seneschal's wife are discussing the nature of "true" love, one can scarcely miss the fact that the treachery of which they speak pertains to them above all. In *Le Fresne*, the wife's envious statement concerning the birth of twins ultimately redounds to her own misfortune, for as Marie notes, "Whoever slanders and lies about others does not know what lies before them" (vv. 87–88).

In other *lais* there are incidental situations which are ironic when considered in light of the principal action of the story. In *Guigemar* Marie describes at length the young lady's physical surroundings, her confinement, and the relationship with her old husband. It is indeed amusing that the old man should have decorated her walls with a scene in which Venus is shown "excommunicating" those who would read Ovid's *Remedia Amoris*. One can only assume that the scene was painted for the girl's edification and that Venus' hostile attitude toward Ovid's book is intended for her benefit. Undoubtedly, the husband intended her unrestrained love (urged by the painting) to be directed toward him. However, given the obvious direction of the story and the husband's cruel treatment of the lady, the reader can only smile at the girl's probable interpretation of the scene, certainly serving an unintended purpose once she has met Guigemar.

There are a number of authorial comments and asides which are charged with ironic overtones. When Guigemar arrives by boat at the castle, he does not awaken until the ladies are on board wondering what to make of the situation. Upon awakening, the first thing Guigemar sees is the young girl:

> The knight, who was sleeping,
> awakened and saw her;
> he was happy about it and greeted her:
> well does he know that he has reached land. (vv. 302–5)

Indeed, to see other humans aboard assures him that he has reached land, but Marie's real intent is cleverly placed in the progressive order of the short half-lines, followed by what can only be a gently ironic understatement. Later in the text Marie again uses understatement in an engaging way to convey the boy's emotion in his first encounter with love. As Guigemar meditates over this new feeling, a sensation he has never felt in his life, he is not sure what it means. The understatement of his naïve conclusion, however, draws a smile from the reader:

> But nevertheless he certainly perceives
> that, if he is not cured by the lady,
> he is sure and certain that he must die. (vv. 396–98)

Marie could scarcely have chosen a more attractive device to express Guigemar's recognition of love.

Even such a cursory discussion of Marie's narrative techniques demonstrates her ability as a writer and serves easily to refute earlier criticism. In her transformation of folk material, in her use of monologue and dialogue, in her ability to create suspense (such as in *Lanval*) and use description, and in her charming use of understatement and ironic language, Marie displays her great talent and originality as a writer.

CHAPTER 9

Conclusion

WITHOUT question, Marie de France has taken her place among the finest writers of the twelfth century. Much of the period can be seen in her poetry. The fact that she was born in France and wrote in England reflects the prominent role played by Norman Frenchmen and England in the Renaissance of French vernacular literature. The importance of the classical heritage, the influence of oral Celtic materials, and the mediaeval transformation of these texts are important aspects of the period which are mirrored in her work. In the three texts generally attributed to her, one finds three types of literature eminently suited to mediaeval taste. In one way or another her work relates to Latin, French, English, and Breton, the four languages which play such a prominent role in the cultural heritage of the age. In the *Lais* one sees the mediaeval interest in the *merveilleux*, the strong didactic inclination, the dominant theme of love, and the intellectual ideals of the period. Moreover, the *Lais* display the mixture of refinement and violence, so characteristic of the period. Her sophisticated and subtle style, narrative sense, and delicate sensitivity have earned her the esteem she deserves.

Notes and References

Chapter One

1. Other *lais* appearing in manuscripts where certain of the twelve texts attributed to Marie have appeared have been ascribed at various times to the poetess as well as a few texts in which the writer calls herself "Marie." These problems will be treated in the course of the book. Recently Richard Baum has sought to prove that there is no basis for attributing the above-mentioned works to a single poetess named Marie de France. He disputes the attribution of the twelve *lais* in the British Museum Harley manuscript 978 to one author, argues that there is no documentation relating the Marie known for writing *lais* with the Marie de France of the *Fables*, nor for linking the Marie who translated the *Espurgatoire* with either of these Maries or with other texts signed by a Marie. Mr. Baum's arguments will be reviewed in conjunction with various problems to which they pertain (Richard Baum, *Recherches sur les oeuvres attribuées à Marie de France*, Heidelberg, 1968).

2. *Al finement de cest escrit,/qu'en Romanz ai traitié et dit, me numerai pur remembrance: Marie ai num, si sui de France.* (*Die Fabeln der Marie de France*, edited by Karl Warnke [Halle, 1898], p. 327, vv. 1–4). All citations from the *Fables* have been taken from this edition, henceforth designated as Warnke.

3. *Jo, Marie, ai mis en memoire/Le livre de l'Espurgatoire: En Romanz qu'il seit entendables/A laie gent e cuvenables.* (*The Espurgatoire Saint Patriz of Marie de France*, edited by T. A. Jenkins [The Decennial Publications of the University of Chicago, 1903], First Series, Volume VII, 303, vv. 2297–2300). All citations from the *Espurgatoire* are from this edition. It should be pointed out that not all extant manuscripts of the *Espurgatoire* contain the lines in which Marie is named.

4. Mr. Baum admirably develops at great length the history of scholarly activity surrounding the attribution of works to Marie. He insists that early scholarly conclusions concerning the subject have dominated inordinately the opinion of subsequent scholars, preventing

them from evaluating properly contradictory evidence and from recognizing the fragility of evidence which exists (Baum, *Recherches*, pp. 59 ff.). While Mr. Baum's accusation concerning the fragility of evidence and the failure to consider contradictory materials has a basis in fact, it will be seen, perhaps, that, given the uncertainties commonly present in the literary history of any mediaeval problem, the assumptions that have been made concerning Marie de France are still likely to be valid. In fact, it may well be that too few texts have been attributed to Marie, a result directly related to the reluctance of scholars over the last hundred years to accept texts for Marie without more authentic proof than linguistic and stylistic evidence. A text which definitely merits more serious consideration is *La Vie Seinte Audree*, edited by Östen Södergård from a fourteenth-century manuscript found in Welbeck Abbey. Although long thought to be a late thirteenth-century translation, Mr. Södergård estimates, based on linguistic evidence, that the text was translated from the Latin in the early thirteenth century. The closing lines of the text bear a striking resemblance to passages in the *Fables, Espurgatoire*, and the *Lais*:

> *Issi ay ceo livere finé,*
> *En Romanz dit et translaté*
> *De la vie seinte Audree*
> *Si com en latin l'ay trové . . .*
> *Mut par est fol ki se oblie.*
> *Ici ecris mon non Marie,*
> *Pur ce ke soie remembree.*

"Thus have I concluded this book of the life of Saint Audree. Just as I found it in Latin, I translated it into romance. He who forgets himself is foolish. Here I write my name, Marie, that I may be remembered" (*La Vie Siente Audree*, edited by O. Södergård [Uppsala, 1955], p. 181, lines 4606–20). If the text is early thirteenth century (it should be remembered that linguistic evidence is virtually the only proof that other works by Marie are late twelfth or early thirteenth century), it perhaps has as much right to be placed among Marie's works as any of the other three. Not only does the author name herself, but the line *En romanz dit et translaté* as well as her reasons cited in the phrases *se oblie* and *soie remembree* are clearly reminiscent. The fact that it is a saint's life should be adduced as further circumstantial evidence rather than the contrary, since one willingly accepts the *Espurgatoire*. A close, comparative linguistic study might prove rewarding.

5. However, the copy of these texts may be some twenty years later than the date of composition (See *Le Couronnement de Renard*, edited by Alfred Foulet, Princeton, 1929).

6. Eduard Mall, *De aetate rebusque Mariae Francicae nova quaestio instituitur*, Halle, 1867.

7. Eduard Mall, "Noch einmal: Marie de Compiègne und das *Evangile aux femmes*," ZRP 1 (1877), 337–56.

8. Gaston Paris, "Lais inédits de *Tyolet*, de *Guingamor*, de *Doon*, de *Lecheor* et de *Tydorel*," *Romania* 8 (1879), 29–72.

9. Baum points out that the dedicatees of all the texts in BN manuscript 1446 are more or less closely associated and that the manuscript was prepared during the lifetime of Gui de Dampierre. Since he would certainly be aware of what had or had not been dedicated to his family, there is little likelihood of an error (Baum, pp. 212–13). It should be pointed out that such an assumption is by no means certain. Was the dedication of a text an event of sufficient importance that Gui de Dampierre (1225–1305) would necessarily know of it, given that the work might have been composed when he was only a child?

10. Six manuscripts indicate that the English translation was the work of King Alfred. Three manuscripts have the name Henri, considered a substitution. No such English version is extant, but scholars have generally seen no reason to doubt Marie's assertion that she translated the text from English, although it is believed that she was mistaken in her attribution of the translation to King Alfred.

11. The *Espurgatoire Saint Patriz* is a translation into French of a Latin text composed by an author designated by the letter *H*, identified as Henry of Saltrey.

12. *La Vie de Seint Edmund le rei*, edited by H. Kjellman, Göteborg, 1935, vv. 25–45.

13. Gustav Gröber and Gaston Paris both placed the composition of the *Vie de Seint Edmund* at the end of the twelfth century. The reference to "Partenopé" (*Partenopeus de Blois*) is somewhat helpful; it is estimated to have been written in the 1180's. The author has not been identified with certainty, but Mr. Haxo, one of the editors of the *Vie de Seint Edmund*, suggested a certain monk named Dionysios who belonged to the Abbey of St. Edmund at Edmundsbury. This particular Dionysios was associated with the abbey as early as 1160 and is last mentioned in 1200, but there is no reference to link him with the literary text.

14. Warnke, vv. 5–8.

15. Though a common feature in many mediaeval texts of the period, it is worth noting that the prologues resemble one another in their didactic tone.

16. Professor Baum believes that the reference to Marie in the prologue to *Guigemar* is a later addition to the text. The lines in which her name is found are not in the Old Norse text, which he considers

to represent the oldest extant version of the *Lais*. Few would accept his challenge to the Harley manuscript.

17. Richard Baum points out that the treatise *Manière et facture des monstres des hommes, qui sont en Orient et plus en Inde*, found in BN manuscript, fonds français, 15106, ends with lines which might indicate that the same author who composed the *Fables* was responsible for this treatise. It is not clear from the lines, however, that the author of the *Fables* is the same person who is making the statement (Baum, *Recherches*, p. 214).

18. U. T. Holmes cites two twelfth-century narrative poems which distinguish Normandy and Beauce from France proper and points out that Marie herself distinguished Frenchmen from Normans in *Chaitivel* (verse 77). He defines the Ile-de-France as the ". . . territory comprised between the Seine, Marne, Oise, Nonette and Therouanne rivers . . ." (U. T. Holmes, "New Thoughts on Marie de France," *SP* 29 [1932], 1–10; "Further on Marie de France," *Symposium* 3 [1949], 335–39). It might be added that Marie makes a precise reference to Normandy in lines 7 and 8 of *Les Deus Amanz: Verité est kë en Neustrie/Que nus apelum Normendie . . .*

19. F. W. Locke, "A New Date for the Composition of the *Tractatus de Purgatorio Sancti Patricii*," *Speculum* 40 (1965), 641–46.

20. Mr. Baum accepts the early date for the *lais* rather readily. In so doing, he points out that Marie's period of creative activity would have to span at least fifty years to allow her authorship of all three texts attributed to her. One must concur with him that such a lengthy literary career, though not impossible, is improbable. However, there is no real evidence linking any of the twelve *lais* to such an early date. For attempts to date the individual *lais* in reference to contemporary literary influence, see E. Hoepffner, "Pour la chronologie des lais de Marie de France," *Romania* 59 (1933), 351–70; 60 (1934), 36–66, and R. N. Illingworth, "La Chronologie des *Lais* de Marie de France," *Romania* 87 (1966), 433–75.

21. Maurice Wilmotte argued, to the contrary, that Marie's *Guigemar* shows a distinct borrowing from Chrétien's *Cliges*. He considered the hind's prediction to be a direct borrowing from Chrétien's text:

> Oï, lase! jeo sui ocise!
> E tu, vassal, ki m'as nafree,
> Tel seit la tue destinee:
> Jamais n'aies tu med[e]cine!
> Ne par herbe ne par racine
> Ne par mire ne par pociun
> N'avras tu jamés garisun . . . (Ewert, lines 106–12)

("Hélas, I have been killed. And you, vassal, who have wounded me, may such be your destiny: Never may you have medicinal remedy!

Neither by herb, root, physician, nor potion will you ever have a cure. . . .") The passage in *Cliges* is indeed similar:

> *Je sent le mien mal grevain*
> *Que ja n'en avrai garison*
> *Par mecine ne par poison*
> *Ne par herbe ne par racine*
> *A chascun mal n'a pas mecine:*
> *Li miens est si enracinez*
> *Qu'il ne puet estre mecinez.* (lines 646–52, quoted from Wilmotte)

("I feel the seriousness of my wound from which I shall never be cured neither by medicine, potion, herb nor root. For each hurt there is not a remedy: Mine is so deeply rooted that there is no medication for it.")

Wilmotte stresses that Marie substituted *mire* for *mecine*, thus eliminating a repetition. He argues that it is unreasonable to think that Chrétien would have added a repetition had he been borrowing from Marie. Although the passages are similar, one must be cautious in concluding from such resemblances that a certain author borrowed from another specific writer. The narrative technique of twelfth- and thirteenth-century writers causes one to find many passages where the wording is similar. This is especially true because of the many stock situations, themes, and motifs common to many of the texts. A good example of this is provided by Wilmotte himself, who believed that the storm-at-sea passage in *Eliduc* was borrowed from the *Guillaume d'Angleterre*. Others have asserted that this same passage was drawn from the *Eneas* or *Brut*. One simply cannot ascertain the exact relationship of these texts, except to note that they belong to the same literary milieu and derive from the same stylistic tradition.

22. Lucien Foulet, "Marie de France et les lais bretons," ZRP 29 (1905), 19–56; 293–322.

23. Ernest Hoepffner, "La Géographie et l'histoire dans les *Lais* de Marie de France," *Romania* 56 (1930), 1–32.

24. One cannot be sure whether or not this was a later addition to the text.

25. Maurice Wilmotte objected stringently to the thesis that *Eliduc* was the source for Gautier's text. He insists that there is no proof to indicate which of the two texts came first and that there is more resemblance between Gautier's *Ille* and his own *Eracle* than there is between *Ille* and *Eliduc*. Wilmotte's arguments underscore the fragility of attempts to date works based on their resemblance to other contemporary texts (Maurice Wilmotte, "Problèmes de chronologie littéraire," *Moyen Âge* 50 (1940), 99–114.

26. Manuscript *P* makes reference to Thiebaut V of Blois who ruled

from 1172–1191. Was this a later addition to the text made after Beatrice's death?

27. Professor Holmes reviews the dispute current in the church concerning the steps necessary before a marriage was considered legal. Both *Eliduc* and *Le Fresne* pose problems concerning the question of a legal marriage and under what circumstances and at which point the union might be dissolved. Unfortunately, one cannot be sure that Marie would know the latest church ruling which would have made the solution in *Eliduc* illegal, nor can one be sure that *Le Fresne* follows the ruling of 1179, which supported consummation as the only validating step in the marriage procedure.

28. E. Levi, "Il Re Giovane e Maria di Francia," *Archivum Romanicum* 5 (1921), 448–71.

29. A. Ahlström, *Marie de France et les lais narratifs*, Göteborg, 1925.

30. Ahlström proposed Guillaume de Gloucester, son of Robert, a natural son of Henry I who raised Henry II. Young Guillaume and the future king were thus close childhood companions. Ahlström notes further that Robert, who owned a large library, was well known for being learned and a patron of letters. Levi suggested William Marshal, tutor of the Young King. However, he did not become Count of Pembroke until 1199, considered late for dating the *Fables*.

31. The acceptance by many of William Longsword stems from his relationship to Henry II and the widely accepted identification of Marie as Henry II's natural sister, the Abbess of Shaftesbury.

32. Sidney Painter, "To Whom Were Dedicated the *Fables* of Marie de France," *MLN* 48 (1933), 367–69.

33. Emile Winkler wrote in support of this identification, asserting that the phrase "de France" referred to the fact that she was a member of the royal family (Emile Winkler, *Marie de France*, Vienna, 1918).

34. John C. Fox, "Marie de France," *EHR* 25 (1910), 303–6.

35. Records indicate that she was no longer abbess in 1216. Since Geoffrey died in 1151, Marie was at least thirty years of age by 1181. Her father was Count of Anjou, hence the likelihood that she was born in "French territory."

36. It has been noted that a fragment of an Anglo-Norman version of the *Espurgatoire* was found written on the cover of a twelfth-century psalter formerly owned by the abbey. However, the text is not that of Marie's translation.

37. Some writers have pointed out that Marie's dedication to the *nobles reis* is too humbly phrased to have been written by the king's sister.

38. E. Levi, "Maria di Francia e le abbazie d'Inghilterra," *Arch-*

ivum Romanicum 5 (1921), 472–93. Noting the limitations imposed by the facts of Marie's place of birth and status of learning, U. T. Holmes hypothesized that Marie de France could have been Marie, the eighth child of Count Waleran de Meulan. Born in an area some sixty kilometers from Pitres, the only area which the poetess seems to have known firsthand, Count Waleran's daughter married one Hugh Talbot, who owned land in England. Waleran's father had been an important figure in the wars against Henry I and Waleran had sided with Mathilde and Henry II against Stephen (U. T. Holmes, "New Thoughts on Marie de France," *SP* 29 [1932], 1–10).

39. Cesare Segre, "Piramo e Tisbe nei *Lai* di Maria di Francia," *Studi Lugli-Valeri* (Venezia, 1961), 845–53. Segre demonstrates that both texts reveal direct knowledge of Ovid's *Piramus and Tisbe* and not indirect influence through the early twelfth-century French version. In the *Deus Amanz* he selects four passages where the language is strongly reminiscent of the Latin text. His arguments for *Laüstic* are even more persuasive. He shows that the first fifty lines of the French text, undoubtedly drawn from the Latin, are really unnecessary to the basic story and are not present in other versions of the same tale. The specific lines which are so strikingly similar to the Latin text are not present in the French adaptation of the story. He suggests that Marie added these lines to her text to provide a frame for the tale.

40. For the principal studies which have developed the influence of these texts on Marie's work, the reader is referred to the studies of Hoepffner, Levi, Pelan, and Illingworth in the Bibliography.

Chapter Two

1. The books and articles written on the subject of the twelfth-century Renaissance are too numerous to list. The student might well begin with C. H. Haskins, *The Renaissance of the Twelfth Century,* Cambridge, 1927, and, for the period leading into the twelfth century, R. W. Southern, *The Making of the Middle Ages,* New Haven, 1953.

2. However, it should be noted that such Byzantine influence is not solely attributable to the Crusades. Some features associated with Byzantine technique in fortification can be seen in pre-Crusade constructions such as the Chateau d'Arques (near Dieppe) and the Tower of London. The Byzantine influence in Southern French churches comes by way of Rome.

3. For an introduction to the Norman contribution, the student is referred to the books and articles of C. H. Haskins and to the recent book of David C. Douglas, *The Norman Achievement 1050–1100,* Berkeley, 1969.

4. See G. Paré, A. Brunet, and P. Tremblay, *La Renaissance du XIIᵉ siècle. Les Écoles et l'enseignement,* Paris, 1933.

5. It is important that the twelfth-century Renaissance be seen in the proper perspective. Certainly the increased intellectual activity in the fields of law (Bologna), medicine (Salerno), and the physical sciences (with the translations from Arabic and the availability of Aristotelian texts, theretofore unavailable, beginning to be felt) indicate that the term Renaissance is appropriate. Yet, the term itself is, in a sense, prejudicial, in that it places everything in a tendentious perspective. One tends to search for those elements in the "awakening" which lead to the modern viewpoint; indeed, our use of the term is predicated on the notion of our own enlightenment. In the twelfth-century one can see a rising interest in many areas of learning and culture. To understand the period, however, one must see the world as they saw it, not as we see it. It is their intellectual understanding of things which is important, not ours, if we wish to comprehend the period for what it really was in its own terms.

6. D. Legge, *Anglo-Norman Literature and its Background*, Oxford, 1963.

7. Adeliza became the wife of Henry I in 1121.

8. Little has been said about the influence of Eleanor of Aquitaine in the development of the vernacular literature. The legend concerning her amorous involvements and her influence as a literary patroness is extensive. The omission is deliberate, in that primary documents contribute little in the way of support for the legend. Professor Labande's careful review of Eleanor's career ("Pour une image véridique d'Aliénor d'Aquitaine," *Bull. Soc. Antiq. Ouest* 2 [1952/54], 175–234) is a sobering reminder of the necessity for consultation and objective evaluation of contemporary documents. Verification of the queen's role as a literary patroness is similarly lacking. Rita Lejeune's extensive article ("Le Rôle littéraire d'Aliénor d'Aquitaine," *Cultura Neolatina* 14 [1954], 5–57) assembles much hypothetical influence but is lacking in documentary evidence. *Chansons de geste* and *romans* set in the South of France and texts bearing the "courtly" love element, etc., are associated with her. It is alleged that she played an important role among *troubadour* poets and that many followed her to Paris and later to England. It has been suggested that she may have been the "faraway lady" of Jaufré Rudel and a Provençal *Vida* links her amorously with Bernard de Ventadour, virtually the only *troubadour* who can be associated with her to any degree of certainty. What is remarkable, given her legendary influence, is the little effect that can be seen from her fifteen years with Louis VII and the lack of evidence there is to support the assertion that she was surrounded by a considerable literary retinue. Given the influence she is reputed to have had, a relatively small number of works is actually dedicated to her. There is really nothing to link her with Thomas' *Tristan*, except the belief

that the treatment of love in the story would have pleased her, and only Layamon's early thirteenth-century statement supports the notion that Wace presented his *Brut* to her. It is possible, of course, that Eleanor of Aquitaine did play a major role in the development of French romance, but the evidence adduced thus far rests on a series of hypotheses under serious challenge: that the love in Northern French romance is related to the love found in *troubadour* poetry (interpreted specifically in "courtly" terms), that this concept of love moved from the South to the North of France and can be seen in Thomas' *Tristan,* Chrétien's *Lancelot,* and Andreas Capellanus' *De Amore,* and that the refined Provençal influence played a major role in changing the mores of society, a change which is reflected literally in the change from epic to romance. The hypotheses important to this development are currently less certain than was once believed. Eleanor's importance as a literary patroness and her alleged influence on the literature of the period are supported more by this theory of development than by evidence found in contemporary documents.

9. A great deal of attention has been given recently to the much needed revision of the literary chronology of the period. For an introduction to the problem and bibliography, see H. Tiemann, "Die Datierungen der altfranzösischen Literatur," *Romanistisches Jahrbuch* 8 (1957), 110–31.

10. It is often stated (See E. Faral, *Recherches sur les sources latines des contes et romans courtois du moyen âge,* Paris, 1913), that the addition of zoological, cosmological, mineralogical, and geographic details in these texts stems from the mediaeval writer's interest in displaying his encyclopedic knowledge and from the mediaeval man's growing interest in the exotic Orient and the *merveilleux.* However, the type of digression in question, far from being a vain display of knowledge, is often closely related thematically to the subject of the narrative and helps elucidate or confirm the meaning of the text. Rarely is the interest in the material objectively scientific. What interested the mediaeval writer and his public was the symbolic interrelationship among things. It is always the hidden qualities or properties of substances, the characteristics of animals and their place in the order of things, and the analogies which illuminated the mysteries of the created order which interested the mediaeval writer. In short, it was the mediaeval philosophical perspective which stimulated interest in these subjects, not an "exotic" or scientific appeal in a nineteenth-century sense. Similarly, it was his sense of thematic unity which accounts for his use of such materials in ways which we consider damaging to the narrative's unity in a linear sense.

11. The traditional description of the development from epic to romance is suspect. I hope to deal with this subject in the near future.

12. L. Foulet, "Marie de France et la légende du Purgatoire de Saint Patrice," *Romanische Forschungen* 22 (1908), 599–627.

13. Modern aesthetic values can hinder our evaluation of the historical development of the period. Philippe de Thaon's allegorized bestiary was later dedicated to Queen Eleanor, a fact which has caused some scholars to suggest that such a dedication must have amused the worldly queen, an assumption which has no basis in fact and which, in my opinion, fails to consider the tastes of the period. It is the fault of dividing secular and religious literature, didactic from what we consider nondidactic literature, and "allegory" from what we consider a more appealing "realistic" literature where the characters are "real" human beings. These distinctions are, I believe, artificial in a twelfth-century context.

Chapter Three

1. For a discussion of sources and the relationship among the manuscripts, see Karl Warnke, *Die Fabeln der Marie de France*, Halle, 1898, and the confirming study of Hélène Chefneux, "Les Fables dans la tapisserie de Bayeux," *Romania* 60 (1934), 1–35; 153–94.

2. M. Ellwood Smith, "A Classification for Fables Based on the Collection of Marie de France," *Modern Philology* 15 (1917–18), 477–89.

3. *Ibid.*, p. 477.

4. *Ibid.*, p. 479.

5. The problem of distinguishing *fabliaux* from fables where there is overlap probably concerns us more than it would the mediaeval author.

6. Needless to say, there are exceptions to this schema.

7. E. A. Francis, "Marie de France et son temps," *Romania* 72 (1951), 78–99.

Chapter Four

1. In his *Topographia Hibernica* (*ca.* 1189), Giraldus Cambrensis discusses the legend but makes no reference to the Irish knight. The same is true of Jocelin of Furness writing soon after 1180.

2. For a detailed discussion of the contents and classification of the manuscripts, see H. L. D. Ward, *Catalogue of Romances in the Department of Manuscripts in the British Museum*, vol. 2 (Longmans, 1893), pp. 435–92; Lucien Foulet, "Marie de France et la légende du Purgatoire de Saint Patrice." *Romanische Forschungen* 22 (1908), 599–627; T. A. Jenkins, ed., *L'Espurgatoire Saint Patriz*, The Decennial Publications, First Series, vol. 7 (Chicago, 1903), pp. 235–327; Karl Warnke, *Das Buch vom Espurgatoire S. Patrice der Marie de France*

und Seine Quelle, Halle, 1938. Additional bibliography can be found in these studies.

3. The table of comparison is drawn from Jenkins, *Espurgatoire.* Foulet, *op. cit.,* concluded that BM Harley 3846 and Bamberg E vii, 59, represent the oldest form of the text, but do not reproduce the original itself. In fact, their inclusion of the First Homily, judged to be one of the additions to the original, indicates that these texts, as well as the manuscript used by Marie, were copied at a time when all the surmised additions had already been made.

4. It may be that the episode concerning the old Irishman who did not realize that homicide is a sin is an addition.

5. L. Foulet, "Marie de France et la légende du Purgatoire de Saint Patrice," *Romanische Forschungen* 22 (1908), 599–627.

6. "Wretched is he who is drawn into such pain by his sins."

7. "Alas, that anyone must deserve that he should suffer such travail."

8. "May God grant that we deserve it, in order that we may come to these joys."

Chapter Five

1. Among the anonymous texts not attributed to Marie, but often referred to as *lais,* are the following: *Amours, Aristote, Epine, Graelent, Cor, Mantel mautaillié, Desiré, Guingamor, Doon, Haveloc, Ignaure, Lecheor, Melion, Nabaret, Narcissus, Epervier, Oiselet, Trot, Tidorel, Tyolet,* Jean Renart's *Lai de l'Ombre,* and Huon le Roi's *Vair Palefroi.* There are many other references to *lais* in various *romans* of the twelfth and thirteenth centuries. Many of these are not extant and one cannot always be sure whether the reference is to a lyric or to a narrative text. For a rather extensive list of such titles found in the Shrewesbury manuscript, see G. E. Brereton, "A 13th Century List of French Lays and Other Narrative Poems," *Modern Language Review* 45 (1950), 40–45. See also Baum, *Oeuvres* . . . , pp. 117ff.

2. For discussion of various aspects of the problem and bibliography, see Jean Maillard, *Évolution et esthétique du lai lyrique* (Fontainebleau, 1961); R. Baum, "Les troubadours et les lais," *ZRP* 85 (1969), 1–44; F. Neri, "La voce 'lai' nei testi italiani," *Atti della R. Accademia delle Scienze di Torino* 72 (1936–37), 105–19.

3. H. d'Arbois de Jubainville, "Lai," *Romania* 8 (1879), 422–25.

4. It is generally agreed that the French word does not derive from the Welsh *llais* (voice, sound) or German *lied.* The Oxford English Dictionary derives the word from Teutonic origin, an adoption of a form of the Germanic *leich* (melody, song, play). However, the primitive *leich* seems to have been abandoned totally by German poets in

the eleventh and twelfth centuries and gains currency again only through influence of the French *lai*.

5. This argument will be developed more fully later in the chapter.

6. Baum doubts the Irish derivation of the word, since the Provençal form ends in *s* and is mentioned by Uc Faidit as a word which is not declined. The Irish *laid* would not ordinarily suffice as an explanation for the Provençal form.

7. F. Wolf, *Ueber die Lais, Sequenzen und Leiche* (Heidelberg, 1841).

8. Even if one were to accept the influence of the Celtic lyric on the Latin sequence, a point which is dubious, this hardly links the twelfth-century lyric, so much later than the beginnings of the sequence, directly to Celtic profane material.

9. Professor Bromwich develops the same argument in an interesting note, but carries the parallel one step further. She compares the French lyric *lais* with the Irish lyrical speech passage and asserts that the *conte* or *aventure*, referred to by Marie and others, would be parallel to the Irish prose narrative. Although a similar tradition cannot be established for Wales and Brittany, she affirms that there was a strong ballad tradition in Brittany concerned with tragic and supernatural events where monologue and dialogue are dominant forms (this is unfortunately attested only by nineteenth-century recordings). She suggests that Marie, in versifying older narratives, was only following a development already taking place in Brittany. She is simply putting into the form of narrative *lais* the *contes* which had developed from the once prose-verse Irish sagas (R. Bromwich, "A Note on the Breton Lays," *Medium Aevum* 26 [1957], 36–38).

10. Maillard considers the term *lai* to be misapplied in the case of Marie's *nouvelles versifiées*, since it should be applied only to the lyric interlude in a narrative poem.

11. One should not overlook F. Neri's study of the Italian thirteenth-century translation of the French word *lai*. In addition to numerous terms which confirm that the French word meant *chanson* or melody to the Italians, the word *lemento* or *laimento* is also used. Commentaries define the word as *i tristi canti* and *versi in forma di lamentazione*, while Chaucer used *compleynt* as a substitute for *lay*. Baum has shown that the term *lays* could mean *chanson pieuse* in Provençal poetry prior to the thirteenth century. The writer of the *Doctrina de compondre dictatz* (beginning of the thirteenth century) gave the etymology of *lays* as *l'ays* (*chagrin, ennui, tristesse*). This would seem to confirm the assertions of Wolf, Spanke, and Handschin that the *lai*, *sequence*, and *planctus* are all closely related (F. Neri, *op. cit.*, pp. 105–19; R. Baum, "Les Troubadours . . . ," *ZRP* 85 [1969], 28–29).

12. The similarity between these prose texts with verse interludes and the *prosimetrum* has been noted. The *Aucassin et Nicolette* is thought by some to represent a form akin to the narrative-lyric relationship in the Breton tradition.

13. It was even thought that these narratives might have been accompanied by music. Although no narrative text has been found with musical notation, in BN ms. fr. 2168 there is an empty bar for music at the beginning of the *Lai de Graelent*. This has tempted some to postulate that, originally, there may have been musical accompaniment.

14. Several scholars have proposed that the Breton narrative *lai* was to the lyric what the Provençal *razo* is to its poem. This is the meaning a number of scholars find in the opening four lines of *Eliduc:* *De un mut ancïen lai bretun / Le cunte e tute la reisun/Vus dirai* . . . That is, Marie's work tells the story or relates the narrative on which the lyric was based.

15. Hoepffner affirmed that the author of the lyric *lai* knew Marie's text and was influenced by it (E. Hoepffner, "Les deux lais du Chèvrefeuille," *Mélanges Paul Laumonier,* Paris, 1935).

16. See principally H. Zimmer, "Bretonische Elemente in der Arthursage des Gottfried von Monmouth," *ZFSL* 12 (1890), 230–56; "Beiträge zur Namenforschung in den altfranzösischen Arthurepen," *ZFSL* 13 (1891), 1–117; E. Brugger, "Über die Bedeutung von Bretagne, breton in mittelalterlichen Texten," *ZFSL* 20 (1898), 79–162; "Die *Lais* der Marie de France," *ZFSL* 49 (1927), 116–55; "Eigennamen in den *Lais* der Marie de France," *ZFSL* 49 (1927), 201–52; 381–484.

17. They are *Guigemar, Eliduc, Fresne, Laüstic, Chaitivel, Bisclavret,* and *Milun* (where the scene of action shifts from Great Britain to the continent).

18. They affirmed that such names as Guigemar, Bisclavret, Laüstic, and Graelent (of the anonymous *lais*) all have specifically Armorican origin.

19. This, of course, is one of the weakest arguments of the continental theory. Zimmer had early argued that it was the Welsh who would have placed Arthur's seat at Carlion in the South. The early Bretons who had migrated to the continent would have remembered that Arthur's principal residence was in the North. He withdrew from this position when it was pointed out that the Bretons who had migrated were from the southern part of Wales and that they had migrated prior to Arthur's exploits. Brugger weakened the position further in attempting to link all the geographical names to place-names on the continent. He also saw in the more famous Arthurian names replacements for continental heroes who were not so well known.

20. Details of Lot's argument can be found in F. Lot, "Le Sens du mot 'breton' au XIIe siècle," *Romania* 24 (1895), 497–528; "La Patrie des lais bretons," *Romania* 28 (1899), 1–48.

21. *"Quand l'oeuvre de Gaufrei de Monmouth vint révéler au public courtois l'existence et les exploits des antiques possesseurs de l'île de Bretagne, le mot* breton *s'entendit au sens archaïque, rétrospectif. Tous les exploits des héros celtiques furent reportés au temps des 'anciens Bretons courtois'"* (F. Lot, "La Patrie des lais bretons," *Romania* 28 [1899], 45).

22. Constance Bullock-Davies has recently argued against the notion that Marie superimposed the Arthurian setting in *Lanval* on her original source. She believes that the *lai* preserves primitive elements which indicate that the tale probably originated among the northern Bretons and was brought south after the defeat of the northern Bretons by the invaders. She asserts that the geographical description in *Lanval* accords with that around Carlisle, that the name of the hero is etymologically related to the geography and his situation in the tale, and that Avalon should be related, not to Glastonbury, but to the nearby ancient town of Avalana or Aballava. She suggests that the tale bears reminiscences of a historical reality which is still present in the oral tale and which Marie preserved without understanding their significance (C. Bullock-Davies, " 'Lanval' and 'Avalon,' " *Bulletin of the Board of Celtic Studies* 23 [1969], 128–42).

23. In an interesting article entitled "Marie de France et son temps," *Romania* 72 (1951), 78–99, E. A. Francis suggests the interest that nobles at Henry II's court who hailed from Brittany and Normandy might have had in Marie's *lais*. Both the geographical setting and personal names in *Le Fresne, Les Deus Amanz, Milun,* and *Lanval* might have held special interest for the Fresneys, the family of Miles de Gloucester, and the family of Willelmus de Lanvaleio.

24. ". . . *le public français des châteaux qui écoutait les jongleurs venus de Grande ou Petite Bretagne appréciait hautement leurs mélodies, les comprenait d'autant mieux que la musique est un langage universel, mais n'entendait point les paroles de ces lais bretons. Certains rimeurs français, notamment d'expression anglo-normande, qui connaissaient les deux langues, eurent l'idée de transcrire dans la forme courante le la poésie narrative—en l'occurrence l'octosyllabe—l'histoire des lais*" (G. Paris, "Lais inédits," *Romania* 8 [1879], 33). There are references to a certain Bledhericus or Bleheri, renowned for his storytelling. Pierre Gallais has recently reinforced the idea that this *conteur*, identified with the Welsh nobleman Bledri ap Cadivor (*ca.* 1070–*ca.* 1140), said to have told stories to the Count of Poitiers, is responsible for the great Arthurian popularity among troubadour poets. Gallais points out that the name Gauvains, certainly not con-

nected with continental Breton traditions, is found in Poitou and Anjou four times in the early twelfth century. Does this not indicate some direct link between the oral tradition of Wales and Poitou prior to the appearance of Geoffrey of Monmouth's *Historia?* (P. Gallais, "Bleeheri, la cour de Poitiers et la diffusion des récits arthuriens sur le continent," *Actes du VII* *Congrès national de littérature comparée* [Paris, 1967], 47–79).

25. Some scholars see Marie's use of titles in more than one language (*Eliduc* or *Guildeluec ha Guilliadun*) and her occasional explanation of a word in more than one language as evidence of bilingual narratives and of the bilingual nature of the British-French audiences. Lucien Foulet wryly noted that anyone not understanding French would scarcely be helped by the explanation of one word in his native English tongue.

26. That many of the anonymous *lais* are imitations of Marie is well established. However, Professor Foulet's attempt to make all the *lais* dependent upon Marie is not entirely successful. If *Graelent* is agreed to be an imitation of Marie's *Lanval* (see C. Segre, "Lanval, Graelent, Guingamor," *Studi in onore di A. Monteverdi* [Modena, 1959], 756–70), and if *Espine, Desiré, Melion, Doon,* and *Tyolet* all show marked influence, it is, nonetheless, forcing the argument to pretend that the entire text in each case can be explained by the thesis of imitation. Professor Foulet's thesis is forced in the cases of *Espine* and *Tyolet* and in his cursory dismissal of the other texts often called *lais.* Professor Levi documents an impressive number of references to an oral Breton tradition (E. Levi, *I lais brettoni e la leggenda di Tristano,* Perugia, 1918).

27. For the view that the "Prologue" is not related to the collection itself, see Baum, *Recherches . . . ,* where the writer seeks to demonstrate that the collection has been attributed to Marie erroneously.

28. It is true that the prologue to *Guigemar* is considerably longer than the introduction to any of the other *lais.*

29. *"Quant au sens poème narratif, il est inconnu . . . avant Marie; c'est elle qui l'a introduit dans la langue, sans dessein bien arrêté, par suite d'une confusion qui devait nécessairement se produire entre le lai breton auquel elle se référait sans cesse et le conte français qui prétendait retracer l'origine de ce lai"* (L. Foulet, "Marie de France et les lais bretons," *ZRP* 29 [1905], 310–11).

30. *". . . jadis, au temps des anciens Bretons, quand une aventure était arrivée parmi les barons, on prenait plaisir à se la raconter, elle circulait de bouche en bouche; puis c'était une mode très en honneur que d'en faire un lai pour en conserver le souvenir; ce lai portait généralement le nom du héros de l'aventure; c'était une mélodie qu'on exécutait sur la harpe ou la rote et qu'on pouvait probablement aussi*

chanter sur des paroles; parfois le lai n'était composé que longtemps après que l'aventure elle-même était arrivée; il pouvait donc y avoir des aventures qui se transmettaient sans donner naissance à un lai" (*Ibid.*, p. 314).

31. It is true that Marie never actually states that she had heard a *lai* herself.

32. His argument that her lack of knowledge concerning the Breton language is manifest in her joining of the French article to the Breton word *austic* is obviously weak. The form *laüstic* may well be the result of scribal error; in any case one could scarcely assume from such a mistake that she did not understand the language. Nonetheless, it is probably a sound assumption that she did not know Breton.

33. For a vigorous attack on Foulet's thesis of imitation, his assertion that the *lais* were only *mélodies* and that the Breton tradition was far removed from Marie's time, see E. Levi, *I lai brettoni e la leggenda di Tristano,* Perugia, 1918.

34. The inclusa motif in *Guigemar* and *Yonec,* and the Putiphar's wife theme in *Lanval* are not specifically Breton. And the hawk-lover visitation in *Yonec,* for example, has closer analogues outside the Celtic tradition, to list only a few instances.

35. In the case of *Milun,* the epilogue refers only to *li auncïen,* but this generally has been understood to refer to the Bretons.

36. See Baum, *Recherches,* and Horst Baader, *Die Lais,* Frankfurt am Main, 1966. It is possible that the Bretons made *lais* to commemorate well-known stories which they had come to know but which were not specifically Breton. There is no need to assume that storytellers would not adopt tales from adjacent regions. In such cases, it is plausible that the names and settings would be adapted. If this were true, there would be nothing incongruous in finding Breton names and settings for non-Breton tales. As a consequence, Marie's statement that the Bretons had made a *lai* about them would then be logical and accurate.

37. E. Hoepffner, "La Géographie et l'histoire dans les lais de Marie de France," *Romania* 56 (1930), 1–32.

38. Martín de Riquer, "La 'aventure,' el 'lai' y el 'conte' de Maria de Francia," *Filologia romanza* 2 (1955), 1–19.

39. *"Issi avient cum dit vus ai./Li Bretun en firent un lai . . ."* (*Equitan,* vv. 311–12).

40. *"Une aventure vus dirai/Dunt li Bretun firent un lai"* (*Laüstic,* vv. 1–2). See also *Yonec,* vv. 559–62, *Deus Amanz,* vv. 1–6, and *Le Fresne,* vv. 533–36.

41. See *Eliduc,* vv. 1181–4, and *Bisclavret,* vv. 315–18.

42.   *Cele aventure fu cuntee,*
        Ne pot estre lunges celee.

> *Un lai en firent li Bretun*
> *Le Laüstic l'apelë hum.* (*Laüstic*, vv. 157–60)

It should, perhaps, be noted that the last two lines could be seen as a restatement of the first two lines. If one considers that the term *lai* could refer to a narrative form, then *lai* could be viewed as that which was *cuntee*.

43. One could probably make a better case for interpreting *faire* as *traiter*.

44. *L'aventure ke avez oïe*
   Veraie fu, n'en dutez mie.
   De Bisclavret fu fet li lais
   Pur remembrance a tutdis mais. (*Bisclavret*, vv. 315–18)

45. Horst Baader objects to Professor Riquer's thesis that Marie intended her texts to be thought of as *contes*. He notes that the term appears in only four of the texts. Moreover, he rejects the argument based on the idea that Marie's audience knew what a *lai* was. If this were so, what is one to say about texts such as *Cort Mantel, Auberée, Piramus, Narcisus, Aristote*, etc., where the term *lai* is unmistakably used to mean the work itself? Is one to suppose that the audience of a generation later no longer knew what a *lai* was and hence accepted the term as a name for these narrative texts?

46. The genre continued in England throughout the thirteenth and fourteenth centuries, its popularity extended probably by the translation into English of Marie's *Le Fresne* and *Lanval*. Professor Donovan classifies the English Breton lay into two groups, those written in the tail rhyme stanza (*Sir Launfal, Erl of Toulous, Emare*, and *Sir Gowther*) and those composed in the octosyllabic couplet (*Lai le Freine, Sir Landeval, Sir Lambewell, Sir Lamwell, Sir Orfeo*, and *Sir Degare*). (Mortimer Donovan, *The Breton Lay: A Guide to Varieties*, University of Notre Dame Press, 1969.)

47. "*Ce sont des contes d'aventures et d'amour, où figurent souvent des fées, des merveilles, des transformations; on y parle plus d'une fois du pays de l'immortalité, où les fées conduisent et retiennent les héros; on y mentionne Arthur, dont la cour est parfois le théâtre du récit, et aussi Tristan. . . . On peut y reconnaître les débris d'une ancienne mythologie, d'ordinaire incomprise et presque méconnaissable; il y règne en général un ton tendre et mélancolique en même temps qu'une passion inconnue aux chansons de geste; d'ailleurs les personnages des contes celtiques sont transformés en chevaliers et en dames*" (G. Paris, *La Littérature française au moyen âge*, Paris, 1890, p. 91).

48. Whether the term *mélancolique* is really apropos is doubtful.

There is more than a little nineteenth-century sensibility involved in using the term to describe the tone of the *lais*.

49. Nearly fifty years later, E. Hoepffner broadened the sense of the *monde féerique* beyond the purely supernatural. Even when the supernatural is not a factor, he argued that the tale was placed in an atmosphere of extraordinary occurrences, striking for their singularity. He elaborates on Paris' reference to the transformation of Celtic characters into *chevaliers*. "It moves [the *lai*] in an aristocratic world and reflects the ideas and feelings of a chivalric society" (E. Hoepffner, *Les Lais de Marie de France*, Paris, 1935, p. 47). This reflection of twelfth-century aristocratic values and their relationship to the *monde féerique* of the texts is extremely important to modern analyses of the *lai* and *roman*.

50. "*Le conte, comparé au roman, est plus bref, plus rapide, plus étroitement noué; les événements, peu nombreux, y concourent tous à préparer une scène principale, qui absorbe en elle l'intérêt essentiel du sujet, toute sa grâce ou tout son tragique; les thèmes poétiques, prestement traités, n'y sont jamais développés pour eux-mêmes, mais sont strictement subordonnés à l'action, qui se hâte vers le dénoûment . . .*" (E. Faral, *Recherches sur les sources latines des contes et romans courtois du moyen âge*, Paris, 1913, p. 392).

51. In his recent book on the *fabliau*, Nykrog disagrees with Bédier's basic social distinction. For the Danish scholar, both genres were written for an aristocratic audience. Instead of reflecting true bourgeois values written for a bourgeois audience, the *fabliau* reflects bourgeois values as they were viewed by the aristocracy. The erotic element appears in the form imagined by the aristocratic world to be typical of the noncourtly society. The humor of the *fabliau* is not that of a bourgeois author writing about his own society in its own terms. Rather, it is the humor of an aristocratic society looking down on a group which does not understand refined ways (P. Nykrog, *Les Fabliaux. Étude d'histoire littéraire et de stylistique médiévale*, Copenhagen, 1957).

52. J. Frappier, "Remarques sur la structure du lai, essai de définition et de classement," *La Littérature narrative d'imagination* (Paris, 1961), pp. 23–39.

53. "*On s'explique ainsi l'union étroite et la synthèse, admirable à tant d'égards, de deux mythologies, l'une primitive et merveilleuse, l'autre de l'esprit et du coeur, dans cette matière de Bretagne*" (*Ibid.*, p. 31).

54. "*Dans cette structure le rôle de* l'aventure, *de l'événement merveilleux ou singulier, est de permettre le passage du plan inférieur au plan supérieur*" (*Ibid.*, p. 32).

55. "*Ainsi, il arrive presque toujours dans nos lais un moment où*

le héros quitte le monde quotidien pour entrer dans un monde ou féerique ou sentimental dont l'accès est permis seulement à des êtres d'élite. Or, le plus souvent, l'aventure se produit dans des régions intermédiaires, qui sont à la fois des frontières et des passages, non sans des analogies, que je ne crois pas tout à fait fortuites, avec la conception celtique de l'Autre Monde" (*Ibid.*, p. 35).

56. See Chapter Two of Elena Eberwein, *Zur Deutung mittelalterlicher Existenz*, Bonn, 1933.

57. In his recent book *The Breton Lay: A Guide to Varieties*, Professor Donovan studies both the French *lai* and the extension of the form in England. In addition to the length, meter, and organic structure which characterize the exterior form of the short narrative, he perceives an interior unity in the *lai* focused around the development of a courtly theme. But within this framework, there are many varieties: ". . . some are realistic, others not; some read like *fabliaux*, others like biography or saints' lives; some have little plot, others, a great deal; but all are concerned with an adventure, a human experience having . . . profound implications" (Donovan, p. 6). The large majority of Breton lays in Marie's collection and in the imitations which follow have a unity in the theme of love. Those texts which are not directly related to this tradition are treated as derivatives and are classified under three headings: (1) the didactic lay (*Lai du Trot, l'Oiselet, Conseil,* and *l'Ombre*); (2) the elevated *fabliau* (*Lai de l'Epervier, Aristote, Cor, Mantel,* and *Nabaret*); (3) nondescript short poems framed as Breton *lais* to attract the reader, such as the *Lai d'Haveloc*. Professor Donovan's groupings are helpful in studying texts which are related to one another in form and content. However, the demarcation between the *lai* and other short narrative forms remains a problem.

58. H. Tiemann, *Die Entstehung der mittelalterlichen Novelle in Frankreich*, Hamburg, 1961.

59. The unity of style in the narrative material can be seen in the development of the *roman*, which Tiemann considers an outgrowth of the short narrative. Instead of a central event developed within the stylistic ideal of *abréviation*, the *roman* extends or amplifies the narrative by including a number of events in a hero's life.

60. H. Baader, *Die Lais*, Frankfurt am Main, 1966.

61. For development and justification of this interesting thesis, see Erich Köhler's works listed in the Bibliography.

62. Professor Baader rejects Bédier's thesis that the *fabliau* was written for a bourgeois audience. Since *fabliaux* and *lais* are found grouped and intermixed within the same manuscripts, they both must have been intended for the same reading audience.

63. Professor Baader contends that the *Lai du Mantel mautaillié*

was never intended to be called a *lai*. Only in BN ms. fr. 1104 is it called a *lai* by a later copyist who wished to take advantage of the popularity of the genre. In the other four texts it is not called a *lai*.

Chapter Six

1. This famous abduction scene has often been offered as proof of the currency of Arthurian legend prior to the available Latin and French written sources. However, the early twelfth- or late eleventh-century date which some would give is a matter of great dispute.

2. Other texts where the motif occurs include the *Didot Perceval*, the Dutch *Lancelot, Peredur, Huth Merlin, Dolopathos,* and the *Naissance du Chevalier au Cygne* of the cycle of poems concerning the First Crusade. For consideration of this theme in Celtic tradition, see R. S. Loomis, *Arthurian Tradition and Chrétien de Troyes,* New York, 1949.

3. *Etudes Celtiques* 9 (1961), 439–74.

4. *Ibid.,* 445. The various forms of the legend of the Hag, the proposed remains of this legend in French literature, and the relationship to Irish mythology cannot be dealt with adequately within the limits of this study. The reader is referred to the study of Miss Bromwich cited above.

5. *Ibid.,* 462.

6. R. N. Illingworth, "Celtic Tradition and the Lai of Guigemar," *Medium Aevum* 31 (1962), 176–87.

7. Mr. Illingworth argues that there are indications in the text that the young lady to whom Guigemar is taken was originally a fairy. In the Breton source material she may have been, but the traces he sees in Marie's text seem to me imagined. He would have the hind's remarks be not a curse, but a helpful indication concerning the means by which Guigemar may be cured. He further suggests that the hero is mysteriously drawn along a path leading to the boat. This would accord with the "original" Celtic motif where a fairy lures a mortal to her kingdom, but such an interpretation seems to violate the Old French text. The doe begins by a lament of her own death, and then pronounces to the one who has wounded her the prediction of his fate, ending with the line, "Go away, leave me in peace." As for Guigemar's departure from his own country, have we not been told that many young ladies would have been pleased to have Guigemar, but that he had no interest in them? It is only logical, then, that he leave the country to seek his love, since there had been none in his own land who had so attracted him.

8. F. Neri proposes that the rendition of the tale included in the fourteenth-century chivalric romance, *Dalla storia di Messere Prodesaggio,* has elements from a version of the story earlier than that used

by Marie. Virtually all the elements and episodes of the *Guigemar* text are present, but in the Italian insert the girl is a fairy named Aventuria and has sent the hind and boat for the hero, who is brought to where she is held captive by the Saracens. Even though the text is late, it is significant to note that the girl has the role of sending for the hero. (F. Neri, "Appunti su 'Guigemar,' " *Annali dell' Istituto superiore di magistero di Torino* 7 [1933], 151–60).

9. E. Hoepffner, "Marie de France et l'*Eneas*," *Studi Medievali* 5 (1932), 272–308.

10. Hoepffner related the hunt of the white hind to the hunt of Ascanius in the *Eneas*. Except for the fact that each episode is a hunt, there is no similarity.

11. See R. Köhler, "Vergleichende Anmerkungen" in Warnke's edition, *Die Lais der Marie de France* (Halle, 1925), p. CVI.

12. Stefan Hofer, "Zur Beurteilung der Lais der Marie de France," *ZRP* 66 (1950), 409–21. In the passage in question (lines 3748 ff.), the king hears of his vassal's wife, goes on a hunting trip, and stays at the vassal's house. Because of his love, the king spends a sleepless night thinking of how he might win her. But here the resemblance ends. The vassal is killed in the end and the woman marries the king.

13. M. Delbouille, "Le Nom et le personnage d'Equitan," *Moyen Âge* 69 (1963), 315–23.

14. D. W. Robertson supports the thesis of condemnation, though from a somewhat different perspective ("Love Conventions in Marie's 'Equitan,' " *Romanic Review* 44 [1953], 241–45).

15. Based on the idea that Provençal influence is present, J. Wathelet-Willem proposed that the reading "Aquitan" should be accepted as Marie's indication of this influence ("Equitan dans l'oeuvre de Marie de France," *Moyen Âge* 69 [1963], 325–45).

16. W. Küchler, "Schön Annie, Fraisne und Griselda," *Neuere Sprachen* 35 (1927), 489–97.

17. For possible interest in the names and locale of *Le Fresne* to twelfth-century families of prominence, see E. A. Francis, "Marie de France et son temps," *Romania* 72 (1951), 78–99.

18. S. Battaglia, "Il mito del Licantropo nel 'Bisclavret' di Maria di Francia," *Filologia romanza* 3 (1956), 229–53.

19. For a recent argument that the Arthurian setting is authentic and appropriate, see C. Bullock-Davies, " 'Lanval' and 'Avalon,' " *Bulletin of the Board of Celtic Studies* 23 (1969), 128–42.

20. C. Segre, "*Lanval, Graelent, Guingamor*," *Studi in onore di A. Monteverdi*, vol. 2 (Modena, 1959), 756–70.

21. The Duke of Cornouaille had raised Guinevere and his son succeeded Arthur. Hoepffner contended that Cardeil, not found as an Arthurian residence in Geoffrey or Wace, was drawn from the Tristan

story known by Marie. In Beroul's *Tristan*, Cardeil is a residence of the king. Lanval may well have been Marie's contribution to the list of Arthurian heroes. He is not among the names of Arthurian knights in Chrétien's *Erec*, although he does figure in the version of *Erec* done by Hartman von Aue (E. Hoepffner, "La Géographie et l'histoire dans les *Lais* de Marie de France," *Romania* 56 [1903], 1–32).

22. T. P. Cross, "The Celtic Elements in the Lays of 'Lanval' and 'Graelent,'" *Modern Philology* 12 (1914–15), 585–644.

23. E. M. O'Sharkey suggests that Lanval's fairy mistress may be equated with Morgain. In *Erec* she is referred to as the mistress of Guingamor, Lord of the Isle of Avalon. Is this the earliest example of the rivalry between Morgain and Guinevere in the thirteenth-century Vulgate Cycle? (E. M. O'Sharkey, "The Identity of the Fairy Mistress in Marie's 'Lai de Lanval,'" *Bulletin Bibliographique de la Société Arthurienne* 21 [1969], 146–47).

24. Recently J. Wathelet-Willem contended that the queen in *Lanval* does not seek Lanval's love, but merely seeks to offer the lonely knight her friendship and consolation. Because of his preoccupation with his love, Lanval misunderstands the queen's offer, takes offense, and insults her. The queen's subsequent accusation of sodomy stems from her own wounded pride (J. Wathelet-Willem, "Le Personnage de Guenièvre chez Marie de France," *Marche Romane* 13 [1963], 119–31). While it is true that the queen makes no direct offer to sleep with Lanval, one must force the text to see the word *druerie* used only in terms of friendship here and to attribute her impatience a moment later to Lanval's silence. It seems certain that Lanval understood her correctly and that the episode fits the tradition. The charge of sodomy, used earlier against Guigemar for not having enough interest in women, would not be entirely foreign to the Hippolytus character associated with this role.

25. R. N. Illingworth, "La Chronologie des *Lais* de Marie de France," *Romania* 87 (1966), 433–75.

26. E. A. Francis, "The Trial in *Lanval*," *Studies in French Language and Mediaeval Literature* (Manchester, 1939), pp. 115–24.

27. E. Hoepffner, "La Géographie . . . ," *Romania* 56 (1930), 1–32.

28. J. Wathelet-Willem, "Un lai de Marie de France: 'Les deux amants,'" *Mélanges offerts à Rita Lejeune*, vol. 2 (Gembloux, 1968), 1143–57.

29. C. Segre, "Piramo e Tisbe nei *Lai* di Maria di Francia," *Studi Lugli-Valeri* (Venezia, 1961), pp. 845–53.

30. For Yonec Brugger proposed *Ediunet*, a cognate of the Welsh *eidduned*, meaning "desire." Holmes suggested a Breton formation from *dihud* through a nonattested *dihudennec*, meaning "one who comforts." Holmes' hypothesis is influenced by the statement in the

text that the son to be born will comfort the mother (U. T. Holmes, "Old French 'Yonec,'" *Modern Philology* 29 [1931–32], 225–29).

31. T. P. Cross, "The Origin of the Lay of 'Yonec,'" *Studies in Philology* 11 (1913), 26–60.

32. R. N. Illingworth, "Celtic Tradition and the 'Lai' of 'Yonec,'" *Etudes celtiques* 9 (1960–61), 501–20.

33. He maintains that her leap from the window without being hurt by the spikes or the fall and her visit to an Other-World-type realm (through the *hoge*), which later turns out to be just a neighboring region, point to a maladroit joining of two different tales. He suggests that the magic ring was invented specifically to reconcile some of the problems of the text.

34. M. B. Ogle, "Some Theories in Irish Literary Influence and the Lay of 'Yonec,'" *Romantic Review* 10 (1919), 123–48. Ogle also attacks the early dates given to the Irish texts found only in later manuscripts. While most scholars accept that the tales are certainly much older than the manuscripts in which they are found, it is nevertheless true that influences from and relationships with Celtic lore are often broadly asserted without adequate proof.

35. P. Toldo, "Yonec," *Romanische Forschungen* 16 (1904), 609–29. In the *Fan Prince*, a young woman summons her lover from a distant land by means of a magic fan (the girl's wish in *Yonec*). Subsequently, the lover is wounded by pieces of glass placed on the bed. The girl later goes in search of her lover, heals his wound, and is married to him. In many respects the resemblance between this tale and Marie's *lai* is as slight as the Irish analogues. The woman is not imprisoned by a jealous husband, the lover is not a bird-man nor even a supernatural being, there is no predicted son, and the lover does not die. Moreover, the accessibility of this tale to Marie is doubtful.

36. For the heritage of Marie's *lai*, see Köhler's comments on pages CLII–CLVI in Warnke's edition of the *Lais*.

37. C. Segre, "Piramo e Tisbe nei *Lai* di Maria di Francia," *Studi Lugli-Valeri* (Venezia, 1961), pp. 845–53.

38. R. Cargo, "Marie de France's 'Le Laüstic' and Ovid's *Metamorphoses*," *Comparative Literature* 18 (1966), 162–66.

39. For numerous citations of the theme, see R. Köhler's comments, pp. CLX–CLXII in Warnke's edition.

40. C. Bullock-Davies, "The Love-Messenger in 'Milun,'" *Bulletin Bibliographique de la Société Arthurienne* 21 (1969), 148.

41. L. Foulet, "Marie de France et la légende de Tristan," *ZRP* 32 (1908), 161–83; 257–89; E. Hoepffner, "Thomas d'Angleterre et Marie de France," *Studi Medievali* 7 (1934), 8–23.

42. The question of what Tristan carved on the *bastun* and whether an earlier letter had been sent has been debated heatedly for more

than half a century. Did he carve only his name, the entire message related in the text, or only the two lines which sum up poetically the essence of their love? For the many interesting suggestions that have been made, see the studies of M. Cagnon, M. Delbouille, L. Foulet, E. Francis, G. Frank, J. Frappier, A. Hatcher, E. Hoepffner, P. Le Gentil, G. Schoepperle, and L. Spitzer listed in the Bibliography.

43. S. Hofer, "Der Tristanroman und der 'Lai Chievrefueil' der Marie de France," ZRP 69 (1953), 129–31.

44. Maria di Francia, *Eliduc*, edited by E. Levi, Firenze, 1924. Levi discusses sources and analogues in his extensive introduction to the text.

45. A. Nutt, "The Lai of Eliduc and the *Märchen* of Little Snow-White," *Folk-Lore* 3 (1892), 26–48. In the tale of Gold-tree and Silver-tree, the second wife revives the first wife from a poison stab which had put her in a lifeless state. The second wife agrees to step aside, but the husband insists they all live together. The two women become the best of friends.

46. G. Paris, *La Poésie du moyen âge*, vol. 2 (Paris, 1895), 108–30. For an analogous tale from the Prussian area, see R. Basset, "La Légende du mari aux deux femmes," *Revue des Traditions Populaires* 16 (1901), 614–16.

47. Such a procedure certainly accords with the general mediaeval method of composition.

Chapter Seven

1. The present chapter appeared earlier in a more extensive format in an article entitled "A Reconsideration of the *Lais* of Marie de France," *Speculum* 46 (1971), 39–65.

2. F. Schürr, "Komposition und Symbolik in den *Lais* der Marie de France," ZRP 50 (1930), 556–82. Schürr believed that both Gautier d'Arras and Chrétien used the doctrine of "courtly love" as an answer to the blind fate in Marie.

3. J. Bédier, "Les Lais de Marie de France," *Revue des Deux Mondes* 107 (1891, 5), 835–63.

4. *Ibid.*, p. 853.

5. *Ibid.*

6. C. Conigliani, "L'Amore e l'avventura nei lais di Maria di Francia," *Archivum Romanicum* 2 (1918), 281–95.

7. *Ibid.*, p. 283.

8. Damon contends that Marie's primary consideration in writing the *Lais* was the analysis of character and the psychology of love. Damon divides the *Lais* into two groups, those which he calls realistic and those which include the supernatural. Using a Freudian approach in his interpretation, Damon sees dreams and subconscious states of

mind in the supernatural occurrences. For example, the prison in which Guigemar's lady is placed really represents her subconscious state of mind, etc. Damon judges the lovers innocent or not based on the question of carnal love and adultery (S. Foster Damon, "Marie de France: Psychologist of Courtly Love," *PMLA* 44 [1929], 968–96). For the most part Professor Hoepffner's literary analysis of each *lai* is conventional; lovers are judged innocent or guilty on the basis of adultery. Hoepffner does not see a consistent purpose throughout the *Lais*, but groups them according to similarities of outcome and circumstances. *Milun* and *Le Fresne* are stories of ideal love and perfect examples of a woman's faithful love. *Equitan* and *Chaitivel* condemn the Provençal love which had recently come north. In *Laüstic* and *Les Deus Amanz,* the *rossignol* and the potion are symbols of the love, etc. (E. Hoepffner, *Les Lais de Marie de France,* Paris, 1935).

9. E. Schiött, *L'Amour et les amoureux dans les lais de Marie de France,* Lund, 1889.

10. Professor Schober sees four principles involved in Marie's love: (1) Love is a natural thing, i.e., it is inherent in nature; (2) Beautiful people belong together; (3) Love commands man's entire being, leaving no "measure"; (4) The tie between two lovers is irrevocable, a love of fate such as one finds in the Tristan story (R. Schober, "Kompositionsfragen in den Lais der Marie de France," *Wissenschaftliche Zeitschrift der Humboldt-Universität zu Berlin* 4 [1954–55], 45–59 and "Weltstruktur und Werkstruktur in den Lais der Marie de France" in *Von der wirklichen Welt in der Dichtung* [Berlin, 1970], pp. 112–36; 383–97).

11. For use of the manuscript of this unedited French gloss (*ca.* 1390–1430) on the anonymous fourteenth-century poem *Les Echecs amoureux,* I am indebted to Mrs. Joan Jones. Mrs. Jones's thesis, a translation and photocopy of the entire text, is in the University of Nebraska library. This extraordinary commentary, over eleven hundred pages in Mrs. Jones's excellent translation, includes a complete mythography from a secular viewpoint and a close commentary on the poem, which imitates rather closely the *Romance of the Rose.* It is to be hoped that a significant portion of Mrs. Jones's text will find a publisher and that a critical edition of the text itself will one day be made.

12. *The Chess of Love,* translation by Joan M. Jones, Ph.D. thesis at the University of Nebraska, pp. 854–55.

13. The first inclination is Venus and the second is her son, Cupid.

14. Mrs. Jones, fol. 283 r.

15. *Ibid.,* fol. 296 v.

16. The author actually divides loyal love into two types, although

the nature of the love is the same. However, the lovers of the third type, recognizing the legal and religious obstacles, deliberately abstain from any relationship which would bring shame and grief. Because they exercise reason, these lovers are placed in highest position.

17. Marie de France, *Lais*, edited by A. Ewert (Oxford, 1965). All citations from the *Lais* are from this edition. Henceforth only the verse numbers will be given in the text.

18. The woman suffers from the same anguish as Guigemar, but her suffering is only indicated and not described (vv. 389–92; 427–30).

19. Although Marie here concentrates on the woman's misery, one must assume that Guigemar is suffering similar anguish, just as the woman's earlier anguish, though not described, paralleled Guigemar's.

20. It is true that the general exterior features, the physical condition of the lovers and the development of their thought patterns, follow a development often associated with "courtly love," but the nature of the love which binds the lovers is far less intellectually determined and controlled.

21. That all love, including the charity of the saint and the love of the mystic, entails suffering is manifest in the religious literature describing the sacrifices and martyrdom of the saints and the anguish of the mystic experience. However, the suffering is only a prelude to the magnificent triumph through love.

22. Unlike the love between Equitan and his lady, the love of Guigemar and his lady is not based on the sole interest of carnal gratification. Hence separation does not signal the end of love as it does in *Equitan*.

23. Just how little the nature of love in Marie's works has to do with the so-called courtly tradition or the Celtic love of fate is manifest in *Le Fresne*. Fresne's love, unquestionably richer in human terms than any yet treated by Marie, transcends the suffering brought by Cupid and the *démesure* which is the *mesure* of love.

24. Apropos of the specific effects of *démesure* described in *Les Deus Amanz*, there is a fascinating passage in Peter of Blois's well-known treatise, *De Amicitia*. Under Chapter LV, entitled "Quod actus noster non est ordinandus secundum affectum spiritualem," the author warns of the results when one's acts are governed by attraction of the senses rather than by *ratio*. The comments of this contemporary are so pertinent to the *lai* that they can virtually serve as a commentary: "But if this attraction alone orders our action, our action will be disordered, because the attraction leads us beyond our physical capacities (p. 532)." In the same text, the author elaborates on the concept that *démesure* can cause one to go beyond his physical capacities:

If, therefore, the exterior act is not tempered by a certain moderation, it will fail or succumb without completing the affair. Too much does the attraction neglect measure; it does not consider the strength of the body. Drawn by the attraction of sweet pleasure, it does not feel what is painful, arduous, harmful, or impossible, in fact, what kills mortal life. (p. 532)

Is this not precisely the case of the young man who becomes so inflamed that he is completely unaware of his failing strength and the impossibility of the task, even to the point that he destroys himself? Thus, he continues, those who follow immoderately and impetuously their desire ". . . in the day of battle, when victory depends on strength (*virtute*), he will succumb because of temerity" (p. 534). (Pierre de Blois, *Un Traité de l'amour du XII siècle*, edited and translated by M. M. Davy, Paris, 1932.)

25. Perhaps the significant element of the story concerning the lovers is expressed by Marie in the last two lines of the poem, when she discloses the *lai*'s purpose:

> Cil que ceste aventure oïrent
> Lunc tens aprés un lai en firent,
> De la pité, de la dolur
> Que cil suffrirent pur amur. (vv. 551–54)

26. It should be noted that, unlike the brutal husband in *Yonec*, the husband in *Milun* is not portrayed as odious and cruel.

27. Eliduc's deliberate abstention from carnal relations reminds one of a third kind of natural love described by the commentator of the *Echecs amoureux*. This love he considered ñobler precisely because reason controlled the "bestial" instinct: "No doubt it sometimes happens that two honorable people love each other loyally and perfectly, and this same end mentioned above, that Nature intends in it, could be attained without baseness. But because it is a thing in the law mentioned above, and from which great bad fame usually results when it becomes known, the people sometimes finally forsake this delight out of great honesty and wish to live until death chastely, and yet to love each other perfectly" (Mrs. Jones, p. 867).

28. Twice in the story Eliduc is deceitful: first, when he fails to tell Guilliadun that he has a wife, and second, when he tells his wife that his grief is due to the fact that he must again leave home. However, in each case the deceit is not perpetrated with an ulterior, selfish motive in mind. They are falsehoods which develop from the dilemma in which Eliduc finds himself. His failure to inform Guilliadun and his lie to his wife are both means of escape from the agony of disclosing the real situation. It is a deceit which derives from human weakness and not evil intent. That Marie considered it as such is shown in the wife's reply to Guilliadun's accusations against Eliduc.

29. For an interpretation of the "Prologue," see my forthcoming article in the 1974 issue of *Romania*.

30. In mediaeval discussions of love, great emphasis is placed on the necessary loyalty between lovers and the desire that the union be undertaken with the intent of progeny. That the lovers would not be dismayed by a fruitful result of their union is proof that they are not concentrating on delight alone. The anonymous commentator of the *Echecs amoureux* is quite explicit in insisting that even lovers out of marriage, if their love be true, would not be unhappy by the result of offspring from their union.

Chapter Eight

1. For a discussion of the legal circumstances in these texts, see E. A. Francis, "The Trial in 'Lanval,'" *Studies . . . Presented to M. K. Pope* (Manchester, 1939), pp. 115–24, and J. R. Rothschild, "A *Rapprochement* Between *Bisclavret* and *Lanval*," *Speculum* 68 (1973), 78–88.

2. Marie also transforms the folk material by allusions and descriptions drawn from her reading: the description of the magic boat and the Ovidian scene portrayed on the walls in *Guigemar*, the elaborate depiction of the tent in *Lanval*, the reminiscences of Ovid's *Piramus* in *Laüstic*, and the careful development of the love-passion in *Guigemar* and *Equitan*, etc. These artistic touches not only contribute to an understanding of the episodes as Marie uses them, but change the basic flavor of the tales. Once again the texts are drawn into a familiar frame of reference, a literary tradition well known to the contemporary reader.

3. E. Köhler, *Ideal und Wirklichkeit in der höfischen Epik*, Tübingen, 1966. Additional studies of particular interest include E. Auerbach, *Mimesis*, Berne, 1946; E. Eberwein, *Zur Deutung mittelalterlicher Existenz*, Bonn, 1933; R. W. Southern, *The Making of the Middle Ages*, New Haven, 1963; E. Vinaver, *The Rise of Romance*, New York, 1971; H. Baader, *Die Lais*, Frankfurt, 1966.

4. Cf. Professor Frappier's comments discussed in Chapter 5.

5. For a discussion of the importance of destiny in the *Lais*, see F. Schürr, "Komposition und Symbolik in den Lais der Marie de France," *ZRP* 50 (1930), 556–82.

6. If Iseult refers to a future pardon from King Mark, the dominant tone of the text is certainly grief, symbolized by the title, their grief at parting, and Marie's reference to their grievous death: "And I put in writing the story of Tristram and the queen and of their love which was so 'fine.' From it they had much grief, then died of it the same day" (vv. 7–10).

7. Leo Spitzer, "The Prologue to the *Lais* of Marie de France and Medieval Poetics," *Modern Philology* 41 (1943), 96–102.

8. Literally speaking, there is a theological problem in reconciling the supernatural elements in the *Lais* and the Christian world. This undoubtedly contributed to Denis Piramus's scornful comment that the *lais* were full of *mensonges*. It is difficult to assess the importance of Marie's acceptance of the supernatural in terms of her theology. It is true that she affirms the veracity of the stories on more than one occasion, but one must be skeptical of such comments, given the stylistic tradition of the period.

9. It should be noted that Marie does not claim such transformations for her own society. She states clearly that "formerly" it happened that men became werewolves.

10. The categories are those of John Frey, "Linguistic and Psychological Couplings in the Lays of Marie de France," *Studies in Philology* 61 (1964), 3–18. Mr. Frey argues that coupling is a basic structural principle in the *Lais*.

11. In *Bisclavret* the misery referred to is that of the wife.

12. Similar questions might be asked concerning *Milun*. Why did he not seek to marry the girl? Why did he go off tourneying when he did? Obviously Marie does not seem to consider such questions important. There is no indication that Milun is to blame for any of his actions.

13. Marie's use of irony is so extensive that only a brief discussion of the subject can be included within the scope of this book. For a more thorough and detailed presentation, the reader is referred to my forthcoming article, "Marie de France's Use of Irony as a Stylistic and Narrative Device," *Studies in Philology* 71 (1974), 265–90.

Selected Bibliography

PRIMARY SOURCES

1. Editions

Das Buch vom Espurgatoire S. Patrice der Marie de France und seine Quelle. Ed. Karl Warnke. Halle: Niemeyer, 1938. Good edition.

L'Espurgatoire Saint Patriz. Ed. T. A. Jenkins. Chicago: University of Chicago Press, 1903. Revised edition, excellent.

Die Fabeln der Marie de France. Ed. Karl Warnke. Halle: Niemeyer, 1898. Only complete edition.

Lais. Ed. A. Ewert. Oxford: Blackwell, 1965. Excellent.

Lais. Ed. Salvatore Battaglia. Napoli, 1948. Good edition.

Die Lais der Marie de France. Ed. Karl Warnke. Halle: Niemeyer, 1925. Still a good edition.

I Lais di Maria di Francia. Ed. Ferdinando Neri. Torino: Chiantore, 1946. Not readily available.

Les Lais. Ed. Ernest Hoepffner. Strasburg: Heitz, 1921. Changes orthography.

Les Lais de Marie de France. Trans. Harry F. Williams. Englewood Cliffs: Prentice, 1970. Useful.

Les Lais de Marie de France. Ed. Jeanne Lods. Paris: Champion, 1959. Use cautiously.

Les Lais de Marie de France. Ed. Jean Rychner. Paris: Champion, 1966. Excellent.

Le Lai de Lanval. Ed. Jean Rychner. Geneva-Paris: Droz, 1958. Excellent.

The Lays Gugemar, Lanval, and a Fragment of Yonec. Ed. Julian Harris. New York: Institute of French Studies, 1930. Useful edition of variant manuscript.

Eliduc. Ed. Ezio Levi. Florence: Sansoni, 1924. Useful introduction.

SECONDARY SOURCES

1.Manuscript Tradition and Chronology

BURGER, ANDRÉ. "La Tradition manuscrite du 'Lai de Lanval.'" *Linguistique et Philologie Romanes* 10 (1965), 655–66. Reviews earlier studies; suggests archetype.

FOULET, LUCIEN. "Marie de France et la légende du purgatoire de S. Patrice." *Romanische Forschungen* 22 (1908), 599–627. Essential study.

FRAPPIER, JEAN. "Une Édition nouvelle des *Lais* de Marie de France." *Romance Philology* 22 (1968–69), 600–613. Pertinent comments.

HOEPFFNER, ERNEST. "Pour la chronologie des lais de Marie de France." *Romania* 59 (1933), 351–70; 60 (1934), 36–66. Tenuous chronology.

———. "Le Roman d'Ille et Galeron et le lai d'Eliduc" in *Studies in French Language and Literature Presented to Professor Mildred K. Pope*. Manchester: Manchester University Press, 1939, pp. 125–44. Possible relationship.

———. "La Tradition manuscrite des lais de Marie de France." *Neophilologus* 12 (1927), 1–10; 85–96. Useful general discussion.

ILLINGWORTH, R. N. "La Chronologie des *Lais* de Marie de France." *Romania* 87 (1966), 433–75. Suggested internal chronology.

LEVI, EZIO. "Sulla cronologia delle opere di Maria di Francia." *Nuovi Studi Medievali* 1 (1923), 40–72. Somewhat dated.

LOCKE, F. W. "A New Date for the Composition of the *Tractatus de Purgatorio Sancti Patricii*." *Speculum* 40 (1965), 641–46. Essential study.

SEGRE, CESARE. "Per l'edizione critica dei *lai* di Maria di Francia." *Cultura Neolatina* 19 (1959), 215–37. Excellent discussion.

WILMOTTE, MAURICE. "Marie de France et Chrétien de Troyes." *Romania* 52 (1926), 353–55. Suggests Marie borrowed from Chrétien.

———. "Problèmes de chronologie littéraire." *Le Moyen Âge* 50 (1940), 99–114. Interesting argument against traditional *Eliduc* and *Ille et Galeron* relationship.

2. General Studies

AHLSTRÖM, A. *Studier i den fornfranska lais literaturen*. Akademisk Afhandlung . . . Uppsala, 1892. Old, but still of some value.

———. *Marie de France et les lais narratifs*. Göteborg, 1925. General discussion.

BAADER, HORST. *Die Lais. Zur Geschichte einer Gattung der altfranzösischen Kurzerzählungen*. Frankfort/Main: Klostermann, 1966. Essential study.

BAUM, RICHARD. *Recherches sur les oeuvres attribuées à Marie de France*. Heidelberg: Winter, 1968. Valuable for questions raised, but conclusions are dubious.

BRUCE, J. D. *Evolution of Arthurian Romance*. Baltimore: Johns Hopkins University Press, 1923. General remarks.

DONOVAN, MORTIMER J. *The Breton Lay: A Guide to Varieties*. Notre

Dame: University of Notre Dame Press, 1968. Readable general discussion.

ECKLEBEN, SELMAR. *Die älteste Schilderung vom Fegefeur des heil. Patricius.* Halle, 1885. Dated.

HOEPFFNER, ERNEST. *Aux Origines de la nouvelle française.* Oxford: Clarendon Press, 1939. General remarks.

————. *Les Lais de Marie de France.* Paris: Boivin, 1935. Good for background.

JAUSS, HANS R. *Untersuchungen zur mittelalterlichen Tierdichtung.* Tübingen: Niemeyer, 1959. Important general study.

KÖHLER, ERICH. *Ideal und Wirklichkeit in der höfischen Epik.* Tübingen: Niemeyer, 1966. Scholarly. Interesting perspective.

————. *Trobadorlyrik und höfischer Roman: Aufsätze zur französischen und provenzalischen Literatur des Mittelalters.* Berlin: Rütten, 1962.

LAZAR, MOSHÉ. *Amour courtois et fin'amors dans la littérature du XIIe siècle.* Paris: Klincksieck, 1964.

LESLIE, SHANE. *Saint Patrick's Purgatory.* London: Burns Oates, 1932. Useful anthology.

LEVI, EZIO. "Maria di Francia e il romanzo di Eneas," *Atti del reale instituto veneto di scienze, lettere ed arti* 81 (1921–22). Conclusions not accepted.

MALL, E. *De aetate rebusque Mariae Francicae nova quaestio instituitur.* Halle, 1867. Dated.

NAGEL, E. "Marie de France als dichterische Persönlichkeit." *Romanische Forschungen* 44 (1930), 1–102. Dated.

PELAN, M. *L'Influence du Brut de Wace sur les romanciers français de son temps.* Paris: Droz, 1931. Slightly overstated.

SCHIÖTT, EMIL. *L'Amour et les amoureux dans les lais de Marie de France.* Lund, 1889. Dated.

WARNKE, KARL. *Marie de France und die anonymen Lais.* Coburg: Ostern, 1892. Superficial.

————. "Über die Zeit der Marie de France." *Zeitschrift für Romanische Philologie* 4 (1880), 223–48. Dated.

WINKLER, EMIL. *Marie de France.* Vienna: Hölder, 1918. Conclusions not accepted.

3. Identity of Marie de France

FLUM, P. N. "Additional Thoughts on Marie de France." *Romance Notes* 3 (1961), 53–56. Related to Holmes' identity of Marie.

————. "Marie de France and the Talbot Family Connections." *Romance Notes* 7 (1965), 83–86. English relationship.

FOX, JOHN C. "Marie de France." *English Historical Review* 25 (1910), 303–6. Interesting suggested identity.

————. "Mary, Abbess of Shaftesbury." *English Historical Review* 26 (1911), 317–26.

HOLMES, URBAN T. "Further on Marie de France." *Symposium* 3 (1949), 335–39.

————. "New Thoughts on Marie de France." *Studies in Philology* 29 (1932), 1–10. Possible identity.

LEVI, EZIO. "Il Re Giovane e Maria di Francia." *Archivum Romanicum* 5 (1921), 448–71. Concerning the Young King Henry.

————. "Maria di Francia e le abbazie d'Inghilterra." *Archivum Romanicum* 5 (1921), 472–93.

PAINTER, SIDNEY. "To Whom Were Dedicated the Fables of Marie de France." *Modern Language Notes* 48 (1933), 367–69. Important note.

RINGGER, KURT. "Zum 'Nobles Reis' bei Marie de France. Eine Richtigstellung." *Zeitschrift für Romanische Philologie* 83 (1967), 495–97. Significant observation.

WHICHARD, ROGERS D. "A Note on the Identity of Marie de France" in *Romance Studies in Honor of W. M. Dey.* Chapel Hill: University of North Carolina Press, 1950, pp. 177–81. Pertinent remarks on Beaumont family.

4. Sources

BASSET, R. "La Légende du mari aux deux femmes." *Revue des Traditions Populaires* 16 (1901), 614–16. Prussian parallel.

BATTAGLIA, SALVATORE. "Il mito del Licantropo nel 'Bisclavret' di Maria di Francia." *Filologia Romanza* 3 (1956), 229–53. Interesting study.

BLONDHEIM, D. S. "A Note on the Sources of Marie de France." *Modern Language Notes* 23 (1908), 201–2. An addition to Warnke.

BROMWICH, RACHEL. "Celtic Dynastic Themes and the Breton Lays." *Études Celtiques* 9 (1961), 439–74. Interesting, but tenuous.

————. "The Character of the Early Welsh Tradition" in *Studies in Early British History.* Ed. N. K. Chadwick. Cambridge: Cambridge University Press, 1954, pp. 83–136. Interesting study.

————. "A Note on the Breton Lays." *Medium Aevum* 26 (1957), 36–38. Important note.

BULLOCK-DAVIES, CONSTANCE. "'Lanval' and 'Avalon.'" *Bulletin of the Board of Celtic Studies* 23 (1969), 128–42. Attractive but doubtful conclusions.

————. "The Love-Messenger in 'Milun.'" *Bulletin Bibliographique de la Société Internationale Arthurienne* 21 (1969), 148 (résumé).

CARGO, ROBERT T. "Marie de France's 'Le Laüstic' and Ovid's *Meta-*

morphoses." *Comparative Literature* 18 (1966), 162–66. Plausible suggestion.

COHEN, GUSTAVE. "Marie de France. Le Lai des Deux Amants." *Mercure de France* 265 (1936), 61–68. Modern vestiges of the tradition.

CROSS, TOM P. "The Celtic Elements in the Lays of 'Lanval' and 'Graelent.'" *Modern Philology* 12 (1914–15), 585–644. Still useful.

———. "The Celtic Origin of the Lay of Yonec." *Studies in Philology* 11 (1913), 26–60. Still useful.

FERGUSON, MARY H. "Folklore in the *Lais* of Marie de France." *Romanic Review* 57 (1966), 3–24. Catalogue.

FOULET, LUCIEN. "English Words in the *Lais* of Marie de France." *Modern Language Notes* 20 (1905), 108–10. Important note.

HOEPFFNER, ERNEST. "La Géographie et l'histoire dans les lais de Marie de France." *Romania* 56 (1930), 1–32. Important study.

———. "Graelent ou Lanval?" in *Recueil de travaux offert à M. Clovis Brunel*. Paris: Société de l'École des Chartes, 1955, pp. 1–8. Compare with Segre below.

———. "Marie de France et l'*Eneas*." *Studi Medievali* 5 (1932), 272–308. Overstated relationship.

———. "Thomas d'Angleterre et Marie de France." *Studi Medievali* 7 (1934), 8–23. Slightly forced parallels.

HOFER, STEFAN. "Zur Beurteilung der Lais der Marie de France." *Zeitschrift für Romanische Philologie* 66 (1950), 409–21. Relationships to Tristan.

HOLMES, URBAN T. "Old French Yonec." *Modern Philology* 29 (1931–32), 225–29. Possible etymology.

———. "A Welsh Motif in Marie's *Guigemar*." *Studies in Philology* 39 (1942), 11–14. Interesting contemporary tale.

ILLINGWORTH, R. N. "Celtic Tradition and the *Lai of Guigemar*." *Medium Aevum* 31 (1962), 176–87. Tempting hypothesis.

———. "Celtic Tradition and the *Lai of Yonec*." *Études Celtiques* 9 (1960–61), 501–20. Useful discussion.

JOHNSTON, OLIVER M. "Sources of the Lay of the 'Two Lovers.'" *Modern Language Notes* 21 (1906), 34–39. Possible folk sources.

———. "Sources of the 'Lay of Yonec.'" *Publications of the Modern Language Association* 20 (1905), 322–38. Still useful.

KOLLS, A. *Zur Lanvalsage, eine Quellenuntersuchung*. Kiel, 1886. Dated.

KÜCHLER, WALTER. "Schön Annie, Fraisne und Griselda." *Neuere Sprachen* 35 (1927), 489–97. Parallel Scotch ballad.

MALL, E. "Zur Geschichte der Legende vom Purgatorium des heil.

Patricius." *Romanische Forschungen* 6 (1891), 139–97. Still useful.

NERI, FERDINANDO. "Appunti su *Guigemar*." *Annali dell'Istituto Superiore di Magistero di Torino* 7 (1933), 151–60. Interesting remarks.

NUTT, ALFRED. "The Lay of 'Eliduc' and the *Märchen* of Little Snow-White." *Folk-Lore* 3 (1892), 26–48. Folk analogues.

OGLE, M. B. "Some Theories in Irish Literary Influence and the Lay of 'Yonec.'" *Romanic Review* 10 (1919), 123–48. Important article.

O'SHARKEY, EITHNE M. "The Identity of the Fairy Mistress in Marie's 'Lai de Lanval.'" *Bulletin Bibliographique de la Société Internationale Arthurienne* 21 (1969), 146–47 (résumé).

PARIS, GASTON. "Le Mari aux deux femmes" in *La Poésie du Moyen Âge*. 2e série. Paris: Hachette, 1895, pp. 108–30. Still useful.

SALVERDA DE GRAVE, J. "Marie de France et *Eneas*." *Neophilologus* 10 (1925), 56–58. Important note.

SCHOEPPERLE, GERTRUDE. "'Chievrefoil.'" *Romania* 38 (1909), 196–218. Important.

SCHOFIELD, W. H. "The Lay of Guingamor." *Harvard Studies* 5 (1895), 221–43. Relationship with *Lanval* and *Graelent*.

———. "The Lays of Graelent and Lanval and the Story of Wayland." *Publications of the Modern Language Association* 15 (1900), 121–80. Still useful.

SCHÜRR, FRIEDRICH. "Das Aufkommen der 'matière de Bretagne.'" *Germanisch-Monatsschrift* 9 (1921), 96–108. Interesting general comments.

SEGRE, CESARE. "*Lanval, Graelent, Guingamor*" in *Studi in Onore di A. Monteverdi*. Vol. 2. Modena: Società Tipografica Editrice Modenese, 1959, 756–70. Excellent study.

———. "Piramo e Tisbe nei *Lai* di Maria di Francia" in *Studi in Onore di Vittorio Lugli e Diego Valeri*. Venezia: Pozza, 1961, pp. 845–53. Important study.

TOLDO, PIETRO. "Yonec." *Romanische Forschungen* 16 (1904), 609–29. Readable.

5. The Narrative *Lai*

BAUM, RICHARD. "Les Troubadours et les lais." *Zeitschrift für Romanische Philologie* 85 (1969), 1–44. Important study.

BRERETON, GEORGINE E. "A 13th Century List of French Lays and Other Narrative Poems." *Modern Language Review* 45 (1950), 40–45. Significant.

BRUGGER, ERNST. "Eigennamen in den *Lais* der Marie de France."

Zeitschrift für Französische Sprache und Literatur 49 (1927), 201–52; 381–484. Significant.

――――. C. R. of Warnke's edition of the *Lais* in *Zeitschrift für Französische Sprache und Literatur* 49 (1927), 116–55. Some worthwhile remarks.

――――. "Über die Bedeutung von Bretagne, breton in mittelalterlichen Texten." *Zeitschrift für Französische Sprache und Literatur* 20 (1898), 79–162. Important study.

FOULET, LUCIEN. "Marie de France et la légende de Tristan." *Zeitschrift für Romanische Philologie* 32 (1908), 161–83; 257–89. Essential study.

――――. "Marie de France et les lais bretons." *Zeitschrift für Romanische Philologie* 29 (1905), 19–56; 293–322. Essential study.

――――. "Thomas and Marie in their Relation to the *conteurs*." *Modern Language Notes* 23 (1908), 205–8. Interesting remarks.

FOULON, CHARLES. "Marie de France et la Bretagne." *Annales de Bretagne* 60 (1953), 243–58. Some excellent remarks.

GALLAIS, PIERRE. "Bleheri, la cour de Poitiers et la diffusion des récits arthuriens sur le continent." *Actes du VIIᵉ Congrès National de Littérature Comparée* (Paris, 1967), pp. 47–79. Interesting study.

HANOSET, M. "Les Origines de la Matière de Bretagne, 2: La légende arthurienne. Chrétien de Troyes et Marie." *Marche Romane* 10 (1960), 67–77. General remarks.

HOEPFFNER, ERNEST. "Les deux lais du Chèvrefeuille." *Mélanges Laumonier*. Paris: Droz, 1935, pp. 41–49. Significant comparison.

――――. "Marie de France et les lais anonymes." *Studi Medievali* 4 (1931), 1–31. Important study.

JUBAINVILLE, H. D'ARBOIS DE. "Lai." *Romania* 8 (1879), 422–25. Still of interest.

LEVI, EZIO. "I lais brettoni e la leggenda di Tristano." *Studi Romanzi* 14 (1917), 113–246. Readable and still important.

LOT, FERDINAND. "La Patrie des lais bretons." *Romania* 28 (1899), 1–48. Significant.

――――. "Le Sens du mot 'breton' au XIIᵉ siècle." *Romania* 24 (1895), 497–528. Important study.

MAILLARD, JEAN. *Évolution et esthétique du lai lyrique*. Fontainebleau, 1961. Good general discussion.

――――. "Le 'Lai' et la 'note' du Chievrefoil." *Musica Disciplina* 13 (1959), 3–13.

――――. "Le Lai lyrique et les légendes arthuriennes." *Bulletin Bibliographique de la Société Internationale Arthurienne* 9 (1957), 124–27. Pertinent comments on lyric *lai*.

————. "Problèmes musicaux et littéraires du 'Lai.'" *Quadrivium* 2 (1958), 32–44.

NERI, FERDINANDO. "La voce 'lai' nei testi italiani." *Atti della R. Accademia delle Scienze di Torino* 72 (1936–37), 105–19. Interesting article.

REANEY, GILBERT. "Concerning the Origins of the Medieval Lai." *Music and Letters* 39 (1958), 343–46. General remarks.

RIQUER, MARTÍN DE. "La 'aventure,' el 'lai' y el 'conte' de Maria de Francia." *Filologia Romanza* 2 (1955), 1–19. Excellent article.

TIEMANN, HERMANN. "Die Datierungen der altfranzösischen Literatur." *Romanistisches Jahrbuch* 8 (1957), 110–31. Interesting discussion.

————. *Die Entstehung der mittelalterlichen Novelle in Frankreich.* Hamburg: Europa-Kolleg, 1961. Interesting remarks.

WOLF, FERDINAND. *Über die Lais, Sequenzen und Leiche.* Heidelberg: Winter, 1841. Old, but still useful.

6. Interpretive Essays

ADLER, ALFRED. "Höfische Dialektik im *Lai du Freisne.*" *Germanisch-Romanische Monatsschrift,* Neue Folge 11 (1961), 44–51. Forced perspective.

————. "Structural Uses of the Fairy Mistress Theme in Certain Lais of Marie de France." *Bulletin Bibliographique de la Société Internationale Arthurienne* 9 (1957), 127–28.

BATTAGLIA, SALVATORE. "Maria di Francia" in *La Coscienza letteraria del medioevo.* Napoli: Liguori, 1965, pp. 309–59. Readable discussion.

BAYRAV, SÜHEYLÂ. "Symbole-emblème chez Béroul et Marie" in *Symbolisme médiéval.* Paris: Presses universitaires de France, 1957, pp. 43–74.

BÉDIER, JOSEPH. "Les Lais de Marie de France." *Revue des Deux Mondes* 107 (1891), 835–63. Still interesting.

CAGNON, MAURICE. "'Chievrefueil' and the Ogamic Tradition." *Romania* 91 (1970), 238–55. Possible solution to the problem.

CONIGLIANI, C. "L'Amore e l'avventura nei *lais* di Maria di Francia." *Archivum Romanicum* 2 (1918), 281–95. Dated.

DAMON, S. FOSTER. "Marie de France, Psychologist of Courtly Love." *Publications of the Modern Language Association* 44 (1929), 968–96. Dated.

DELBOUILLE, MAURICE. "Ceo fu la summe de l'escrit. . . ." in *Mélanges J. Frappier.* Geneva: Droz, 1970, pp. 207–16. Event related to well-known Tristan episodes.

————. "Le Nom et le personnage d'Equitan." *Le Moyen Âge* 69 (1963), 315–23. Worthwhile comments.

Selected Bibliography

DONOVAN, MORTIMER J. "Priscian and the Obscurity of the Ancients." *Speculum* 36 (1961), 75–80. Interesting.

EBERWEIN, ELENA. "Die Aventure in den altfranzösischen Lais" in *Zur Deutung mittelalterlicher Existenz.* Bonn: Köln, 1933. Significant.

FRANCIS, ELIZABETH A. "A Comment on 'Chevrefoil'" in *Medieval Miscellany Presented tc Eugene Vinaver.* Manchester: Manchester University Press, 1965, pp. 136–45. Argues for plausibility of preceding letter.

———. "Marie de France et son temps." *Romania* 72 (1951), 78–99. Important.

———. "The Trial in 'Lanval'" in *Studies . . . Presented to M. K. Pope.* Manchester: Manchester University Press, 1939, pp. 115–24. Excellent article.

FRANK, GRACE. "Marie de France and the Tristram Legend." *Publications of the Modern Language Association* 63 (1948), 405–11. Message is on stick, perhaps in cryptic form.

FRAPPIER, JEAN. "Contribution au débat sur le 'Lai du Chevrefeuille'" in *Mélanges Istvan Frank.* Universität des Saarlandes, 1957, pp. 215–24.

———. "Remarques sur la structure du lai, essai de définition et de classement" in *La Littérature narrative d'imagination.* Colloque de Strasbourg, 1959. Paris, 1961, pp. 23–39. Interesting comments.

FREY, J. A. "Linguistic and Psychological Couplings in the Lays of Marie de France." *Studies in Philology* 61 (1964), 3–18. Somewhat superficial.

FUCHS, W. *Der Tristanroman und die höfische Liebe.* Rohrschach: Lehner, 1967.

HATCHER, ANNA G. "'Le Lai du Chievrefueil.'" *Romania* 71 (1950), 330–44. Romantic extension of Spitzer.

HOEPFFNER, ERNEST. "Le Lai d' 'Equitan' de Marie de France" in *Miscellany . . . Presented to Leon E. Kastner.* Cambridge: Cambridge University Press, 1932, pp. 294–302. Conclusions forced.

HOFER, STEFAN. "Der Tristanroman und der 'Lai Chievrefueil' der Marie de France." *Zeitschrift für Romanische Philologie* 69 (1953), 129–31. Interesting comments on the origins of Marie's text.

LE GENTIL, PIERRE. "A Propos du lai du Chèvrefeuille et de l'interprétation des textes médiévaux" in *Mélanges H. Chamard.* Paris: Nizet, 1951, pp. 17–27. The stick had Tristan's name and the two famous lines.

MARTINEAU-GÉNIEYS, CHRISTINE. "Du 'Chievrefoil,' encore et toujours." *Le Moyen Âge* 78 (1972), 91–114.

MÉNARD, PHILIPPE. "La Déclaration amoureuse dans la littérature arthurienne au XIIe siècle." *Cahiers de Civilisation Médiévale* 13 (1970), 33–42. General remarks of interest.

MICKEL, EMANUEL J. "A Reconsideration of the *Lais* of Marie de France." *Speculum* 46 (1971), 39–65.

———. "Marie de France's Use of Irony as a Stylistic and Narrative Device." *Studies in Philology* 71 (1974), 265–90.

———. "The Unity and significance of Marie's 'prologue.'" *Romania* 95 (1974).

NOLTING-HAUFF, ILSE. "Symbol und Selbstdeutung: Formen der erzählerischen Pointierung bei Marie de France." *Archiv* 194 (1962), 26–33. Interesting.

RIBARD, JACQUES. "Le Lai du 'Laostic.' Structure et signification." *Le Moyen Âge* 76 (1970), 263–74.

ROBERTSON, D. W. "Marie de France, *Lais*, Prologue, 13–15." *Modern Language Notes* 64 (1949), 336–38. Possible interpretation.

———. "Love Conventions in Marie's *Equitan*." *Romanic Review* 44 (1953), 241–45. Interesting observations.

ROBERTSON, HOWARD S. "Love and the Other World in Marie de France's 'Eliduc'" in *Essays in Honor of Louis Francis Solano.* Chapel Hill: University of North Carolina Press, 1969, pp. 167–76.

ROHLFS, G. *Vom Vulgarlätein zum Altfranzösischen.* Tübingen: Niemeyer, 1960.

ROTHSCHILD, JUDITH R. "A *Rapprochement* Between *Bisclavret* and *Lanval*." *Speculum* 68 (1973), 78–88. Further on Marie's knowledge of legal matters.

SCHOBER, RITA. "Kompositionsfragen in den Lais der Marie de France." *Wissenschaftliche Zeitschrift der Humboldt-Universität zu Berlin* 4 (1954–55), 45–59. Useful discussion.

———. "Weltstruktur and Werkstruktur in den Lais der Marie de France" in *Von der wirklichen Welt in der Dichtung.* Berlin: Aufbau-Verlag, 1970, pp. 112–36; 383–97. General remarks of interest.

SCHÜRR, FRIEDRICH. "Komposition und Symbolik in den Lais der Marie de France." *Zeitschrift für Romanische Philologie* 50 (1930), 556–82. Interesting.

SPITZER, LEO. "La Lettre sur la baguette de coudrier dans le 'Lai du Chievrefeuil.'" *Romania* 69 (1946–47), 80–90. Important article.

———. "Marie de France—Dichterin von Problem-Märchen." *Zeitschrift für Romanische Philologie* 50 (1930), 29–67. Significant.

———. "The Prologue to the *Lais* of Marie de France and Medieval Poetics." *Modern Philology* 41 (1943), 96–102. Important remarks.

Selected Bibliography

VALERO, ANNA M. "El lai del 'Chievrefueil' de Maria de Francia." *Boletin de la Real Acad. de Buenas Letras de Barcelona* 24 (1951–52), 173–83. Dubious reading of text.

WATHELET-WILLEM, JEANNE. "La Conception de l'amour chez Marie de France." *Bulletin Bibliographique de la Société Internationale Arthurienne* 21 (1969), 144–45 (résumé).

———. "Equitan dans l'oeuvre de Marie de France." *Le Moyen Âge* 69 (1963), 325–45. Belongs to collection, but early work.

———. "Un lai de Marie de France: 'Les Deux amants'" in *Mélanges offerts à Rita Lejeune*. Vol. 2. Gembloux: J. Duculot, 1968, 1143–57. Interesting discussion.

———. "Le Mystère chez Marie de France." *Revue Belge de Philologie et d'Histoire* 39 (1961), 661–86. Remarks of interest.

———. "Le Personnage de Guenièvre chez Marie de France." *Marche Romane* 13 (1963), 119–31. Strained reading of text.

WIND, BARTINA H. "L'Idéologie courtoise dans les lais de Marie de France" in *Mélanges Delbouille*. Vol. 2. Gembloux: J. Duculot, 1964, 741–48. Courtly influences are superficial.

WOODS, WILLIAM S. "Femininity in the *Lais* of Marie de France." *Studies in Philology* 47 (1950), 1–19. Dubious observations.

———. "Marie de France's 'Laüstic.'" *Romance Notes* 12 (1970–71), 203–7. Interesting note on structure.

Index

Abbey of Reading, 16, 21
Adeliza of Louvain, 30, 150n7
Aeneid, 26
Ahlström, Axel, 19, 148n30
Ailred de Rievaulx, 30
Alice de Condet, 31
Andreas Capellanus, 93, 99, 100, 116, 151n8
Annales Cambriae, 55
Aphthonius, 34, 37
Archbishopric of Dol, 19
Archbishop Theobald, 26
Armorica, 55-56
Ars Amatoria, 26
Auberée, 159n45
Aucassin et Nicolette, 155n12
Avalon, 62, 110, 126, 156n22, 164n23

Baader, H., 67-71, 125, 159n45, 161n62, 161n63
Battaglia, S., 80
Baum, R., 14, 51-52, 143n1, 143n4, 145n9, 145n16, 146n16, 146n20, 154n6, 154n11, 157n27
Beatrice de Bourgogne, 19
Beauvais, 26
Bec, 26
Becket, Thomas, 19, 26, 29
Bédier, Joseph, 64, 99-100, 104, 160n51, 161n62
Benoit, 30
Bernard de Ventadour, 150n8
Beroul, 164n21
Bestiaire, 30

Bisclavret, 56-61, 66, 70, 79-81, 97, 100, 109-10, 118, 121, 123-24, 126, 128-32, 134, 136, 155n17, 171n9, 171n11
Bishop Florentianus, 46
Bledhericus, 156n24
BM Harley manuscript 978, 14, 16, 34, 143n1, 146n16
BN manuscript 1446, 14, 145n9
Boethius, 104
Book of Leinster, 83
Bromwich, R., 74, 154n9
Brugger, E., 55, 155n19, 164n30
Brut, 17-18, 22, 30, 51, 59, 73, 75, 83, 147n21, 151n8
Bueve de Hamtone, 97
Bullock-Davies, C., 92, 156n22
Byzantine Empire, 24-25, 149n2

Cambridge Song Book, 66
Canterbury, 26
Canterbury Tales, 14
Cargo, R., 91
Chaitivel, 56, 58-59, 62, 66, 68, 70, 93, 97, 99, 116-17, 121, 124, 130, 131, 133-34, 146n18, 155n17, 167n8
Chanson de Roland, 84
Chartres, 26
Chevalier au Cygne, 74, 98, 162n2
Chevrefoil, 22, 55-56, 58-59, 62, 93-95, 97, 117-18, 121-22, 127-28, 130-33, 136, 170n6
Chrétien de Troyes, 13, 18, 22-23, 48, 50, 63, 74, 75, 100, 146n21,

Chrétien de Troyes (*Cont.*)
151n8, 164n21, 166n2
Cicero, 27
Clemence of Barking, 31
Cliges, 146n21
Compendium in Job, 31
Conigliani, C., 100
Conqueste de Constantinople, 29
Constantinople, 25
Conte del Graal, 74
Cort mantel, 159n45
Couronnement, de Renard, 14-15
Cross, T. P., 83
Crusades, 24-25, 98, 149n2

Dair le Roux, 84
Damon, S. F., 166n8
D'Arbois de Jubainville, H., 51-52
De Amicitia, 168n24
De Amore, 99-100, 104, 109, 116, 151n8
De Consolatione Philosophiae, 104
Delbouille, M., 77
De Naturis rerum, 97
De Rebus gestis regum Anglorum, 29
Dolopathos, 162n2
Donovan, M., 161n57
Dutch *Lancelot*, 162n2

Eberwein, E., 65, 125
Echecs amoureux, Les, 101-103, 113, 167n11, 169n27, 170n30
Eilhart von Oberg, 7, 94
Eleanor of Aquitaine, 20, 26, 30-31, 150n8, 152n13
Eliduc, 18-19, 22, 56, 58-59, 70, 95-97, 100, 118-21, 124, 126, 127-31, 135-36, 147n25, 148n27, 155n17, 157n25, 169n28
Equitan, 23, 56, 58-59, 62, 66, 68, 70, 75-77, 97, 99-100, 103-109, 111, 121, 124, 126, 130-31, 134-38, 167n8, 168n22, 170n2
Eracle, 147n25
Erec et Enide, 18, 48, 63, 74-75, 100, 164n21, 164n23

Estoire des Engleis, 22, 30, 75-76, 84
Evangile aux femmes, 14
Ewert, A., 103

Fair Annie, 79
Fan Prince, 89, 165n35
Fantosme, Jordan, 30
Faral, E., 63
Fauchet, Claude, 13
Fitz-Baderon, Gilbert, 32
Flamenca, 86
Fotha Catha Cnucha, 89
Foulet, L., 18-19, 47-49, 57-59, 67, 94-95, 153n3, 157n25, 157n26, 158n33
Fourth Eclogue, 26
Fox, J., 20-21
Francis, E. A., 39, 84, 98, 156n23
Frappier, J., 64-65, 71
Frederick Barbarossa, 19
Frey, J., 171n10

Gaimar, Geoffrey, 22, 30, 75-76, 84
Gallais, P., 156n24
Ganelon, 84
Gautier d'Arras, 18-19, 147n25, 166n2
Geoffrey of Monmouth, 22, 29-30, 50, 55-56, 59, 68, 73, 83, 97-98, 157n24, 163n21
Gervais de La Rue, 14
Gervase of Louth, 42
Gilbert of Louth (Basingwerk), 42-43, 46-47
Giraldus Cambrensis, 29-30, 97, 152n1
Godefroy de Bouillon, 25
Godwine le Danois, 84
Gormont et Isembart, 92
Gottfried von Strasbourg, 77
Graelemuer, 75
Graelent, 73, 83, 155n13, 157n26
Gregory of Tours, 85
Griselda, 79
Guernes de Pont-Sainte-Maxence, 31
Gui de Dampierre, 14, 145n9

Index

Guigemar, 22-23, 56-59, 62, 65, 72-75, 97, 100, 103-10, 121, 123-31, 133-36, 138-39, 145n16, 155n17, 157n28, 158n34, 162n7, 163n6, 170n2
Guillaume d'Angleterre, 147n21
Guillaume de Dampierre, 14-15
Guillaume de Dole, 19
Guillaume de Gloucester, 148n30
Guinevere, 73, 163n21
Guingamor, 74-75, 157n26
Guiot de Provins, 20
Guiron le Courtois, 86
Gröber, G., 145n13

Henry I of England, 25, 30, 148n30, 149n38, 150n7
Henry II of England, 19-21, 25, 28-31, 148n30, 148n31, 149n38, 156n23
Henry III of England, 21
Henry of Huntingdon, 30
Henry of Saltrey, 17, 42-43, 46, 145n11
Henry of Sartis, Abbot, 17, 42
Henry the Young King, 19
Hertz, Wilhelm, 20
Hippolytus, 74, 103
Histoire de Gilion de Trasegnies, 97
Historia Francorum, 85
Historia naturalis, 80-81
Historia regum Britanniae, 22, 29-30, 59, 73, 83, 97, 157n24
Hoepffner, Ernest, 18, 22, 59, 75, 77, 84-85, 94-95, 98, 155n15, 163n10, 163n21
Hofer, S., 76, 95
Holmes, U. T., 146n18, 148n27, 149n38, 164n30
Horace, 27
Horn, 97
Hue de Roteland, 32
Hugh de Saint-Victor, 97
Huth Merlin, 162n2

Ille et Galeron, 18, 63, 97, 147n25
Illingworth, R. N., 75, 84, 89, 162n7

Innocent III, 19
Ipomedon, 32

Jaufré, 86
Jenkins, T. A., 43
Jocelin of Furness, 152n1
John of Salisbury, 30

King Alfred, 16, 21, 34, 145n10
King Arthur, 50, 55-56, 62, 81
King Hoilas, 72
King Stephen, 25, 149n38
Köhler, E., 124

Lai d'Aristote, 64, 68-70, 159n45, 161n57
Lai de Desiré, 157n26
Lai de Doon, 157n26
Lai de l'Epervier, 64, 68-69, 161n57
Lai de l'Espine, 157n26
Lai de l'Oiselet, 161n57
Lai de l'Ombre, 68, 161n57
Lai de Melion, 63, 68, 157n26
Lai de Nabaret, 64, 68, 161n57
Lai de Tyolet, 74, 157n26
Lai d'Haveloc, 161n57
Lai d'Ignaure, 64, 68-69
Lai des Deus Amanz, 54
Lai du Chevrefueil, 54
Lai du Conseil, 68, 161n57
Lai du Cor, 63, 69, 161n57
Lai du Lecheor, 64, 69-70
Lai du Palefroi, 64, 68
Lai du Trot, 161n57
Lancelot, 48, 151n8
Lanval, 19, 22, 55-56, 58-59, 62, 65, 68, 81-84, 97, 110, 121, 123, 126-128, 130, 131, 133, 135, 140, 156n22, 156n23, 157n26, 158n34, 159n46, 164n23, 164n24, 170n2
Laüstic, 22, 56, 58-60, 62, 90-91, 97, 113-14, 121-22, 127-28, 130-35, 149n39, 155n17, 158n32, 167n8, 170n2
Layamon, 151n8
Le Fresne, 19, 56, 58-62, 77-79, 97, 100, 103-10, 120-21, 124, 127-28, 130-31, 135-39, 148n27, 155n17,

156n23, 159n46, 163n17, 167n8, 168n23
Legrand d'Aussy, J. B., 14
Lejeune, R., 150n8
Les Deus Amanz, 17, 22, 56, 58-59, 62, 66, 70. 84-86, 97. 110-13. 115, 121-22, 127-32, 134-36, 146n18, 149n39, 156n23, 167n8, 168n24
Levi, Ezio, 19, 21, 75, 97, 148n30, 157n26, 166n44
Locke, F. W., 17
Lot, F., 55-56
Louis VII of France, 20, 26, 150n8

Maillard, J., 52-53
Mall, E., 14, 17
Mantel mautaillié, 70, 161n57, 161n63
Map, W., 30
Marie de Champagne, 20
Marie de Compiègne, 14
Marie de Meulan, 149n38
Mary, abbess of Shatesbury, 21, 148n31, 148n35
Mathilda, mother of Henry II, 25, 149n38
Melusine, 83
Meriadus, 73
Metamorphoses, 22, 26
Milun, 55-56, 58-59, 62, 91-93, 97, 100, 114-16, 121, 124-28, 130-33, 136, 155n17, 156n23, 158n35, 167n8, 169n26, 171n12

Narcissus, 32, 159n45
Neckam, A., 97
Neri, F., 154n11, 162n8
Nutt, A., 97
Nykrog, P., 69, 160n51

Ogle, M. B., 89, 165n34
Oridials, lord of Liun, 72
Orléans, 26
O'Sharkey, E. M., 164n23
Ovid, 22, 26-27, 32, 50, 86, 91, 139, 149n39, 170n2
Owein, 33, 42-49

Painter, Sidney, 20
Paris, G., 15, 17, 54, 56, 62-63, 145n13
Partenopeus de Blois, 15, 145n13
Peredur, 162n2
Peter of Blois, 30-31, 168n24
Petronius, 80
Philippe de Thaon, 30, 152n13
Philomela, 91
Piramus and Tisbe, 22, 86, 91, 149n39, 170n2
Piramus, Denis, 15-16, 18, 68
Piramus et Tisbe, 32, 66, 75, 86, 159n45
Plantagenet, Geoffrey, 21, 25, 148n35
Pliny, 80-81
Priscian, 22
Protheselaus, 32
Psychomachia, 48
Putiphar's Wife, 83, 158n34

Queen Maud, 30

Remedia Amoris, 22, 26, 139
Resplendent Falcon, 89
Richart de Fournival, 97
Riquer, Martín de, 60-61, 159n45
Robert of Gloucester, 29
Robertson, D. W., 163n14
Roman de la Violette, 52
Roman d'Eneas, 22, 32, 75, 77, 147n21, 163n10
Roman de Renard, 38
Roman de Rou, 30
Roman de Thebes, 22, 32, 75, 84, 100
Roman de Troie, 22, 75, 100
Romulus Nilantii, 34
Rudel, Jaufré, 150n8

St. Anselm, 28
St. Augustine, 43
St. Bernard, 28
St. Gregory, 43
St. Malachias, 17
Saladin, 25
Salerno, 40

Index

Sallust, 27
Salverda de Grave, J., 75
Sanson de Nantuil, 31
Satyricon, 80
Schiött, E., 100
Schober, R., 167n10
Schürr, F., 99
Segre, C., 83, 86, 149n39
Seneca, 27
Smith, M. E., 34-36
Södergård, Östen, 144n4
Spitzer, L., 127
Station Island, 41

Terence, 27
Thiebaut V of Blois, 147n26
Thomas, 150n8
Tiemann, H., 66, 71, 161n59
Togail Bruidne Da Derga, 88-89
Toldo, P., 89
Topography of Ireland, The, 97, 152n1
Tours, 26
Tractatus de Purgatorio Sancti Patricii, 17, 42
Tristan, 22, 32, 100, 150n8, 164n21
Tuatha da dannan, 41
Tyrwhitt, T., 14

Venus, 22, 101-102, 139
Vie de Saint Alexis, La, 31, 66
Vie de Saint Thomas le martyr, La, 31

Vie Seint Edmund le rei, La, 15, 145n13
Vie Seinte Audree, La, 15-16, 144n4
Villehardouin, G., 29
Virgil, 26
Voyage of Saint Brendan, 30-31

Wace, 17-18, 22, 29-31, 50-51, 55, 59, 68, 73, 75, 83, 85, 98, 151n8, 163n21
Warnke, K., 15, 17, 20, 76
Wathelet-Willem, J., 86, 163n15, 164n24
Wauchier continuation, 74
William Conches, 30
William Longsword, 19-21, 148n31
William Marshal, 148n30
William of Malmesbury, 29
William of Mandeville, 20
William of Orange Cycle, 31
William the Conqueror, 56
Wilmotte, M., 146n21, 147n25
Winkler, E., 16, 148n33
Wolf, F., 52

Yonec, 22, 55-56, 58-59, 62, 65, 86-90, 97, 112-16, 121-23, 126, 128-33, 135-36, 158n34, 164n30, 165n35

Zimmer, H., 55, 155n19